Columbia Books on Architecture, Engineering, and Materials

A series edited by Michael Bell

Other books in this series:
Engineered Transparency—
The Technical, Visual, and Spatial Effects of Glass
978-1-56898-798-9

Published by
Princeton Architectural Press
37 East Seventh Street
New York, New York 10003

For a free catalog of books, call 1-800-722-6657.
Visit our website at www.papress.com.

Cover credits:
Front: photograph by Christian Richters
Back: photograph © Brigida Gonzalez

This book was made possible through the generous sponsorship of Lafarge

Editor: Laurie Manfra
Designer: Jan Haux

Special thanks to: Nettie Aljian, Bree Anne Apperley, Sara Bader, Nicola
Bednarek, Janet Behning, Becca Casbon, Carina Cha, Tom Cho, Penny (Yuen
Pik) Chu, Russell Fernandez, Pete Fitzpatrick, Linda Lee, John Myers, Katharine
Myers, Dan Simon, Steve Royal, Andrew Stepanian, Jennifer Thompson, Paul
Wagner, Joseph Weston, and Deb Wood of Princeton Architectural Press
—Kevin C. Lippert, publisher

Library of Congress Cataloging-in-Publication Data

Solid states : concrete in transition / Michael Bell and Craig Buckley, editors.—
1st ed.
p. cm.—(Columbia books on architecture, engineering, and materials)
Includes bibliographical references and index.
ISBN 978-1-56898-895-5 (alk. paper)
1. Concrete construction—Congresses. 2. Architecture, Modern—21st
century—Congresses. I. Bell, Michael, 1960– II. Buckley, Craig. III. Title: Concrete
in transition.
NA4125.S65 2010
721'.0445—dc22

2009046626

Solid States
Concrete in Transition

Michael Bell and

Craig Buckley, editors

Princeton Architectural Press

New York

Contents

6   Foreword   Mark Wigley

8   Preface   Christian Meyer

10   Introduction   Michael Bell

Essays

21   Earth as Urban Laboratory   Jean-Louis Cohen

27   Pervasive Plasticity   Detlef Mertins

39   Concrete: Dead or Alive?   Sanford Kwinter

47   Modelmaking Rangers: Form-Makers in Action at Eero Saarinen & Associates   Pierluigi Serraino

61   Reinforced Concrete and Modern Brazilian Architecture   Carlos Eduardo Comas

73   Notes on Weight and Weightlessness   Steven Holl

Projects

89   Horizontal Skyscraper: Continuous City / Continuous Garden   Steven Holl

Vanke Center, Shenzen, China

102   Concrete, or the Betrayal of Geometry   Preston Scott Cohen

Nanjing University Performing Arts Center, Nanjing, China

Tel Aviv Museum of Art, Tel Aviv, Israel

116   Tower and Temperament   Jesse Reiser + Nanako Umemoto

O-14, Dubai, United Arab Emirates

124   A Circular Journey   Stanley Saitowitz, Mason Walters, and Stephen Marusich

Congregation Beth Sholom, San Francisco, California

130   São Paulo: A Reinforced Context   Angelo Bucci

Houses in Ribeirão Preto and Ubatuba, São Paulo, Brazil

Structural Engineering + Material Science

137 Exposed Concrete: Design, Engineering, and Performance   Werner Sobek + Heiko Trumpf

143 Magical Structuralism   Guy Nordenson

147 From Wire Mesh to 3-D Textiles: Progress in New Reinforcements for Ferrocement and Thin-Cement
Composites   Antoine E. Naaman

158 Engineering in Cuba   Ysrael A. Seinuk

168 Nanotechnology in Concrete   Surendra P. Shah

175 Ultra-High-Performance Concrete in Highway Transportation Infrastructure   Benjamin A. Graybeal

177 Form Over Mass: Light Concrete Structures   Hans Schober

Energy + Sustainability

187 Concrete and Sustainable Development   Christian Meyer

193 An Integrated Energy and Comfort Concept: Zollverein School of Management and Design,
Essen, Germany   Matthias Schuler

200 Green Concrete and Sustainable Construction: A Multiscale Approach   Paulo Monteiro

202 The Hypergreen Path   Jacques Ferrier

Cultural Effects

209 Materialization of Concepts   Bernard Tschumi

218 The State of Concrete: An Investigation of Concrete in China   Qingyun Ma

227 Living with Infrastructure   Marc Mimram

234 Opportunity in Transition: The Reinventing of Concrete   Toshiko Mori

242 Implicit Performance: Exploring the Hybrid Condition   Juan Herreros

250 Solidifications   Fernando Menis

255 A Building and its Double   Mabel Wilson

259 Cloaked Transparency: Land Port of Entry at Massena, New York   Laurie Hawkinson

264 Artificial Natures / New Geographies   Kate Orff

267 Concrete Becoming Plastic, Then Graphic   Neil M. Denari

272 Acknowledgments

274 Contributors

276 Credits

280 DVD Contents

Foreword

We live in a concrete world—literally. Concrete is by far the most pervasive and resource-intensive man-made material on the planet. It is therefore the single biggest form of evidence of our species's existence. Concrete is our default setting. Its solidity and apparent inertness support our fragile flesh, psychology, and social life. We treat it as a given and identify it with unchanging basic conditions, most obviously with the infrastructural world of foundations (e.g., floors and roads). It is so fundamental to our sensibility that we use the word "concrete" to refer to reality itself, to the world of facts, tangibility, and specificity. Even ideas are considered concrete if they have precise relationships with the given world.

Yet concrete is far from a given. It is always made. The very substance of its internal organization is designed or more precisely, cooked. A particular recipe is mixed to launch a chemical reaction that generates considerable heat, as liquid turns to solid. From ancient Rome to today, ever-more sophisticated recipes have released new technical and spatial potentials. Concrete has never simply been the worker in the background laying the inert foundations of human life. The miracle of its metamorphosis allows it to represent liquidity just as fully as solidity. As it evolved from the unreinforced dome of the Roman Pantheon to the implausibly thin decks of contemporary bridges, concrete's unique, fluid ability—to take or make any shape—seemingly knows no limit. For all of our routine associations of concrete with tangible facts, what is truly specific to concrete is its lack of specificity. Far from fixed, it moves within a continuous spectrum, from raw infrastructural power to the most sophisticated dance. It is no longer associated just with solidity, the factual, or the given, but equally with flow, intricacy, experimentation, and playfulness. Pervasive and unpredictable, it has no inherent dimension, no fixed properties. It almost always exists in partnership with other materials, each opening up new spectrums of possibility. Concrete is always about the mix, even if its monolithic surface veils its source of strength in internal hybridity.

As the ingredients of this remarkable material are distributed, mixed, poured, vibrated, and cured in unimaginable quantities, concrete is being continuously reengineered into multiple levels of technical performance. As thousands of years of technical evolution accelerate, endless testing and retesting is relocated from buckets on building sites to sophisticated research laboratories.

Complex flows of materials, with precise technical performance and intellectual infrastructure, are changing so rapidly that leaders in the fields of architecture and engineering are increasingly finding themselves side by side within an ever-wider research community. When the properties of materials can be custom designed to address an extraordinarily wide range of parameters, there is no longer such a thing as an ordinary material. Iwan Baan's photographs of the cable-stay structure under construction at Steven Holl's Vanke Center in Shenzhen show the massive forces at work in this new regime. Concrete is employed in its most essential role as compression device but is now laced with a new, linear steel partner. The ordinary is launched into the extraordinary, and a horizontal skyscraper is able to levitate above the newly freed landscape below it. Concrete is no longer the prosaic solidity beneath us. We are pulled up by the new hybrid. Within this suspended world, concrete is called upon to provide a calming backdrop for daily life, with subtle recesses in its surface setting up an abstract play of light and shadow that quietly echoes the diagonal geometry of the supercables. It moves seamlessly along an unprecedented spectrum, from massive infrastructural effort to delicate domesticating effect.

As more and more of our world is made of concrete, we must look at it more closely than ever. This collaborative project is the second in a series examining materials across a broad range of scales, from the nanoscale of chemical engineering to the global scale of resource flows. Armed with the resulting reflections, concrete no longer appears as a solid and inert fact but as an ever-evolving set of relationships that are decisively changing our world and calling for new forms of creativity and responsibility.

—Mark Wigley

Preface

Concrete is by far the most important construction material for the built environment. It has been around in some form or another for thousands of years, but needed to be rediscovered in the nineteenth century following the invention of Portland cement. It has been estimated that we produce over 12 billion tons of concrete worldwide each year. In the United States, this translates into some two tons for each man, woman, and child every year. With the exception of water, mankind uses no other commodity in such vast quantities.

So what is so special about this age-old, all-too-familiar and seemingly utilitarian building material that it warrants such intense investigation? To be specific, this is the second of what hopefully will be a continuing series of books published by Columbia University's Graduate School of Architecture, Planning, and Preservation and the Department of Civil Engineering and Engineering Mechanics, in collaboration with Princeton Architectural Press. Using modern construction materials as the building blocks for bridging the gap between architects and engineers—a gap that has become all too prevalent on many university campuses—seemed to be a logical choice. By bringing together architects, engineers, and scientists to address topics of common interest, we intend to identify the latest advances in science and technology, not only for the sake of fostering mutual learning and understanding, but also to inform architects of the novel tools available to them for realizing their visions of the built environment. Whereas the technical, visual, and spatial effects of glass formed the basis of *Engineered Transparency*, concrete was the logical choice for the second.

It has been said that more progress has been made in the technological development of concrete during the last 25 years than in the preceding 150 years. Concrete is the quintessential "engineered" material. In other words, it can be designed to satisfy almost any reasonable set of performance specifications. The breathtaking scientific and technological breakthroughs of recent years have given us cement composites as strong as steel, lighter than water, and as beautiful as natural stone. Although some of these new materials have not yet reached full-scale application in practice, we feel it our duty as educators to inform the building community of not only what is already available, but what lies ahead. The contributions in this volume, by leaders in their respective fields, provide ample examples and illustrations.

—Christian Meyer

Introduction

Preconcrete Futures

Michael Bell

Bound by the physical and financial constraints of materials, architects and engineers are beholden to the intricate layers of today's global commodity practices. The nature of our profession is more tightly woven into and responsive to investment than it has ever been. Frequently design is less inclined toward characteristics of place; it focuses instead on translocations and interconnected matrixes of development and the input of consultants and partner practices. In fact, over the past twenty years, architectural commissions often seemed to be indexed by way of a constellation of world cities and their particular relations; in this way, the city has superseded the nation as the primary nexus of exchange. Trade barriers between emerging economies continue to change dramatically, reinforcing the role of national relations in development and design. It is within this context that the roles of architect and engineer are merging, both in terms of the large-scale planning of cities and the more general themes of urban life.

This book seeks to raise as many questions as it answers: What new forms of practice have emerged in today's economic arena? How has the conceptual reorganization of architectural space and technique allowed us to operate at levels that were previously the domain of international contractors and state organizations? What is the role of "the architectural concept" in an era of deeply engineered materials and complex economic demands on design?

Solid States: Concrete in Transition brings together a group of leading architects, scholars, and engineers to discuss the implications of new concrete technologies within architecture and engineering, at the scales of building and infrastructure, and within the contexts of new forms of measurement, coordination, and production.

International to Global
Generations of architects since the 1930s have defined the scope of international and then global practice. Avant-garde firms such as Archigram (in London) or Superstudio (in Florence) in the 1960s depicted infrastructural worlds that borrowed industrial metaphors from the turn of the twentieth century while promoting new modes of social life that registered a deep ambivalence to both the material and financial underpinnings of the modern city. But how can we evaluate today's architectural practices when they are so fully realized within the economic procedures and global flows of information and money that form them? In this context, what role does the image of infrastructure and its material techniques now play? What is the role of space, of event, or of nonmaterial design in the present era of such deeply coordinated materials-based value?

Practitioners that began their careers in the 1970s and 1980s—working on disinvested and neglected urban sites—often built on the frayed and forgotten edges of cities, in zones where ambivalence toward the financial center was possible. Today these firms are re-emerging as global participants in the rise of a new city. New means of capitalization and distribution of resources and building materials are affecting design practice, including the global exchange of real estate, high-tech forms of construction and material management (both relatively new), and the need to reexamine the city as the central frontier of social life. Far from being an out-of-control economic and material engine threatening the discrete terms of architectural and engineering practice, the city is becoming a new form of material practice that may look incoherent and fragmented but is increasingly organized and interconnected. This is a condition that produces novel material conceptions in which new forms of urban life are emerging, where the gaps between the imagined and the conditions are not fully understood and where many of the writers in this book are operating.

Concrete and Urbanism
In its existing roles, concrete has remained at the heart of theories of urbanism, and it has been seen as a form of civil life in itself. From its chemical engineering to its formal

aesthetics and plasticity, it has been the source of ingenuity and pragmatic beauty. Basic and essential, concrete has improved social life and has been banished as the substrate of overwhelming forms of infrastructure. It has served as an indicator of public progress, carrying the perceived weight of urban success or failure. It is also expected to provide a sense of the ineffable, while its properties have long conveyed the perception of permanence.

Ironically it is also the least likely material to impart permanence. Intrinsically based in concepts of time and movement, of flow and the formalization of flow, it is a temporal medium, and its use can perhaps be renewed as such. It is both fixed and perpetually in transition; solid, but only as a stage indicative of the shifting attributes of solidity. In this sense, concrete has historically been understood as a "substrate" and as a material of the cities of antiquity, but it has also been conceived as an inevitable, robust, and vigorous agent of the modern urbanization of metropolitan life.

While capable of establishing a city's foundations, concrete can also be molded into the newest of instruments. The differences between how it has been applied in the past and how it is utilized today is immense; nevertheless, concrete continues to dominate not just architecture and infrastructure but the imaginations of practicing architects and engineers and their aspirations for claiming a stake in the construction of civil society. Concrete, it seems, is understood as the building material that virtually assures the rise of modern engineered cities. Reinforced concrete, a composite of concrete and steel, instigated decades of invention in building form and structure over the twentieth century, during which the technology was greatly refined. It defined architecture anew as a deeply plastic art, and it remains the predominant system in use today. Techniques of reinforcement were continually modified during this period, and the mechanics and capitalization of concrete's design and implementation also changed in regular cycles.

Concrete's diverse history constitutes the "preconcrete nature" of much of the built world today. Its past projects into its future: toward uses of concrete in infrastructure, waterworks, airports, military installations, and within the rapid development of established and emerging cities.

Concepts of Flow

In the early 1990s, spatial and temporal concepts of movement and flow were widely discussed and redefined in architectural design, theory, and criticism, and they were reinvigorated within broader discussions of urbanism. In the midst of these conversations, fine-grained distinctions were made regarding the meaning of "flow" and what one might expect from counter-readings of the term.* In that context, social aspects of population migration and monetary flow within newly liberalized economies—in particular, the emergent role of China on the capitalist stage—were vividly seen against the backdrop of declining economies and places, as well as groups of people who were nonparticipants in the newly liquid, "flowing" conditions. In this realm and in the context of Solid States, it is evident that there were immense increases in the liquidity of these new financial and material relationships, but that within those conditions the predominance of nonlinear transactions—disruptions, disparities, and discontinuous modes of exchange and transfer—made for a world that was far from liquid, and often experienced as immutably static and resistant to change.

The title Solid States emerged from these discussions, both in the 1990s and again in 2008 as we organized the authors of the assembled work and reconvened the architects, historians, engineers, and scholars who were instrumental in defining the phrase. "Solid State Architecture" was also the title of a lecture and paper by Jesse Reiser and Nanako Umemoto in the late 1990s. The paper described a simultaneous quality of flow and solidity—of change that pulses through an otherwise stable form—and it attempted to describe a divide between aspects of continual change and apparent stillness in their aspirations. Theoretically it sought to describe architecture in a colloquial sense, as something that moves, changes, and flows at variable rates; it also suggested that stillness was the final and often unavoidable aspect of architectural design. What was radical about Reiser and Umemoto was the degree to which they ultimately were refining (and in some sense defining) an architecture capable of intuiting the variable aspects of flow and change. Arguably, this was also true of their broader generation, a generation that included the writing and design of Greg Lynn, Foreign Office Architects, UNStudio, and many others. This was perhaps (but not fully) evident to the authors and their audience, who usually focused on the architectural work itself. One could see this work as ultimately more accountable to a subject (an inhabitant) capable of comprehending latent and perhaps prior modes of movement and processes of becoming. In this case, aspects of a project's history—its processes of becoming and its eventual presence in the world—were less obvious; where this was not the case, nonlinearities and disruptions of these processes were brought into view. Instead of flows being seamless and laminar, they were evidently non-laminar and, barring completely opaque information, began to provide new levels of awareness and thus a critical capacity to the inhabitant.

As a collection of design, theory, history, and engineering innovations, *Solid States* presupposes what would inevitably involve a return to issues of material flow, phase change, liquidity versus solidity, and the determinant role of time in construction, form, and space. It also proposes a "preconcrete state" as the diagrammatic stage of events leading up to the final realization of form. Within the context of this book, what is dramatically different is the broader focus on urbanism and the potential of nonlinear, fragmented systems of commodity distribution, within processes of economic flow and political and social organizations, as well as within major market practices in the production and sale of concrete. *Solid States* (rather then "solid state") refers to governments, economic and political borders, and the companies and new transnational entities that design, finance, and realize many of the works shown here.

In addition to conceptual work on movement and aspects of imminence, which run counter to the formal and metaphysical histories of architecture, much of this work conflates notions of motion and stillness, change and form, and it does so by describing a subject capable of intuiting the simultaneity of contravening tendencies.

A comprehensive overview of the historical distinctions of the phrase "solid states" is beyond the scope of this introduction. A set of contemporary boundaries regarding concepts of "flow" and the term's relation to material and physical attributes is what underlies the organization of work presented here. In the case of long-term contributors to this discussion and the academic network that has sustained them collectively since the early 1990s, it is also about how concepts of "flow" appear to manifest in solid forms; that is, flows that are either imminent within otherwise motionless forms or recoverable, knowable, or capable of being redirected toward critical goals.

What is the state of the term "flow" today? How do we address resolutely nonflowing manifestations in architecture—entire zones of dislocated and isolated social life—such as the immense architectural forms that produce distance, segregation, and anomie? At times, "flow" refers to something highly liquid or virtual and electronic, and at other extremes it signifies a new inert state or virtual solid with barely perceptible degrees of change. *Solid States: Concrete in Transition* has a broad agenda of showing that both aspects of what we might call "flow" are central not only to concrete but also to its wider application and distribution in the urban world. Solid "states" are manifest within a several-century-long flow of ideas and concepts, from plastic arts and formations of mass and volume to the study of technical and material aspects of concrete, such as chemical composition and the roles of aggregates, plasticizers, and superplasticizers; formwork and releasing agents; and post- and pretensioning. Quite literally, it is a project about flow and phase changes within concrete.

Reinforced Professions

Within the matrix of reinforced concrete, the primary focus is the concrete itself. The role of steel, even as reinforcement, is essential and integral but has less value in the broader discussion of building practices. The ability to realize new forms for the plastic shaping of buildings and space—both today and historically—would not be possible without reinforcement. The rationalization of structure lies in the fusion of these two materials and the parallel actions between them and their properties.

Solid Sates explores concrete in its literal and conceptual realms, examining its future not only in terms of reinforcement but also its chemical engineering, capitalization, geographic production, and installation, and its role in energy expenditure and the environment. What are the new idealized relations between engineering and architecture with respect to concrete? Is architectural practice changing the material or is the material changing practice? How is the gap—between the new capacities of materials and their historically imagined roles—being reshaped?

In the past decade, the concept of a "composite" (or what constitutes concerted but segregate behaviors between materials) has come under a new lens of evaluation and opportunity. The discussion of reinforced concrete changes in this realm. The operative word "reinforced" must be replaced by a more complex interaction; our thinking about material coordination has been changed by this research. Is concrete still reinforced—for example, by fibers—or can we supplant that term with a new, more accurate one that speaks to the distributed nature of reinforcement? Coordinated material action is now deeply affected by the reinvention of the control and subcontrol of structural assemblies, both before and after construction. The limits of modeling the coordinated behaviors of structural form have changed as well. In the case of fiber reinforcement, the mathematical modeling of the fiber is as important as the chemical engineering of cements and compositions of aggregates.

Aspects of time and duration are central to the work included here, from chemical interactions within the curing process to the changing nature of the material, including the effects of thermal action or long-term deterioration. In recent years, such processes have been more carefully examined due to new monitoring capacities, including embedded electronic sensors that track changes endemic to concrete, such as cracking or incremental damage. Engineers, architects, and materials scientists are better equipped to predict and anticipate the interactions and dynamic relationships between materials with a level of accuracy that was not possible even ten years ago. The potential of these new means of examining material behavior constitute the cutting edge in architecture and engineering, more so than the materials themselves. Techniques of measurement and prediction represent new modes that are changing the basis of design today. The work of Benjamin A. Graybeal, for example, in testing ultra-high-performance concrete for use in federal highway programs, and Antoine E. Naaman in establishing parameters for 3-D fabric and textile reinforcement, point toward new material techniques but also new levels of testing and control. In this regard, we begin to see materials as approaching or differentiating themselves from each other as forms of behavior rather than as intrinsic differences. The capacity to model material attributes is becoming the new substrate for spatial, structural, economic, and social practice.

Even if a material cannot be segregated easily, it persists in isolation; a material offers innovation at its own inherent levels and within its own chemical engineering. Industries remain segregate, and their locations, means of capitalization, labor practices, and economies all contribute to how something gets built.

A-plastic Space

Attributes of stillness, permanence, and movement have always been in some ways added to concrete. Recall the use of concrete in the banked test tracks at the Fiat factory in

Turin, Italy (1923); concrete was the substratum upon which acceleration and centrifugal forces were played out, above a factory in which the span of columns was an important component of production, labor, and efficiency. Compare this to the expansive spans and fragile lofted interiors of Auguste Perret's Notre Dame du Raincy (1922), completed at almost the same time as the Fiat factory, or the concave modeled surfaces of Le Corbusier's Ronchamp chapel (1955). Concrete, as we have historically received it, has always been concrete plus form, but also concrete plus speed, aesthetics, and abstraction. Today's infrastructural work changes in light of what we know about evolving economies and demand. The civil aspects of concrete and infrastructure are contravened and supported by an arena of expanding technologies and a more prevalent awareness of new means and methods, from leveraging economic potentials to controlling parameters for off-site work, embedding digital technologies that monitor life span and repair, and applying smart materials. In other words, what is being added to concrete today changes its very nature and reconvenes its qualities in every sense. These new attributes affect the qualities and applications of concrete, and they leave us seeking a new architecture for concrete, one that is decidedly less plastic than its predecessors.

The history of concrete architecture and infrastructure is laced with compelling trajectories that continue to inspire and feed innovation today. In this regard, an approach to the use of concrete, presented as fundamental to modern architecture and the modern city, is demonstrated in the architecture of Perret, even if his work was far more respectful of historical typologies than the heroic works of the twentieth century. Reinforced concrete in Perret's architecture is situated as a rational, pragmatic material, given tenuous balance and tremendously delicate installation. It pushes the limits of structure, formwork, and execution, and it weaves between the rationalized aspects of a modern society and the signifiers of historical programs and building types. Perret's work was plastic, but it left only light traces in space, with little disturbance or effect.

Perret showed a deeply restrained relationship to the visceral and plastic aspects of concrete commonly seen in the work of Le Corbusier, Paul Rudolph, or even Oscar Niemeyer. "Plasticity of form" and "the rationalization of construction" dominate architectural thought throughout the twentieth century, and Le Corbusier's architecture made both cases emphatically. Perret may be more of a touchstone in today's work; however, his more tenuous works are deserving of reexamination in light of advances in concrete that show it to be a material capable of more technical refinement and therefore delicate deployment.

Antecedents for this can be found in Giuseppe Terragni's work in concrete. Terragni replaced robustness with a thin surface quality, planarity, and an a-plastic lack of material thickness. Richard Neutra's Lovell Health House (1928) used light-steel-framing technologies that made concrete seem as planar and as liquid as glass. It was a hybrid steel structure, stiffened by the diaphragm action of concrete; the compressive strength of the concrete increased the ductility of the steel. Today concrete is increasingly ductile in its properties and by way of fiber reinforcement, superplasticizers, and innovations in nanotechnology and chemistry. Concrete is seen as less overtly robust and its potential applications far more subtle in scale and proportion. Terragni and Le Corbusier both used ferrocement for thinner, more planar installations in stair balustrades and other details, making walls narrower in structure or smaller in building volume than typical installations. These can be seen as precursors to newer problems in concrete, and as Naaman notes in his essay, ferrocements trace back to patents in 1855 for *Ferciment* and to the use of mesh reinforcements that are more evenly distributed compared to standard reinforced concrete. In this context, the history of concrete—considered through the lens of plasticity—is only narrowly understood. The effects of these applications are not only sculptural but also strategic with respect to seismic reinforcement and quality control during and after installation, on-site and off.

Aside from its plastic qualities, other questions that are key today include: How do concrete and construction materials integrate with other systems in use today, such as steel? How are concrete works dismantled, and could innovations in the expected life spans of materials affect design? Do we still expect material properties to influence architectural and engineered space? And in what ways are materials understood as plastic and expressive?

Perret revealed two worlds and he offered a delicate balance between them—an equipoise of tenuous spatial extension achieved by way of rational construction. By the end of the twentieth century, his version of reinforced concrete had acquired countless new capabilities, and increasingly it became a different kind of spatial engine, as well as structural system. It offered an entirely new economic commodity and means of urbanization. Nonetheless, reinforced concrete was seen as similar, if not identical, to earlier concrete forms, either in terms of its plastic capabilities, techniques of reinforcement, or its role in environmental crises. The cleft between techniques and the imagined capacities of concrete has grown wider over the past one hundred years, yet one could say that it still involves concrete plus some other attributes, even as the concrete itself is increasingly becoming different on its own terms.

For all of its weight, concrete has almost always been an indicator of empty space (by way of surface and volume) and lightness. These ideas are renewed as we reexamine concrete, not only in terms of surface and form, but also as integral to and coordinated with other materials, such as composite alloys—new materials with entirely new potentials. These potentials are evident in the work of the authors, including SANAA's use of radiant heating with Matthias Schuler and the resulting porous structure in Essen, Germany, the Zollverein School of Management and Design (2006). Steven Holl's Vanke Center (2010) in Shenzhen, China, appears to weightlessly levitate over an absent mass (what he sees as a "receding sea"). The expansive spanning capacities and steel cable-stay systems employed at the Vanke Center use concrete as the compression medium, and essentially they lace the concrete lattice system with highly tensioned but visually absent steel cables. The effect is an uncanny building that seems to stand without any evidence of support. The negative space within and beneath the structure appears surprisingly empty. Void of expectant structural mass, it is newly freed and transformed into a shaded and extensive garden. The concrete work is reinforced at a superscale, and the building operates as a form of spatial infrastructure.

Restraining Flow

Advanced work in admixtures and plasticizers has allowed for new methods of formwork and newly extensive pours, but to build in concrete is still to build twice: one builds the formwork prior to the pour, and the resulting work holds residual if not explicit references to the absent formwork. Formwork has changed in light of new concrete mixtures; the architects and engineers of *Solid States* address these issues in multiple ways. In particular, one witnesses new innovations and the sustenance of architectural space in the work of Stanley Saitowitz, where methods of formwork directly coincide with and provide spatial possibilities. Saitowitz calibrates methods of formwork—its costs, availability, and quality—with sublime spatial ambitions. Far from the historically heroic aspects of Eero Saarinen's full-scale mock-ups presented by Pierluigi Serraino, Saitowitz achieves a mode of monumental architecture in the current realm of budgets and procedures that seems to have thwarted a generation.

Evolution in formwork (e.g., precast concrete) allows Preston Scott Cohen to realize the curved surfaces of the Tel Aviv Museum of Art (2010), while parametric capabilities in formwork modeling have changed the potential of on-site concrete work. Werner Sobek with Heiko Trumpf achieved the double curvature in the exposed surfaces of UNStudio's Mercedes-Benz Museum (2006) by using parametric modeling to create the molds. Sobek and Trumpf are researching how to achieve greater degrees of surface detail by parametric means. In this regard, does formwork constitute the same degree of absence often sought in the eradication of imperfections? Toshiko Mori's focus on the nature of formwork having a reciprocal relationship to the concrete pour—in the work of Mark West—brings into focus the trace of an outward force and the restraint and control of flow that formwork provides.

How is formwork's significance established today? Is it less or more critical compared to its use by previous generations? The work of Fernando Menis is aggressively modeled and roughly cast, recalling an international aspect of brutalism, yet it's done in a site-specific way, rooted in the geologic formation of his home territory of the Canary Islands. Far from universal, his use of concrete and formwork is specific and local. Mabel Wilson focuses on the casting process itself and the otherness of the result, pointing to Rachel Whiteread's large-scale sculptures to explore the revelatory aspects of how a casting exposes a building's interior.

Which aspects of formwork can be seen as essential or intrinsic to a work, and how is formwork designed and understood as a temporal medium as opposed to an unacknowledged prestructure? What role will cementitious structural insulated panels (SIPs) play in future work, not only in relation to sustainability but also to labor, the organization of construction, and architectural space itself (its lack of formwork and presence of concrete)?

Recent advances in the workability and flow of concrete dramatically alter what we can achieve in construction and design. Self-consolidating concrete has revolutionized the field in recent years, and these changes coincide with concepts of flow in a wide range of disciplines.

Woven into existing circumstances, concrete requires focus, precision, and an ultimate willingness to see the work last. When the forms are removed, it is no longer a temporary liquid sustained by applied force. Its execution requires a view to the next century, but some aspects of concrete persist. How do we measure doubt and apprehension in light of a long-lasting material? What concepts of "flow," present in the formation of concrete, can be applied to themes of use, space, or other aspects of the life of a building? How do the means and techniques of admixtures dramatically affect the liquidity of concrete? New innovations also allow for more contiguous pours and therefore newly continuous surfaces and elastic forms.

Concrete and Sustainability

It has been estimated that more than ten billion tons of concrete are produced worldwide each year. In the United States this translates to a ratio of approximately two tons of concrete per person, per year. This requires an unrivaled amount of natural resources for providing the aggregate and raw materials for cement production. Of equal concern is the fact that the production of Portland cement has historically released large quantities of carbon dioxide into the atmosphere, making not only advancements in the design of production plants critical, but also the use of recycled aggregates. The cement industry is believed to account for five to seven percent of all carbon dioxide released worldwide, but as major innovations are made in cement production, these advances are measured against their respective locations and regions. There are advantages in the regional aspects of production—such as levels of modernization and investment at plants, production demands, and levels and speeds of urbanization—indicating that the production of concrete as a geographic entity is uneven (e.g., where it is made versus where it is implemented). In many cases it is being sourced from heavily polluting plants.

The concrete industry is addressing sustainability on several fronts. Advances are measured against global concrete production and also against smaller regional and local dimensions. As with all building materials, questions of embedded energy, eventual use, and local advantages—such as proximity to a building site (for shipping purposes)—are global and local in nature and contingent on immediate detail. The degree of modernization at plants worldwide affects wider sustainability goals and emissions, and the nature of aggregates as recycled versus newly mined minerals combines with issues of life span and use, such as expected thermal mass, rapidity of urbanization, or the sourcing of materials. Sustainability in this regard is far from a direct equation; even if direct action is possible, it is increasingly embedded in issues like carbon trading and global markets. But the question remains: What role can we add to this equation to deal with concrete's technical and sociopolitical dimensions?

Approximately one billion cubic meters of water are used each year in producing concrete. Regions that lack a readily available supply can be inordinately affected by the amount of water needed to produce concrete.

Another immediate issue is the successful development of Portland cement substitutes, typically by-products of other industrial processes, such as fly ash and slags. Aggregate can be partially replaced with recycled materials, such as construction debris, recycled concrete aggregate and glass, paper mill residues, and tires. These efforts not only result in value-added secondary uses of what otherwise would become waste materials (often transported to landfills at high costs), they often improve the properties of the end product. Christian Meyer's research offers an analysis for further reducing the industry's environmental footprint.

Postproduction is also a central issue. The demolition and disposal of concrete structures and pavements constitute an environmental question that has unique parameters compared to other building materials. Construction debris contributes a large fraction of our solid-waste disposal problem, with concrete being its single largest component.

The Globalization of Concrete Production

The history of concrete seems to be revealed by a range of connected but distinct realizations of mid-twentieth-century works. Cultural and technical histories collide in works realized by State-sponsored infrastructural or industrial projects by international contractors such as Bechtel or Brown & Root. Concrete's mass, its plastic presence, and its semipermanence were deployed in works that, despite their spatial expansiveness, were later critiqued as being of a scale that precludes human habitation. When concrete becomes an apparatus of the State, institutions such as the World Bank

and global corporations emerge as memories coexisting with the cubism of Le Corbusier or the sun-shaped masses of Niemeyer. What then do we say about the expanses of freeways, the tremendous network of deeply structured roads that lead to ephemeral, nearly a-material houses within the sprawling suburbs; or the network of signs and inscriptions of postcode spaces that exceed anyone's spatial imagination? Is this a postductile era, one in which the elastic values of material are inextricably lost in the wider urban space, even as the determinants of their immediate value are more assured than ever in history? *Solid States* proposes that material knowledge will lend a new level of control to social and economic spaces, and that new levels of material innovation will reconvene architectural and engineering goals, relinking material and design to social life.

Conclusion

Solid States: Concrete in Transition reveals the newly formed arena of dramatically altered material limits and orchestrations in which architectural work can possibly recover or decipher the mathematics of allocation. The authors of this text interpret the spaces resulting from material allocation and the aftermath of its preconcrete motors and diagrams—of money and material; of engineering, materials science, and architecture; of politics and economies; of global trade and immediate circumstance. They testify to material potentials rather than diminish the potential damages of its uneven trade and application, and they ultimately seek—for space and material— new zones of experience and modes of practice arising from the known and projected potentials of a once circumscribed material. Weighing heavily on this content is the material consumption of emerging nations and economies: the sheer mass of concrete allocated within China's new construction and the historical aspects of concrete as a heroic material orchestrated by the spatial imagination of the engineer and architect, within the social and political experiments coincident with its major urban transformations. These aspects of concrete are here reconstituted from within material science, to its overt shape-making capacity, to its final role and potential as a civil and political realization within works of architecture, infrastructure, and finally as a pliant receptor of our profession's intentions and research.

*To be more specific about our intellectual debts, it's necessary to look closer at one key source and its primary contributors. In the context of the architectural journal *ANY*, edited by Cynthia Davidson and published between 1992 and 2003, "flow" was a recurring theme and concept in the writing and architectural theory of the contributing architects: Greg Lynn, Alejandro Zaera Polo, Ben van Berkel, and Sanford Kwinter. Use of the term "flow" was by no means isolated in its applications, and its recurrence in architectural history is almost as ubiquitous as it is underexamined. One could just as easily reference the term as applied in the network theories and urbanism of Manuel Castells, in large part in relation to sociological goals or a more colloquial use in terms of "flows of information" or "flows of traffic."

Essays

21

Earth as Urban Laboratory

Jean-Louis Cohen

27

Pervasive Plasticity

Detlef Mertins

39

Concrete: Dead or Alive?

Sanford Kwinter

47

Modelmaking Rangers: Form-Makers in Action at Eero
Saarinen & Associates

Pierluigi Serraino

61

Reinforced Concrete and Brazilian Modern Architecture

Carlos Eduardo Comas

73

Notes on Weight and Weightlessness

Steven Holl

Earth as Urban Laboratory

Jean-Louis Cohen

The new geography of the world seems at first sight to be nothing but an archipelago of cities. Seen on a global map of building production, the deployment of architectural firms sometimes resembles the distribution of embassies of major political powers throughout the world's capitol cities. | fig. 1 This pattern will probably survive the economic crisis, which started in 2008 and touches many issues relative to design research and construction. In this changed context, the following commentaries develop not from a direct involvement on the building "front," but rather from my primary position as an historian of ideas, buildings, and cities.

The rapid diffusion of concrete in the early twentieth century derived not only from the sheer qualities of the material, but also from its potential to standardize construction elements and for reconceptualizing the design process itself. In his fundamental book *Bauen in Frankreich, bauen in Eisen, bauen in Eisenbeton* (Building in France, Building in Iron, Building in Ferroconcrete) published in 1928, Sigfried Giedion defined concrete as a "laboratory material."[1] | fig. 2 It is true that through the interplay of patents, regulations, and also the nomadic expertise of engineers travelling to remote countries, by 1914 concrete had become a universal product, used according to scientific procedures established through the first experimental episodes.[2]

The internationalization of concrete was almost instantaneous. Hardly a decade after the first patents, the Paris-based firm founded by François Hennebique could proudly display hundreds of projects built in dozens of countries. Thomas Alva Edison's former partners, George E. Small and Henry J. Harms, applied the process to the construction of houses in France and the Netherlands, while the extraordinary Swiss engineer Robert Maillart worked in Petrograd during most of World War I.[3]

The rapid circulation of concrete—and evidence of the liquidity that characterizes the early stages of its making—is illustrated by the success of the Ingersoll-Rand cement gun. | fig. 3 In his 1926 *Almanach d'architecture moderne* (Almanac of Modern Architecture), Le Corbusier reproduced an image of shotcrete at work in the "reconstitution" of Tokyo, after the 1923 Great Kanto earthquake.[4]

This process of internationalization and of the diffusion of concrete technologies did not, however, imply the disappearance of distortions and divides induced by competition between nations. At times, nationalism also took a concrete face. The material became a bone of contention between France and Germany prior to World War I, replacing iron and steel as the emblematic substance of modernity. Auguste Perret's Théâtre des Champs-Élysées would be dismissed as "hun" and considered, rather strangely, a "Zeppelin."[5] | fig. 4 On the other side of the Rhine, after having called the new material *Monierbeton* after the French pioneer Joseph Monier, whose system they adopted (rather than Hennebique's), the Germans would also try to plant their flag on it and claim excellence, if not anteriority.

These conflicts underline the fact that concrete has never been a peaceful, innocent material. Its appropriation for fortification started in the nineteenth century and found its acme between the two World Wars, with the erection of the partly underground Ligne Maginot in France and the Czech fortifications. The Nazi occupation of Western Europe led to the construction of the bunkers of the Atlantikwall, spread over a line extending from Norway to Spain.[6] The sculptural qualities of the materials were at the time made less conspicuous by the camouflaging of the structures but would be revealed in their ruins.[7] The military use of concrete has remained through the Cold War, and to this day it remains a considerable part of worldwide consumption.

The concrete infrastructure of the military sometimes played an ambiguous role. The strategic *Autobahnen* built by the Third Reich were first used by civilians, and later by more bellicose users. As World War II drew to an end, they saw contradictory flows: a memorable photograph shows the two parallel and inverted convoys of American tanks headed for

fig. 1 | Map of нок's regional offices worldwide, circa 2000

fig. 3 | Ingersoll-Rand cement gun, from *Almanach d'architecture moderne*, by Le Corbusier, 1926

fig. 2 | The current state of reinforced concrete, from *Bauen in Frankreich, bauen in Eisen, bauen in Eisenbeton*, by Sigfried Giedion, 1928

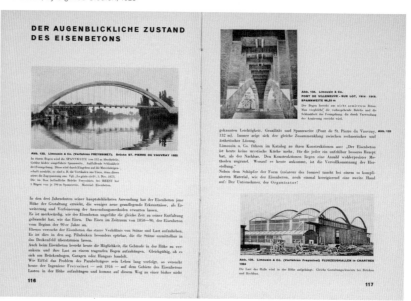

Earth as Urban Laboratory

Jean-Louis Cohen

fig. 4 | Théâtre des Champs-Élysées, axonometric view of the structure, by Auguste Perret, Paris, France, 1913

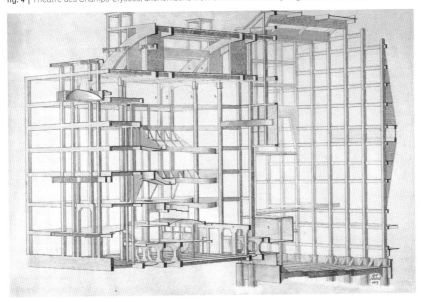

fig. 5 | German prisoners of war walking down an autobahn near Giesen, Germany, as trucks and tanks of the U.S. 6th Armored Division pass in the other direction, 1945

fig. 6 | Système Camus, first used by Henri Loisel, Le Havre, France, 1950

Berlin, and German prisoners of war walking to their detention camps. | fig. 5

Once these martial episodes were forgotten, concrete became, in the second half of the twentieth century, the fetish material of both modernization and modernism. Its apotheosis coincided with the massive diffusion of heavy, panel-based prefabrication, which took place from the1950s to the 1970s. | fig. 6 Systems initially invented in Weimar, Germany, for instance by Ernst May's team in Frankfurt, were industrialized by the French. Building technologies like the système Camus were then patented and exported to the USSR and the Soviet Bloc, and re-exported as far as Cuba, where they got "tropicalized." The prefabricated panel, or *Platte*, became a synecdoche of the entire East German building system, if not of the party-state system at large.[8]

Concrete also became a key technology in modernism and in the modernization of Latin America, with the imaginative structures of Félix Candela in Mexico, and the innovative conjunction of materials in the work of Eladio Dieste in Uruguay. The Brazilian scene was probably the most significant from the late 1930s onward, among all those of the continent. The work of Oscar Niemeyer and Affonso Eduardo Reidy, in Rio de Janeiro | fig. 7 ; João Batista Vilanova Artigas and, more recently, João Filgueiras Lima (usually known as Lelé), in Salvador; and Paulo Mendes da Rocha in São Paulo has been totally defined by the use of concrete, with discrete contributions by remarkable engineers such as Joaquim Cardoso, who was also a poet.[9]

Concrete is inserted in several fields of tension characteristic of today's world. Using another metaphor borrowed from the realm of static, one might say that the material undergoes flexion both geographically and conceptually, as it is deployed in new territories and adjusted to new design principles. It remains the fundamental material of the urbanization process at all scales, from the building of roads to the erection of bridges and buildings. The geography of concrete is not homogeneous, but is strictly determined by the changing economic assets of the Earth, as demonstrated by the fact that roughly half of the world's production of cement is consumed in China. To use Guy Nordenson's suggestive notion, China is one of the most exciting stages where the "concrete theater" unfolds.[10] | fig. 8

Two aspects seem to characterize current trends. The first one, mentioned by Sanford Kwinter, is *biomorphic temptation*. Indeed, this is an old idea that met a playful and rudimentary shape in the early twentieth century, for instance with Robert Mallet-Stevens's concrete trees, built at the 1925 Paris Exposition Internationale des Arts Décoratifs et Industriels Modernes. In contrast with this early and rather literal use of the material, a dialectic relationship between the visible and invisible appeared with the concept of the exoskeleton, which developed initially in the shape of steel structures, beginning with Renzo Piano, Richard Rogers, and Ove Arup's Centre Georges Pompidou (referred to locally as Beaubourg) in the 1970s. It is finding a new materialization with high-performance concrete, as used, for instance, by Marc Mimram with his bonelike elements connecting surfaces. | fig. 9 Another early ideal of concrete is returning to the forefront: infrastructure. One of Auguste Perret's breakthroughs at the Théâtre des Champs-Élysées was the imaginative use of bowstring bridge arches borrowed from Eugène Freyssinet; they became the main load-bearing structure carrying the cupola. The paradigm of the bridge is present today, not only in new megastructures but also in projects of other scales, such as Steven Holl's Linked Hybrid scheme in Beijing.

Vast networks of practice are now intertwined at the global scale. Investors, architects, engineering firms, landscape architects, and contractors are deployed, with the production of structures requiring entire armies of mobile laborers. This frantic activity, which has been seriously challenged by the depression that began in 2008, is based on a complex collection of patents, regulations, norms, and insurance requirements. Questions to be discussed in this respect are the following: how do concrete designs in this networked planet articulate generic or standardized concerns, ideals, and procedures with specific sites and production contexts?

fig. 7 | Pedregulho Low-Income Housing Complex, by Affonso Eduardo Reidy, Rio de Janeiro, Brazil, 1950

fig. 8 | Model of Shanghai at the Shanghai Municipal History Museum, Shanghai, China

fig. 9 | Rendering of a bridge at La Courneuve, France, by Marc Mimram, 2008

What is the meaning of the material in this intense process of modernization and how does it differ from previous concrete ages? In the globalized process of production, what happens to the relationship between imported and local labor?

The work process seems to have become a sort of black box, located somewhere between the laboratory (or the design studio) and the finished building. To paraphrase the main thesis of Karl Marx's *Das Kapital*—a book that seems to have regained popularity—concrete is a social relationship. If technology seems to be providing convincing answers, questions remain open as to the social flexion of concrete today.

1 | Sigfried Giedion, *Bauen in Frankreich, bauen in Eisen, bauen in Eisenbeton* (Berlin, Leipzig: Klinkhardt & Biermann, 1928), 66.

2 | Cyrille Simonnet, *Le Béton, histoire d'un matériau* (Marseille: Parenthèses, 2005), np.

3 | Olga Kirikova, "Robert Maillart in St. Petersburg," *Werk, Bauen + Wohnen* 60, no. 4 (2005): 70–72.

4 | Le Corbusier, *Almanach d'architecture moderne* (Paris: G. Crès & cie, 1926), np.

5 | Jean-Louis Forain, "L'inauguration du théâtre des Champs-Élysées," *L'Illustration*, no. 3658 (April 1913): 302.

6 | J.E. and H.W. Kaufmann, *Fortress France: the Maginot Line and French Defenses in World War II* (Westport, CT: Praeger Security International, 2006), np; and George Forty, *Fortress Europe: Hitler's Atlantic Wall* (Surrey, United Kingdom: Ian Allen, 2002), np.

7 | Paul Virilio, *Bunker Archeology* (New York: Princeton Architectural Press, 1994), np. Originally published as *Bunker archéologie* (Paris: CCI/Centre Georges Pompidou, 1975).

8 | Werner Durth, Jörn Düwel, Niels Gutschow, *Ostkreuz. Personen, Pläne, Perspektiven. Architektur und Städtebau der DDR* (Frankfurt/Main: Campus Verlag, 1999), np.

9 | Elisabetta Andreoli and Adrian Forty, *Brazil's Modern Architecture* (London: Phaidon, 2004), np.

10 | Guy Nordenson, "Concrete Theater," in Jean-Louis Cohen and G. Martin Moeller Jr., *Liquid Stone: New Architecture in Concrete* (New York: Princeton Architectural Press, 2006), 62–63.

Pervasive Plasticity

Detlef Mertins

The material we call *concrete* is remarkable not only in the plasticity of the forms it can take, but equally in its mutability and ever-growing pervasiveness. The last session of the Solid States conference, held at Columbia in the fall of 2008, addressed concrete's role in the unprecedented scale of global building production, while other discussions reported on its current technical innovations and the new formal and spatial opportunities that they open up. Isn't it telling that concrete turns out to be as malleable technically as it is formally? And that much of today's innovation is driven by environmental issues that have become urgent, due to the material's pervasive use: reducing carbon-dioxide emissions, even sucking it out of the air and expanding the recycling of it. What I do in this essay is consider, through the lens of history and admittedly with an orientation more formal than chemical, what happens when plasticity becomes normative.

In his landmark book, *Bauen in Frankreich, bauen in Eisen, bauen in Eisenbeton*, historian Sigfried Giedion provided vivid evidence that iron construction had been the locus of great engineering in the nineteenth century but was superseded in the early twentieth by reinforced concrete.[1] He pointed to Le Corbusier's work on standardized housing to suggest that it would be through concrete rather than steel that the new spatial paradigm of modernity would be widely generalized. If Le Corbusier's Maison Dom-ino (1914–5) captured this potential in a diagram, public housing programs in Germany demonstrated its realization at the urban scale, linking the modernization of technology with the reconstruction of urban territories, albeit without Le Corbusier's internal spatial complexity. | fig. 1 For the public housing program in Frankfurt during the late 1920s, Ernst May ramped up the technology of precast concrete to build some 15,000 units of workers' housing in five years, in new garden settlements on the city's periphery. | fig. 2 Achievements like these were formidable for the time and commensurate with the emergence of mass society, yet they pale in comparison with the scale and speed of urban growth in China today.

China's use of concrete in recent years has become the stuff of legend, accounting for half the world's total production and continuing to grow by 5 percent annually. | fig. 3 Before the economic downturn of 2008, output was expected to reach 1.3 billion metric tons by 2010. In 2007 alone, some 5.5 million units of housing were realized in concrete. If we can say that Le Corbusier's Dom-ino concept now rules the day, it is not only because of the efficiency with which such structures can be produced—the radical reduction in material, time, and labor and the radical expansion of scale they achieved—but also because of the flexibility with which this constructive system can adapt to different sites, scales, programs, configurations, tastes, and cultural desires. While appearing to delineate a rigid rationality, the Dom-ino system, in fact, possesses a plastic logic of variation and adaptation. The abandoned construction sites for hotels on the Sinai Peninsula, documented by Sabine Haubitz and Stefanie Zoche, illustrate how easily the Dom-ino system has incorporated non-Western cultural motifs, producing the kind of kitsch that has always been part of modernity. | fig. 4 It is a system that mutates so easily that it often disconcerts the purists, exchanging Le Corbusier's cylindrical piloti for piers, sheer walls, or other kinds of elements, and producing results that are structurally hybrid, like most commercial buildings or the more extreme "turbo architecture" of Serbia.[2] | fig. 5

During the twentieth century, concrete became celebrated, more typically, not for its systemic applications but for enabling the realization of unique sculptural forms—expressionist, biomorphic fantasies of a post-Symbolist, post-Art Nouveau, post-Futurist world to come—that would supersede and correct mechanization. | fig. 6 So strong was the desire for formal plasticity, complexity, and alterity in the cultural imagination—for the organic, libidinal, Dionysian, delirious, and dark—that concrete acquired a second material logic, directly at odds with its rationalist Dom-ino superego and the modernist ethos of honest construction. In 1919,

fig. 2 | The use of precast-concrete panels at the Praunheim housing estate in Frankfurt am Main, by Ernst May with Eugen Kaufmann, reprinted from *Das Neue Frankfurt*, no. 2, 1927

fig. 1 | Maison Dom-ino, by Le Corbusier, 1914

fig. 3 | "Suzhou Jie, Daoxiang Yuan, Haidian District, Beijing," chromogenic color print from the History Images series, by Sze Tsung Leong, 2004

Pervasive Plasticity

Detlef Mertins

fig. 4 | Seaview Palace, from the Sinai Hotels series, by Haubitz+Zoche, Egypt, 2004

fig. 5 | An example of "turbo architecture" under construction in Serbia, photo by NAO (Normal Architecture Office)

fig. 6 | Trans World Airlines Terminal, by Eero Saarinen and Associates, Queens, New York, 1956–62

for instance, when concrete was still in scarce supply after World War I, Erich Mendelsohn's Einstein Tower in Potsdam (1919–21) appeared to be made of concrete, when it was built in brick and merely parged with cement.

A few years later, the theosophist, educator, and designer Rudolf Steiner did use cast-in-place concrete for his Second Goetheanum in Dornach, Switzerland (1928), a building that remains inadequately recognized. | fig. 7 It was immediately criticized and suppressed—together with other manifestations of apparent irrationality and Gothic desire— by so-called rationalists, such as Giedion and Walter Gropius, both of whom advocated for a moralizing embrace of industrial standardization (although Giedion flirted with Surrealism, as did his friend Le Corbusier).

Steiner had been a scholar of the writings of Johann Wolfgang von Goethe and sought to demonstrate a design approach based on natural principles identified in Goethe's new science of plant morphology (1790): principles of form-generation and growth through an internal mechanism, the details of which remain a mystery. Barry Bergdoll recently observed, in an essay appearing in the *Nature Design* catalog for the Museum für Gestaltung Zurich, how widespread Goethe's influence was throughout the nineteenth and early twentieth centuries.[3] Taking up the question of what natural and artistic beauty might share in common, he launched a search for laws of generation and development that were common to the works of nature and humanity. Goethe was a *monist*; he saw the human being as necessarily part of nature, which is a principle that underlies today's theories of deep ecology. In a similar though more idealist spirit, Karl Friedrich Schinkel had considered architecture the continuation by man of the constructive activity of nature.

The same year that Steiner's Second Goetheanum opened, 1928, Ludwig Karl Hilberseimer and Julius Vischer published a book on concrete titled *Beton als Gestalter* (Concrete as Form-Creator).[4] | fig. 8 As one might expect from Hilberseimer, it featured many examples of industrial buildings with column grids and expressed structural frames, but also domes such as Max Berg's powerful and pioneering Centennial Hall in Breslau (1911–13, in present day Wroclaw, Poland) | fig. 9 ; long-span structures such as Erich Mendelsohn's Hat Factory in Luckenwalde, Germany (1919–20); and vaults such as Bruno Taut's exhibition hall in Magdeburg, the market hall in Reims, and the airplane hangar by Eugène Freyssinet under construction in Orly, France, which was widely admired at the time. Hilberseimer pointed out that the first patent for reinforced concrete had been filed in 1867 by the Parisian gardener Joseph Monier, who had used it to make vessels such as garden pots and tubs. While Hilberseimer dismissed expressionist plasticity as arbitrary just as sternly as he rebuked historicist cladding of concrete skeletons, he commended the disciplined plasticity of cooling towers for following the laws of regularity, functionality, efficiency of means, and for a structural integrity also attributed to nature.

In the 1970s, the historian Manfredo Tafuri characterized this schism within the avant-garde in terms of a dialectic between rigorism and expressionism: Hannes Meyer's League of Nations (1927) versus Johann Friedrich (Fritz) Hoeger's Chilehaus in Hamburg (1924); and Gropius's Bauhaus at Dessau (1925–6) versus Erich Mendelsohn's Schocken department store in Chemnitz (1927–30).[5] He mapped this opposition of forms onto what Theodor Adorno and Max Horkheimer had called the dialectic of Enlightenment in their 1940s analysis of cultural production under capitalism. It was the great insight of these critical theorists to recognize that the Enlightenment objective of banishing myth and superstition—regrounding knowledge and society strictly in reason and science—entailed the unacknowledged construction of new myths. Rather than vanquishing them, it was shot through with myths, dark sides, irrationalities, and violence. Rationality and myth turned out to be flip sides of the same coin, linked in an economy of repression and false consciousness.

But was this transposition of critical theory into formal terms in fact warranted? Weren't both sides of the

fig. 7 | Second Goetheanum, by Rudolf Steiner, Dornach, Switzerland, 1928

fig. 9 | Page depicting Centennial Hall, by Max Berg, Breslau, Germany, 1911–13,
from *Beton als Gestalter*

antagonism between Apollonian and Dionysian form equally enmeshed in the dialectic of Enlightenment? Did they not both manifest reason and myth at the same time? While expressionists emphasized the process of form-generation, functionalists, too, pursued organic principles as the way to supersede mechanistic rationality, although filtered through engineering. Few in architecture followed Freud's search for reason, for understanding the interplay of conscious and unconscious, ego and id, waking and dreaming.

Strangely, the antagonism of formal systems continues to structure architectural discussion today and is registered in competing approaches to concrete. On the one hand, Kazuyo Sejima and Ryue Nishizawa of SANAA continue to employ the Dom-ino system, usually with simple or slightly inflected geometries in plan, pushing its material logic to extremes of thinness and transparency. | fig. 10 Many other firms, large and small, use concrete planes, columns, and tubes in the spirit of the modern tradition that Giedion promoted at midcentury as a new vernacular for industrial society. On the other hand, Zaha Hadid and many others—Coop Himmelb(l)au, Toyo Ito, UNStudio, Asymptote, Daniel Libeskind, and Santiago Calatrava—treat concrete as an inherently plastic material to be shaped at will, like clay, into forms that are irregular, complex, and often hybrid. | fig. 11 New computational tools have made their work easily mathematized, buildable, affordable, and increasingly pervasive. Leveraging celebrity fame and the globalization of practice, many of these firms have likewise grown to corporate scale, seeking to become at least as pervasive as the rigorists.

As this kind of experimental and highly individuated work enters mainstream development, mutations are emerging with greater frequency. Frank Gehry's InterActiveCorp building in New York (2007) achieved its wavelike forms, not with concrete shells but with rather minor inflections of the Dom-ino system's orthogonal frame, relying on shaped glass to produce its complex forms. | fig. 12 Tall buildings, such as the Infinity Tower in Abu Dhabi by Skidmore, Owings & Merrill, have become a favorite vehicle for architects to experiment

with mutating normative structural systems to achieve plastic expressivity.

In his book *Liquid Stone: New Architec-ture in Concrete*, Jean-Louis Cohen outlines a host of dichotomies that concrete has both sponsored and participated in. Expanding on the notion that both rigorists and expressionists alike have employed organic analogies, he writes:

> The first model [Perret's rationalist cage] used finite vertical and horizontal elements assembled to produce a rigid concrete frame that evoked animal skeletons or vegetal stems. The second model [Niemeyer's lyrical shells] used continuous single- or double-curvature surfaces to produce thin vaults that evoked shells or membranes. [6]

Cohen calls the opposition between these systems simplistic and commends instead the hybridization pioneered by Perret, in collaboration with his brother Gustav, in their Notre Dame du Raincy church (1922–3), with its columnar, grid-and-shell roof. Of course, many more hybrids of this kind could be identified—just think of the work of the Manichean, Le Corbusier—but is it possible to go beyond dualisms all together?

Certainly that is one of the promises of parametric design, which has become so central to design research in recent years that Patrik Schumacher delivered a manifesto for *parametricism* at the Dark Side Club during the opening of the 2008 Venice Biennale. He calls parametricism the "great new style after modernism" and suggests that, following a long wave of research and innovation, it has now "achieved pervasive hegemony."[7] The great virtue of parametric design is continuous differentiation within an otherwise uniform formal system, the results of which are systemic and unique, simple and complex, one and many.

The use of parametric tools and thinking was prompted initially by architects, like Norman Foster, wanting to make complex two-dimensional surfaces for facades and roofs, such as the glass roof over the courtyard at the British Museum, and then progressing into three-dimensional forms

fig. 10 | "Bildraum S104," by Walter Niedermayr, 2006

fig. 11 | Phaeno Science Center, during construction, by Zaha Hadid Architects, Wolfsburg, Germany, 2003

fig. 12 | InterActiveCorp, during construction, by Gehry Partners, New York, 2007

fig. 14 | Palazzo della Sport, by Pier Luigi Nervi, Rome, Italy, 1958–59

fig. 13 | *dune*house, parametric study, by su11 architecture + design, commissioned by the Vitra Design Museum for Open House: Architecture and Technology for Intelligent Living, 2007

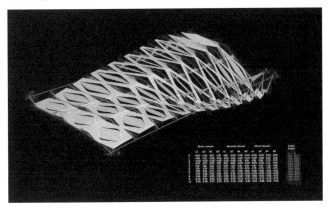

fig. 15 | Unbuilt cathedral, by Pier Luigi Nervi, New Norcia, Australia, 1959–61

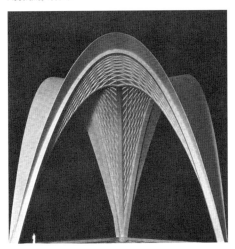

fig. 16 | Glass Pavilion, construction drawing showing the concrete structure of the cupola, by Bruno Taut, for the German Werkbund Exhibition, Cologne, Germany, 1914

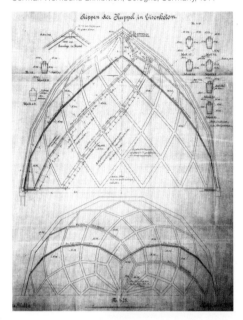

fig. 17 | *Architecture: Its Natural Model*, by Joseph Michael Gandy, 1838

like his famous Gherkin tower in London, where the structure remains relatively conventional and the complex form is achieved once again by shaping the glass envelope.

More recently, younger architects such as Ferda Kolatan and Erich Schoenenberger of su11 architecture + design have explored the potential of parametric three-dimensional structures, which offer a more synthetic way of merging the systematic and the plastic. Their *dune*house for the desert of Nevada was commissioned by the Vitra Design Museum for Open House: Architecture and Technology for Intelligent Living, an exhibition in 2007. | fig. 13 Inspired by the root of a cactus, the designers used Bentley Systems's Generative Components software to extrapolate two-dimensional pattern into a three-dimensional, buildable, and occupiable structure. Their digital model is sufficiently robust and malleable to incorporate all the formal inflections needed to accommodate the functions of domestic life (kitchens, bathrooms, closets, furnishings) and to achieve environmental performance appropriate to local ecology, and also exist as a realizable structure.

Research like this might be seen to follow some of Calatrava's recent work with precast concrete, such as the Valencia Science Center (2000), although this project does not incorporate the variation and customization of components that Kolatan and Schoenenberger seek.

For them, it was Pier Luigi Nervi's work in the 1940s and '50s that showed the way. His Exhibition Hall in Turin (1948–49) and the Palazzo della Sport in Rome (1958–59) used complex precast forms to create intricate patterns and structures of almost hypnotic beauty. | fig. 14 His design for an unbuilt cathedral in New Norcia, Australia (1959–61) already demonstrated that the sizes and shapes of the units could be varied to create complex curvatures. | fig. 15

An even earlier example of this may be found, surprisingly, in Taut's familiar Glass Pavilion of 1914. | fig. 16 While known for its play with glass, the structure is, in fact, concrete, including a cupola of tiny reinforced-concrete ribs, which, as in the work of Nervi and su11, was inspired by

natural models. With Taut's project, we come back to the topic of glass architecture; for Taut and Paul Scheerbart, this encompassed not only glass but other synthetic materials, including concrete and iron, and a host of other new technologies.[8] For Scheerbart, such advances promised to achieve a second nature with which to remake the crust of the Earth, neither in opposition to nature nor in domination of it, but as an extension of it in the sense suggested by Schinkel. It was an optimistic vision of designers learning from nature in order to re-enchant a world that had been disenchanted by science and technology, not by rejecting it but by superseding the opposition of mechanical and organic in a new paradigm that would later be called *biotechnic* or *bionic*.

While parametric design may indeed yield a synthesis of the dialectic of rigor and expression, perhaps it would benefit from being released of that burden, freed of the dialectics of form, even residual ones, and resituated within a much larger, more diverse and polymorphous field of architectural research and experimentation. If we follow Goethe's monistic parallels between human and other natures, might we not leave behind entirely the habit of mind that turns events into categories and pitches them against one another in such reductive ways? Perhaps it would be preferable to explore more freely the world depicted by Joseph Michael Gandy in 1838 in his image *Architecture: Its Natural Model*, updated to incorporate contemporary understandings of living processes and the dynamics of continuously constitutive behavior. | fig. 17

In that world, we might find that mutability is already pervasive. We might also find glorious puzzles, inspiring paradoxes, and unfathomable totalities that caution against claims to definitive knowledge or formal systems, even parametric ones. We might even find that some of the most remarkable things in the world have already been made through human ingenuity, including concrete, whose plastic logic seems entirely at home here, producing unending variations, adaptations and transformations, and refusing to be pinned down.

1 | Sigfried Giedion, *Building in France, Building in Iron, Building in Ferroconcrete*, trans. J. Duncan Berry (Santa Monica, CA: the Getty, 1995).

2 | See Srdjan Jovanovic Weiss, "Evasions of Temporality," in *Urban Transformation*, eds. Ilka and Andreas Ruby (Berlin: Ruby Press, 2008), 208–17.

3 | Barry Bergdoll, "Nature's Architecture: The Quest for the Laws of Form and the Critique of Historicism," *Nature Design: From Inspiration to Innovation*, ed. Angeli Sachs (Baden: Lars Müller Publishers, 2007), 46–59.

4 | Julius Vischer and Ludwig Hilberseimer, *Beton als Gestalter* (Stuttgart: J. Hoffmann, 1928).

5 | Manfredo Tafuri, *Architecture and Utopia: Design and Capitalist Development*, trans. Barbara Luigi La Penta (Cambridge, MA: MIT Press, 1976); and Manfredo Tafuri and Francesco Dal Co, *Modern Architecture*, trans. Robert Erich Wolfe (New York: H. N. Abrams, 1979).

6 | Jean-Louis Cohen, "Modern Architecture and the Saga of Concrete," in Jean-Louis Cohen and G. Martin Moeller Jr., eds., *Liquid Stone: New Architecture in Concrete* (New York: Princeton Architectural Press, 2006), 23–24.

7 | Patrik Schumacher, "Parametricism as Style—Parametricist Manifesto," http://www.patrikschumacher.com/Texts/Parametricism as Style.htm.

8 | See Detlef Mertins, "Bioconstructivisms," *Engineered Transparency: The Technical, Visual, and Spatial Effects of Glass*, eds. Michael Bell and Jeannie Kim (New York: Princeton Architectural Press, 2009), 33–38.

Concrete: Dead or Alive?

Sanford Kwinter

Concrete is an extraordinary material that depending on use can impart the nobility of stone or the humbleness of timber, adobe, or tin. It exhibits the strength and obduracy of stone and the flexibility and robustness of steel, yet it begins its life as a liquid, a river—slurry that is flowed into form and place. Its components are carried by water, which also provides the substrate and medium for the mysterious chemical processes and interactions that, following the curing process, lend its astounding and sudden emergent strength. Concrete is a composite of grains, fluids, gases, and solids of widely different sizes and sorts. It generates and emits heat—the telltale sign of a secret metabolism—and a wide variety of effects and behaviors during its short, prefossilized life. It is a hybrid material that defies classification. Is it colloidal; is it held in suspension? Is it a precipitate, mineral, cement, metal, or organic compound? Or, is it just a strange state of water, since the water one mixes into it remains there, never to be released. No matter, the process works; the material performs. Concrete is tunable, modifiable, specifiable, customizable, and programmable. Indeed, as one philosopher (to whom we will later return) would say, it is a material that endlessly passes out of phase with itself. Concrete is always definable in gradient; even as it ages, it never ceases to grow stronger. Its "being" is trapped in the throes of an endless cure. It responds to modification, signaling, or input by generating its own signals, a range of qualities. I don't understand this change. Is it correct? Experienced workers are known to taste the flowing admixture to identify what stage of development it is in and what properties the hardened end product will bear. Alas, the concrete to which we refer when we picture it to ourselves (and hold conferences about it) is only a very precise and limited phase of concrete's rich life cycle. The phase following hydration is a largely but not completely inert one, a twilight of strict performance, determined by intelligences scarcely understood but empirically encoded into it—the product of decades, perhaps millennia of mostly folk knowledge. It represents, in fact, a bonafide alchemy. I use the term *millennia* here in deference to steadily mounting evidence that the Great Pyramids of Giza are themselves products of cementitious operations and sciences, and not the stone-cutting and hauling efforts as legend has it.[1] But the point I wish to make first is that concrete remains largely a mystery in terms of the details of why it works and how it acquires, then exhibits, the properties it has. And yet, in this, it is no different than the even more common empirical practice that long predates it and serves at the center of daily life: cooking. Similarly, we know next to nothing about the chemistry of the culinary arts, and yet our best chefs achieve levels of precision, originality, and greatness that borders on witchcraft. (Even the well-known Maillard reaction, first isolated no earlier than 1910, continues to undergo refinement, elaboration, and controversy today.[2]) There are also many incompletely understood variables that determine the outcomes of concrete. The fact that concrete owes everything to its fluid, or rather its rheological phase, and especially to water as its necessary vehicle and substrate, alerts us to the fact that for at least one phase of its life it may be just that: a protolife of sorts, like our own living tissues, dependent on the mysteries of electrical bonds, organic chemistry, and nested gradients of order and disorder.

Yet concrete is a thoroughly technological material, more rational than any board or worked metal. In fact, concrete belongs to the same technical world that gave us the first metallic alloys, and with these, the first knowledge that certain mixtures produce properties that are not reducible to those found in their component parts. Many of the mysteries of concrete belong rightly, and perhaps only, to the metallurgical laboratory and arts. Or, perhaps these mysteries will be unlocked by the wet labs of biochemistry. African termites, for example, produce a compound by mixing their saliva and excrement with sand to build cooling towers that approximate the strength and qualities of concrete. | fig. 1

Even in its dry, hardened, post-rheological phase, concrete—more specifically, ferroconcrete—continues principally to manage and administrate flow. Concrete hides within itself not only the reinforcing bars that supply its tensile integrity but infinite micropathways and routes of loads that travel freely to its various ground points, just as an electrical charge propagates and then tunnels through the atmosphere in a thunderstorm. The following image is a beautiful example of how so-called inert and homogeneous matter manages the more accurate reality of distributed differences transiting through it. | fig. 2

It is true that concrete, from its inception, was principally conceived as a kind of ductile and programmable stone, but its labile chemical nature soon lent it to the operations, control, and specification of civil and chemical engineers. In recent years, a further set of determinations has taken hold of it. An important one is the extension of its latent properties by incorporating electronic and electromechanical components, so that the ripe transmissive activity taking place invisibly inside of it has increasingly come to be expressed in feedback loops and communicative channels; concrete is not only a highly active material but it is becoming rudimentarily sensate. Another development to which I would like to briefly call attention in more detail is the new determination, whose accompanying transformations of uses and formal languages are drawn from the biological sphere.

It is arguable that new design motifs are emerging from the evolving marriage between modifiable materials and numerical techniques and control. I will limit my consideration to what could be called *osteomimicry*, which entails an espousal of the unusual logic of the biological structural members we call bones. Two examples are the coming Taichung Metropolitan Opera House by Toyo Ito & Associates | fig. 3 and the Shenzhen Bao'an International Airport by Reiser + Umemoto | fig. 4 as well as their O-14 office building currently under construction in Dubai. I hold these to be among the defining buildings of the present era, on par perhaps with Frank Lloyd Wright's Guggenheim Museum (1956–59) during its era. Both Ito and Reiser + Umemoto deploy an anticlassical, nonmetaphoric, nonanthropomorphic approach

to the perennial skeleton theme, in which structural parti is no longer conceived as torque- and load-bearing rigid members, interconnected with joints and relays to form a cooperative self-sustaining whole; in other words, as derivations of post-and-lintel tectonics, abetted with performing skins and musculatures. On the contrary, the structures are conceived "of a piece," as unitary, essentially componentless entities that manage and distribute forces in the manner of a single osseous structure or bone. | fig. 5 As it turns out, according to biomechanical research of the last five to ten years, bone is a complex and dynamic cementitious element, diverse in its deployment of structures, enormously active, plastic, malleable, and fully and absolutely alive.

The remainder of my presentation is drawn from the work of a former student, Ned Doddington, who developed these themes in research in form during an independent study course with me in 2006. The structures we focused on were part of the bone matrix known as *trabecular* or networked and spongiform bone (the prefix "trab" derives, ironically, from "beam," as in *trabeated*). Recent work in biomechanics has sought to reverse the nineteenth-century model of bone as a static material arranged for optimal handling of mechanical stresses and loads. Today, attention has turned to two other structural aspects embodied in the term *lacunocanalicular*, with "lacuna" referring to the distribution of holes or cells to describe its porosity and "canalicular" referring to the network of channels and blood vessels that permeate trabecular bone and that drive both its shape and evolving performance in a variety of unexpected ways. In an article titled, "Whither Flows the Fluid in Bone?" a prominent biomechanic presents bone as a porous composite composed of a fluid phase, a solid matrix, and cells (intelligent manufacturing centers); she proceeds to demonstrate how forces from within and without the bone cause fluid to move or pressurize and, in so doing, to transmit chemical and biomechanical signals to receptor tissues and organs, which respond by continually remodeling the matrix.[3] In this way, the lacunocanalicular network continually processes load-input from the environment,

fig. 1 | A *Macrotermes* mound, Okavango Delta, Botswana

fig. 2 | From "Visible Signs of Strain," *The Engineer*, C. C. Furnas, Joe McCarthy, and the editors of *Life*

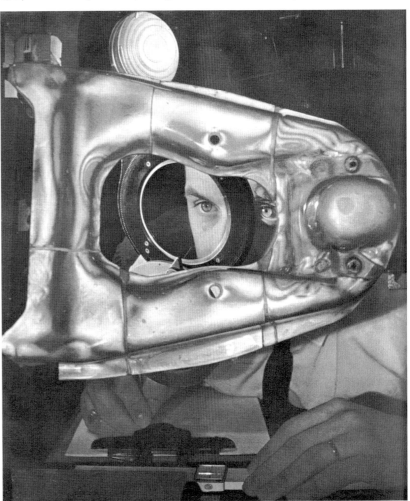

fig. 3 | Taichung Metropolitan Opera House, competition model, by Toyo Ito & Associates, Taichung, China, 2005

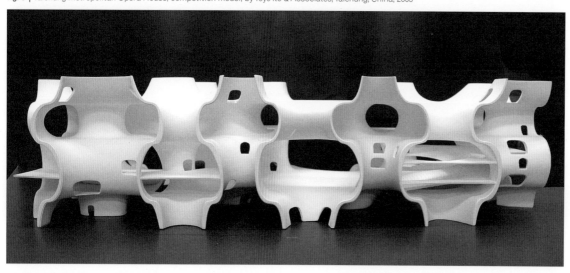

fig. 4 | Shenzhen Bao'an International Airport, by Reiser + Umemoto, Shenzhen, China, 2007

fig. 5 | O-14, perforated concrete shell under construction, by Reiser + Umemoto, Dubai, United Arab Emirates, 2009

fig. 6 | Catenary study (left) and section through a human femur, by Reiser + Umemoto

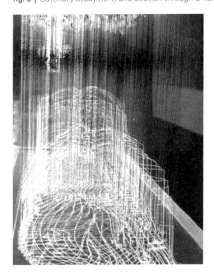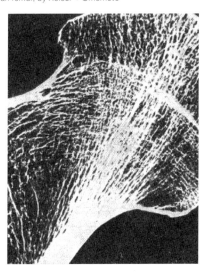

fig. 7 | Schematic diagram of the biomechanics of cortical and trabecular bone

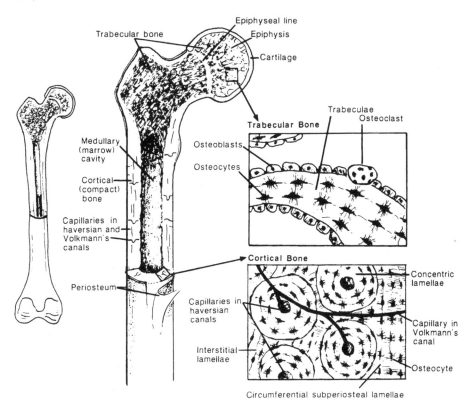

as well as from within. The central role of hydraulics in bone performance is perhaps the most surprising of all (although the system includes significant labor at the cellular and sub-cellular levels, at the level of osteoblasts and osteocytes that serve as sensors and actuators that determine the modifications and self-updating functions of structures). The second most surprising thing is the role played by the network behavior, which not only processes signals but is responsible for everything from armoring and damping functions to filtering solutes from the blood and lymphatic system for use in remodeling the bone, both by addition and by re-absorption of previously deposited solids. | fig. 6 While processes of this subtlety are not yet within the reach of industrial concrete, general reconceptualizations of its possibilities are already underway. (Echoing a term coined by biologist Jacques Loeb, we are entering what one could call a *tropistic stage* in materials science, and furthermore in concrete in general.[4]) In the mislabeled "exoskeletal" projects of Ito and Reiser + Umemoto, one sees a newly integrated structural-material approach; efficiencies are harvested from integral or unitary mold forms, extending the very idea of the cementitious composite to the form and structure (and macroscopic scale) of the building itself. Its performing agents are fully distributed throughout the structure, rather than expressed as distinct components (a direct result of rheological thinking). Second, efficiencies are derived from the foamlike deployment of the matrix, full of empty cells, perforations, and lacunae that both lighten the structure and distribute the stress in a highly manageable way by positing a three-dimensional mesh with internal trusses that simply waits to be thickened or otherwise modulated and have forces assigned to them. | fig. 7 And third is the conception of the trabecular mesh as a fluid and circulatory fabric, capable of transiting information and energy in a highly flexible and efficient way. As in the 45-degree rotated grid in O-14, the carapace operates more as a foam, which is to say, it implicitly operates through the deployment of arches rather than through a network of beams.

Back in the first decade of the twentieth century, Thomas Edison developed an industrial process for foamed concrete. An initial problem in realizing his better-known single-pour concrete houses was to solve an issue of rheology: how to flow the matrix into every nook and cranny, from a single spout, and how to force the slurry to rise upward within a mould under pressure. This specific challenge seems to have been directed primarily at solving the problem of creating concrete pianos; Edison claimed to produce a concrete that was no more than 150 percent the weight of wood and other household materials. | fig. 8 It should be of no surprise that the piano performed poorly in terms of sound, yet this research has hardly been abandoned. Today, researchers at the California Institute of Technology (CalTech) are developing highly springy metal foam, with a view to producing what they call *trabecular metal*. | fig. 9 Virtually all newly developed concretes employ composite recipes such as rubber to impart palpable flexibility and micro-form-imparting processes that, in turn, release novel global traits of concrete expression.

In closing, I would like to return to the philosopher of technology, mentioned earlier in this essay, whose idea of "moving out of phase with itself" served as a defining condition of being: Gilbert Simondon. His principle work, *L'individu et sa Genèse Physico-Biologique: L'individuation à la Lumiere des Notions de Forme et d'Information* (The Individual and his Physical-Biological Genesis: Individuality in Light of the Notions of Form and Information), an immensely rich study aimed principally at expunging Aristotelian, or hylomorphic, thinking from our theory of knowledge. Roughly translated, the aim was to expunge a model of thinking that degraded the putative creativity of matter by continually subjugating it to the idea of the necessity of a superadded agency or form. His contrasting account of the relation between matter and form included an important concept that he called *transductive unity*, which stressed the importance of seeing the unities of our world as including the trajectory of their coming-into-being, or their *formation* as such. In this approach, as he states it, "Notions of substance, form and matter are replaced by the

fig. 8 | Three concrete phonograph cabinets, by Thomas Edison, circa 1912

fig. 9 | Detail of trabecular metal, developed by researchers at CalTech

more fundamental notions of primary information, internal resonance, potential energy, and orders of magnitude."[5] He asks us to abandon the indefensible posture that objects, as they present themselves to the senses and exist in space, are real, and to do so in favor of a broader theory of modalities. The mysterious but dynamic example of concrete therefore provides an object lesson in the theory of knowledge and in the building arts: *it is nothing if not modal in its essence, and this modality is what we must strive to think today*.

1 | Joseph Davidovits, *Ils ont bati les pyramides* (Paris: Éditions Jean-Cyrille Godefroy, 2002). See also Linn W. Hobbs's ongoing experiments at MIT (since 2006) to test the hypothesis that Egyptians used concrete to assemble the pyramids.

2 | A poorly characterized and only partly understood chemical reaction named after Louis Camille Maillard that lies at the basis of nearly all flavors and odors associated with browning processes in cooking. Hundreds of flavor compounds are routinely produced—reactions between amino acids and carbohydrates—that have been used in controlled ways in practical cooking for centuries but have only in recent years begun to be studied in any systematic way.

3 | Melissa L. K. Tate, "Whither Flows the Fluid in Bone?," *Journal of Biomechanics* 36, no.10 (October 2003): 1409–24. (Courtesy of Ned Doddington's research)

4 | Jacques Loeb, "Die Tropismen," in *Handbuch der vergleichenden Physiologie*, bearb. von E. Babák et al., ed. Hans Winterstein (Jena G. Fischer, 1910).

5 | Gilbert Simondon, *L'individu et sa Genèse Physico-Biologique: L'individuation à la Lumiere des Notions de Forme et d'Information* (Paris: PUF, 1964); "The Genesis of the Individual," in *ZONE 6: Incorporations*, eds. Jonathan Crary and Sanford Kwinter, trans. Mark Cohen and Sanford Kwinter (New York: Zone Books, 1993).

Modelmaking Rangers: Form-Makers in Action at Eero Saarinen and Associates

Pierluigi Serraino

Extensive modelmaking informed the last six years of Eero Saarinen's involvement in the design of his projects at Eero Saarinen and Associates (ESA). | fig. 1 From the completion of the General Motors Technical Center in Warren, Michigan, in 1955 until his premature death due to a massive brain tumor in 1961, his practice produced a vastly expanded number of working and finished presentation models at all scales. This shift toward a greater reliance on models in the design process occurred in parallel to Saarinen's embrace of a highly sculptural architecture whose material of choice was poured-in-place concrete. | fig. 2 The factors contributing to this conjunction—between a particular technique of architectural representation and the architect's formal experiments with concrete construction—are multiple and extraordinarily fascinating.

While the extensive use of models as a working method emerges in full force at the tail end of Saarinen's short but intense career, conflicting accounts are available about when such a far-reaching use of models became routine in the firm. Although the D. S. Ingalls Hockey Rink at Yale University (1958) appears to have spurred the production of mock-ups at an ever-increasing rate, other records show that this custom had already gained prominence in the design process before the completion of the General Motors (GM) Technical Center. Thirty models of the water tower at the Technical Center, for instance, were generated before the final version was built. In addition to various study models, full-size mock-ups of its curtain walls were also produced. As early as the late 1940s, full-size drawings of wall sections of the manufacturing plant as well as blueprints of furniture populated the surfaces of Saarinen's office. This practice of assessing design through representations at a 1:1 scale—to study each architectural element both as part of a larger context and as a background for smaller components—was a direct offshoot of the teaching tenets of the architect Eliel Saarinen, Eero Saarinen's father as well as the founder and head of the Cranbrook Academy of Art.

To date, the visual record has been equally scarce. Occasional snapshots of the large cardboard model of the Trans World Airlines (TWA) Terminal at JFK International Airport in New York City taken by the photographer Balthazar Korab during his residence at ESA from 1955 to 1958 have appeared in publications. Our fragmented knowledge of the use of models in the design process at ESA has been greatly expanded by the recent discovery of new photographic sources and personal testimonials of untapped informants. | fig. 3 Invaluable in this regard is a cache of more than 600 photographs of office life at ESA, recently unearthed by architect and author Richard Knight, who as a young designer worked with Saarinen from 1957 until 1961. | fig. 4 The photographs were taken on his own initiative, he recalls: "I am not sure how conscious Eero was, really. It was not part of a public relation scheme."[1] Aline Bernstein Saarinen, the architect's second wife and communication guru for ESA, supported Knight's photography; Saarinen was not always happy to hear the loud clicking of the camera while engrossed in the evaluation of a model. | fig. 5 In reappraising Saarinen's work today, these photographs give an insider's perspective of the office's day-to-day work as it was unfolding, providing a very different image of the architect than was presented in the considerable publicity that Saarinen enjoyed in the media during these years. These new variables add greatly to a reassessment of the legacy of Saarinen, an architect whose critical appraisal still falls outside of the canons of twentieth-century architecture. The images and testimonials also cast light on a design process that has silently but steadily percolated in the signature design practices of our time, which have been committed to form-making with an eye on tectonics. It is with the innovative use of these large-scale models that Eero Saarinen took an adventurous leap in the investigation of compound shapes, whose realization so heavily relied on the formless malleability of concrete. | fig. 6 It was precisely the lack of geometric constraints of concrete that held an irresistible appeal for Eero, who was committed to

fig. 1 | Eero Saarinen

fig. 2 | Steel rebar cage of the sloped supports of Dulles International Airport

Modelmaking Rangers

Pierluigi Serraino

fig. 3 | Simulation of driver's arrival at Washington Dulles International Airport

fig. 4 | Self-portrait of Richard Knight, with the Airport
Traffic Control Tower in the foreground

fig. 5 | Eero reacting to unsolicited picture taking

unraveling the definition of space and construction beyond the ABC principles that Mies gave to modern architecture.

If the endless permutations of boxy volumes could be regarded as the dominant paradigm of the modern movement prior to World War II, organic forms nonetheless appear intermittently in the repertoire of many architects. In the case of Erich Mendelsohn's Einstein Tower in Potsdam, Germany, (1919–21) or in the work of Antoni Gaudí, modelmaking was essential to the design of such organic forms, allowing the formal resolution of the design to be assessed in three dimensions. Yet it was the postwar work of Le Corbusier that marked a renewed engagement with plasticity. In the organic profile of the pilotis as well as in the rooftop of the Unité d'Habitation in Marseilles, France (1946–52), and the chapel of Notre Dame du Haut in Ronchamp, France (1955–56), Le Corbusier actualized a spatial potential that had been fiercely repressed in the dogmatic application of first principles of space-making that characterized the rise of modern architecture. Images of an early study model made of plaster and a more precise wire-and-paper model reveal a process of formal investigation similar to what Eero Saarinen later undertook with the TWA Terminal in New York, a commission earned shortly after the chapel at Ronchamp was completed.

Despite their proximity in time, there is a stark contrast between the Cartesian forms of the manufacturing plants for GM and the fluidity of the concrete shells at TWA. | fig. 7 Metaphorically speaking, following the completion of the GM Technical Center, Saarinen began to chisel space. In his lectures and speeches, he admitted that individual intuition rather than the optimization of the structural scheme drove his designs. One source for this shift could be the early and enduring presence of sculpture in his life. Among his most influential points of contact with the creation of freeform shapes were his studies in sculpture at Académie de la Grande Chaumière in Paris and his experiments in furniture design while at Cranbrook, as well as his father Eliel's friendship with sculptor Carl Milles and his own marriage with sculptress Lily Swann. At Cranbrook he also developed a familiarity with clay

through the ceramist Maija Grotell. Besides sculpture, one can argue that the shift from the orthogonal character of the GM Technical Center to the flowing forms of TWA reflects the impact of concepts of automobile styling on Saarinen's design sensibility. Even prior to his work on the technical center, he had been exposed to the compound geometries of car design and ocean liners through his brief stint with celebrated designer Norman Bel Geddes in 1936, with whom he worked on the Futurama design for GM for the 1939–40 New York World's Fair. As Saarinen would later do in the 1950s, Geddes took on the gargantuan task of conceiving, from the ground up, the formal and plastic expression of movement and modernity in the built environment.

With the death of Albert Kahn in 1942, the automotive industry in Detroit lost its most prized architect. The favorable reception of the Cranbrook campus captivated the attention of the GM executives, who turned to Kahn's friend Eliel to design their compound using similar urban planning principles. Eero progressively took over the design of the complex as his father released control of the practice to his son; Eero's direction was to produce an architecture of precision, in line with the technology that the industrial giant symbolized. At GM he met Harley Earl, the automobile stylist, whose claim to fame was the idea of fusing the discrete mechanical parts of the chassis into a single, continuous form. Through this one-of-a-kind commission, the young Saarinen started working in reciprocity with his client and internalized its engineering and aesthetic practices.

In this process, Earl consolidated Eero's confidence in form-making and deeply affected the design expression of his subsequent work. It was through witnessing Earl's pioneering use of clay models to mold automobile bodies—a practice the competing manufacturing giants quickly adopted—that Eero performed a classic technological transfer from the realm of car design to that of architecture. Both the TWA Terminal and the Tulip Chair embody Earl's concept of blending—in a single suave silhouette—the disconnected components of the frame. The eye, rather than structural reasoning, shaped the

fig. 6 | Formwork for the pouring of the sloped supports of Washington Dulles
International Airport, circa 1961

fig. 7 | The sculptural concrete support for the TWA Terminal, under construction, Queens, New York

fig. 8 | Section model in fiberglass of the TWA Terminal

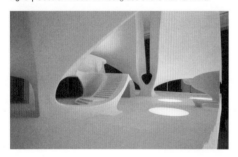

fig. 9 | Model of half of the TWA Terminal held against a mirror to produce the complete shape

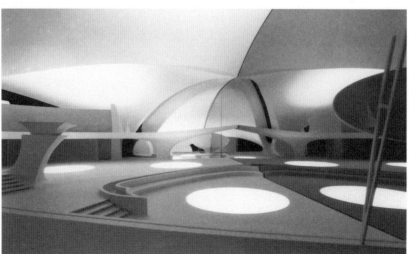

final outcome. Saarinen was interested in the appearance of things regardless of their structural behavior; once the structural demands were taken care of, the oversizing of elements for expressive ends became the leitmotiv of his work. While he admired the Italian engineer Pier Luigi Nervi for his command of form via the logic of building science, formal laws ruled Saarinen's projects.[2]

Intensive modelmaking was used to determine the stretched surfaces of the TWA Terminal. About thirty maquettes of the two columns on the entrance side were made before settling on the final built version. A different office was given the onerous task of producing construction drawings from the models. The organic volumes were transcribed as drawings using the technique of contour lines, a standard system used to produce topographic maps. By connecting points of equal height, these complex forms could be adequately described. The first models were made out of clay, initially red clay and later the gray clay used in the process of automobile design. The next iteration involved models made out of fiberglass. | fig. 8 Since the TWA Terminal was symmetrical, only half of the model was built and a mirror was used to complete the space. | fig. 9 Over the course of the design, the most important model was at a 0.75":1' scale. (It was large enough for a person to crawl inside.) The structural skeleton was cut out of medium-density fiberboard, with the infill made out of convex or concave cutout cardboard strips of different thicknesses. The ribs were fabricated on the basis of sections generated in drawings.

These models accrued at an extraordinary rate, leaving a lasting impression on whoever came by the office.[3] According to Knight, it was Kevin Roche's idea to magnify the scale of the models to enable Saarinen to focus on multiple projects at the same time, something of an imperative for the functioning of the office, as architectural commissions rapidly accumulated after the mid-1950s. | fig. 10 Knight recalls, "The models served every purpose. To build a big model was predicated on some studies having preceded it. Having these models around the office was a marvelous thing to keep Eero engaged." Full-scale

mock-ups were built for the tellers' window of the Irwin Union Bank in Columbus, Indiana; for the exterior wall and office space of the John Deere Headquarters in Moline, Illinois; for the units and the exterior walls of the Ezra Stiles and Samuel Morse Colleges at Yale University; and for the stairs of the Gateway Arch in St. Louis, Missouri, among others. | figs. 11–13

Knight recalls that for Washington Dulles International Airport in Chantilly, Virginia, models were done for the columns, for the bases of the columns, for the layout of the mullions, as well as for the study of how to light the space, something that Eero Saarinen had learned from the TWA project.[4] | fig. 14 Knight also remarked that different scales were used for models that were built for different purposes: 0.5":1' scale models were the smallest; models of 0.75":1' scale were typical for a project such as Dulles; while the largest scale, 1.5":1', were used more for design than for study, such as for the Bell Laboratories interior.[5]

From the TWA project on, modelmaking at the 0.75":1' scale became the norm in the firm's practice for many practical reasons. The models enabled Saarinen to empirically test his ideas and draw reliable findings from them. Despite the fact that they were time-consuming to build, the models enabled decisions to be made quickly, prompting further models to be built. As such, they were surrogates of true spatial statements, where the method of verification could be carried out to its ultimate consequences. Because they required intensive teamwork, models also played a central role in the social dynamics of the office; their social function may have been as important as their status as design aids. Models were created for office parties that contained elaborate settings as well as caricatures of the people being celebrated. Around the models, Eero Saarinen would set up de facto focus groups, asking anyone to express opinions about the merit of every idea and making it part of a public review, even if in the end he was the only one with the power to decide upon the direction of the design. | fig. 15

Despite this sense of community, it was understood that all of the staff had to support Saarinen. Being in Saarinen's

fig. 10 | Kevin Roche holds a model of the Ezra Stiles and Samuel Morse Colleges
for Yale University

fig. 11 | Facade model studies of the Ezra Stiles and
Samuel Morse Colleges for Yale University

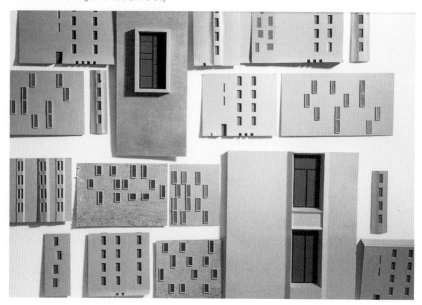

Modelmaking Rangers

Pierluigi Serraino

fig. 12 | Mock-ups of the tellers' windows for Irwin Union Bank in Columbus, Indiana

fig. 13 | Aline Saarinen descends the stairs of the full-size-mock-up for the Gateway Arch in St. Louis, Missouri

fig. 14 | Model of the Washington Dulles International Airport in Chantilly, Virginia

fig. 15 | Inside the office of Eero Saarinen and Associates, Bloomfield Hills, Michigan

fig. 16 | Eero Saarinen inside the model of the Washington Dulles International Airport, circa 1959

fig. 17 | Detail model studies for the John Deere Headquarters

fig. 18 | Fiberglass model of half of the TWA Terminal

fig. 19 | The slanted piers of the Washington Dulles International Airport under construction, Chantilly, Virginia, circa 1961

fig. 20 | TWA Terminal: A metaphor of flight?

fig. 21 | The concrete sheet of the Washington Dulles International Airport under construction, circa 1961

office was already part of a social contract. The employees had to reach Bloomfield Hills and make a concerted effort to move their families there. This logistical test was a powerful mechanism of self-selection for those who would embrace Saarinen's adventure. Even with his closest collaborators, he remained the final arbiter of all design decisions. At a fundamental level, ESA remained a hierarchical organization, using teamwork as an extension of Eero's design power, as opposed to distributed authorship. Even though people in the office were called by their first names, there was no ambiguity whatsoever about who was in command. Nonetheless, candidates eager to become part of Saarinen's office knew that they were about to work under an ongoing regime of charrettes.

Despite its top-down structure, Saarinen's office—under the leadership of both Eliel and Eero—produced a remarkable number of designers: Ralph Rapson, Harry Weese, Edmund Bacon, Edward "Chuck" Bassett, Gunnar Birkerts, Cesar Pelli, Anthony Lumsden, Kevin Roche, and George Matsumoto, among many others. That was not the case for Kahn's firm or Paul Rudolph's. It is not a coincidence that so much talent converged at ESA. While its members felt they were part of the legacy of modern architecture by sheer proximity to Eero himself, the uniqueness of the design exploration, the tour-de-force to meet project schedules per Eero's standards and the collective effort in making these large-scale models—so time-consuming and yet so effective in maximizing the iterative process of form-finding—were the bond that even to this day keeps that community, orphaned of its leader for almost fifty years now, together still. | fig. 16 In concrete, Saarinen saw the potential to challenge universally accepted assumptions in modernist circles about scale, opening, proportion, massing, span, joinery, and order. | figs. 17–19 This plastic architectural language was definitely in formation at ESA. If the TWA Terminal is ambiguous in its final outcome—is it a blown-up Möbius strip? Is it the giant chassis of a car? Is it the caricature of an airplane?—the Dulles Airport displays a remarkable command of design intention. | figs. 20–21 Here the ground condition and the termination of

the building in the sky define the endpoints of a coherent design statement standing on its own architectural terms.

Poured-in-place concrete was for Eero what clay was for Earl. Both designers were so steeped in their own metaphors—flight for the former, speed for the latter—that the formal versatility of the chosen material was the prerequisite to achieving that sought-after dynamism in celebration of postwar technology.

1 | Interview with Richard Knight, March 2, 2007. The author would like to express sincere thanks to Richard Knight and Judith Lynch for sharing their memories and material from their archive.

2 | There are noteworthy parallels between Saarinen's work and the work of Japanese architect Kenzo Tange, both of whom visited each other's offices during these years. Tange's sculptural column at the Golf Club House in Totsuka, Japan, shares some similarities in form with the Terminal. 3 | Aline Saarinen recorded her impression of ESA's office packed with models: "One of the characteristic things about this office is the extensive use of models—rough study models from the very start, up through models of details, and finally a presentation model for the client, the fancy kind that is a child's dream of a landscape for an electric train. Incidentally, the model shop is right in the office, and the model shop men, who are extraordinarily good craftsmen, are respected by everyone." Letter from Aline Saarinen to Cranston Jones of Time magazine, May 2, 1956. Eero Saarinen Collection, Yale University Library.

4 | Interview with the author, March 2, 2007.

5 | Ibid.

Bibliography
Bayley, Stephen. Harley Earl. New York: Taplinger Publishing Company, 1990.
Gartman, David. "Harley Earl and the Art and Color Section: The Birth of Styling at General Motors." Design Issues 10, no. 2 (Summer 1994): 3–26.
Janke, Rolf. Architectural Models. New York: Frederick A. Praeger, Inc., 1968.
Mills, C. Wright. "Man in the Middle: The Designer." In Power, Politics and People: The Collected Essays of C. Wright Mills, edited by Irving Louis Horowitz. New York: Oxford University Press, 1963.
Powell, Tracy. General Motors Styling, 1927–1958. Genesis of the World's Largest Design Studios. Charlestown, IN: Powell House, 2007.
Price, Cathy, ed. Saarinen Swanson Reunion Proceedings. Bloomfield Hills, MI: Cranbrook Educational Community, 2001.
Searle, John R. Philosophy in a New Century: Selected Essays. New York: Cambridge University Press, 2008.
Slaton, Amy E. Reinforced Concrete and the Modernization of American Building, 1900–1930. Baltimore, MD: The John Hopkins University Press, 2001.
Sloan, Alfred. My Years with General Motors. New York: Random House, Inc, 1990.
Smith, Terry. Making the Modern: Industry, Art, and Design in America. Chicago: University of Chicago Press, 1993.

Reinforced Concrete and Modern Brazilian Architecture

Carlos Eduardo Comas

Reinforced-concrete construction was the handmaiden of modernization in the beginning of the twentieth century for many nations lacking a steel industry. Originating in France, Great Britain, Germany, and the United States, it was a global affair from the outset, involving the licensing of techniques and the establishment of subsidiaries in South America by firms such as Hennebique from France and Wayss & Freytag Ingenieurbau from Germany. Expertise was rapidly achieved in Brazil, where reinforced concrete construction was associated with modern architecture since the mid-1930s.[1] Indeed, the history of Brazilian modern architecture can be read in terms of a series of changing attitudes concerning the structural uses and material qualities of reinforced concrete. It can be said that balance and earnestness gave way to different forms of mannerism, from the late 1950s to the 1970s, when criticisms prompted an estrangement that only began to dissipate in the mid-1980s. Most recently, hybrid approaches are suggesting a new and imaginative realism at work.

Early Achievements, 1913–45

The first reinforced concrete building in São Paulo was the seven-story Guinle Building (1913), designed by Hyppolito Pujol Jr. Almost every reinforced concrete structure built after 1924 was designed by engineers such as Pujol, who graduated from the Escola Politécnica in São Paulo, or his contemporary, Emilio Baumgart, who graduated from Escola Politécnica do Rio de Janeiro and trained at the local subsidiary of Wayss & Freytag Ingenieurbau. Baumgart gained an international reputation for the engineering of the A Noite Building (1928), the world's tallest reinforced concrete skyscraper of the 1920s, and the Peixe River Bridge, a pioneering effort in balanced cantilever construction (1930). The Associação Brasileira de Concreto published the first Brazilian reinforced concrete building code in 1931. That same year, Baumgart taught structural design in the architecture course of Rio's Escola Nacional de Belas Artes at the invitation of then dean Lucio Costa. From the appointment of Costa as dean in 1930 to the inauguration of Brasilia as the new capital in 1960, Rio was the base of modern Brazilian architecture, and concrete served as its privileged medium. In the hands of Costa, Oscar Niemeyer, Affonso Eduardo Reidy, the Roberto brothers, and other architects assisted by Baumgart, Joaquim Cardozo, and other engineers, Carioca-style concrete was typically stuccoed or clad and made to appear weightless.

Although built work represents only a fraction of the published projects from 1930 to 1945, it is impressive. The expansion of Rio's central business district in the esplanade, created by razing Castelo Hill, brings about the greatest group of midrise modern office buildings anywhere so far. Baumgart worked on two headquarters that stand out: the crystalline Ministry of Education Building (1945) by Costa, Niemeyer, Reidy, Carlos Leão, Jorge Moreira, and Ernani Vasconcellos, as well as the opaque Brazilian Press Association Building (1939) by Marcelo and Milton Roberto.[2] Both are slab buildings and flat-plate structures that develop the scheme first proposed by Le Corbusier for the Maison Dom-ino project (1915). If the independent skeleton could be considered the normative condition of twentieth-century construction, the normative condition of reinforced-concrete modern architecture was a specific type of independent skeleton with parallel, flat slabs cantilevering over a grid of vertical supports to free both plans and facades.[3]

Dom-ino was a schematic reference rather than a model. Baumgart proposed different solutions for the flat slabs at the Ministry of Education Building, a clever 10-inch (26-centimeter) thick mushroom slab variant spanning 20 by 29 feet (6.16 by 8.85 meters) | fig. 1 ; and at the Brazilian Press Association Building, a 12-inch (30-centimeter) thick waffle slab filled with clay bricks, spanning 22 feet (6.8 meters) square. Moreover, since resistance against horizontal stresses was not an issue in the domestic scale of the Dom-ino scheme, Baumgart's duplication of columns in front of glass bricks in the Ministry Building's public lobby testifies to

fig. 1 | Brazilian Press Association Building, by the brothers Marcelo and Milton Roberto, Rio de Janeiro, Brazil, 1936–39

the Brazilian understanding of modern architecture as quali-fied construction. A generic, geometric, and unitary reason-ing informs the configuration of the grid of supports. Spatial enclosure results primarily from particular topological and circumstantial considerations. Bracing is visually suppressed throughout. | figs. 2–3

This dual logic is made explicit in Rio's Castelo Esplanade through the use of tripartite elevations, whose bases may be expanded or contained in relation to the body of the building but which always display externally apparent columns or colonnades. Colossal colonnades are a recurring feature; they veil shops with mezzanines or public facilities next to imposing, open-hypostyle halls. Brackets connect col-umns to mezzanine slabs; the monumental aura justifies the expense. Balanced symmetries enhance truly porous bases traversed by public routes and articulated with sidewalks. Landscaping and taller colonnades increase the monumen-tality of the Ministry Building. Gridlike concrete sun-breakers shield the mostly transparent bodies. The blank, narrow-end walls and the expanded thickness of the second-floor slab serve as bracing. Superstructures are composed of either setback volumes or a crowning blank band. The vaulted roof of the Ministry Building's auditorium and the curvilinear walls of its water tanks do not detract from the idea of an architec-ture of sheets; rather, they emphasize the plasticity of con-crete, while indicating that the counterpoint of general order and particular circumstance also has volumetric and struc-tural dimensions.

Close to the Castelo Esplanade, the Roberto broth-ers designed a low-rise structure much in the same vein: the Santos Dumont Airport (1947) with Glebe Zaharov as the structural engineer. | fig. 4 The sinuous cutouts of the mezza-nine slab reiterate the interplay of orthogonal norm and cur-vilinear particularity. Curves are wholly absent in Niemeyer's Grand Hotel (1944) at the colonial town of Ouro Preto, where duplex suites obviate the need for elevators. A monopitch tiled roof, trellised balconies, and brown-painted pillars—instead of stone-clad columns—defer to the historic setting and lend

a note of rusticity to the indented volume. Excitement and drama derive from the two- to three-story porous base, whose giant frontal stockade is alternately cut by protuberances and backed by recesses.

A reinforced-concrete butterfly roof, cylindrical stair-cases, and curving screens enliven the dominant orthogonal layout of a yacht club (1940–45) by Niemeyer. A pyramidal composition that evokes an angular cabin cruiser and a cross between Le Corbusier's Maison Citrohan and Maison Errazuris, it integrates a complex of public leisure facilities and equip-ment around Pampulha Lake, designed with structural engi-neers Cardozo and Albino Santos Froufe. A contemporary version of the aristocratic eighteenth-century circuit park, the complex commissioned by then mayor Juscelino Kubitschek anchors a garden-suburb development in Belo Horizonte. The single-story colonnaded dance hall next to the yacht club is all curves and comes across as a circular primitive hut or steam-boat. A box and a drum make up the stately casino, a villa belvedere that recalls Le Corbusier's picturesque Maison La Roche and the spiritual Villa Savoye.

Obvious formal differences between Niemeyer's three buildings reiterate the versatility of the Dom-ino structure, yet parabolic shells shape his Saint Francis of Assisi Chapel, where the facades can be seen as ideograms of spiritual and topographic elevation, while also evoking Maillart's Zurich Cement Hall and Freyssinet's Hangar d'Orly as well as Leon Battista Alberti's triumphal arch at Rimini. Load-bearing, straight masonry walls support the combination of concrete vault and inclined slabs of the golf club, just as they do for the asbestos-cement roofs of Kubitschek House. The latter is an exception to the use of reinforced concrete during this period, similar to the Brazilian Pavilion at the New York World's Fair of 1939 by Costa and Niemeyer, as well as Costa's Park Hotel in Nova Friburgo (1945), done respectively in steel and wood in function of their temporariness.

Brazilians present modern architecture as an inclu-sive proposition. Costa often remarked that two conceptions of form and kinds of beauty therein meet and complete each

figs. 2–3 | Ministry of Education Building, by Lucio Costa, Oscar Niemeyer, et al., Rio de Janeiro, Brazil, 1936–45

fig. 4 | Santos Dumont Airport, by the Robertos, Rio de Janeiro, Brazil, 1942–47

fig. 5 | Copan Building, by Oscar Niemeyer, São Paulo, Brazil, 1951–62

figs. 6–7 | Details of the Copan Building

other.[4] One of them, the *plastic-ideal*, is static, contained like a crystal; the other, the *organic-functional*, is dynamic and blossoms like a flower. In a particular work, either of them may rule alone, prevail, or counteract the other. Ambivalence and diversification enrich the vocabulary and syntax of modern architecture, facilitated by reinforced concrete to a degree that steel and wood cannot match. On the other hand, Brazilians show that the normative Dom-ino-type independent skeleton did not rule out programmatically justified, extraordinary structures; as long as constructional elements kept their essential geometry, even retrograde structures were acceptable when economically justified. Modern architecture appears as a tri-articulated system. Incidentally, slenderness was encouraged at every level, as Arthur Boase observed in the articles he wrote for *Engineering-News Record* after visiting Brazil to report on local practices for the American Concrete Institute.[5] The Brazilian building code for reinforced concrete was much less restrictive than those under which North American engineers were working.

Brio, Bravura, and Brutalism, 1946–75

Modern architecture became hegemonic in Brazil in the years following the end of World War II. São Paulo and Belo Horizonte underwent urban renewal by typological replacement: houses and walk-up buildings gave way to taller structures. The expansion of Rio's urban core continued; Costa's headquarters for the Brazilian Jockey Club (1974) is the outstanding office building of this period.[6] Executed by contractors Christiani & Nielsen, it is a single-loaded corridor perimeter block whose patio is taken up by an eleven-story, steel-framed garage, both crowned by leisure facilities. Yet, housing produced during this period provokes the most excitement. Two buildings draw attention to the bent-slab typology. One is the crescent with a mostly open ground floor that dominates Reidy's Conjunto Residencial Pedregulho (1958), a low-income neighborhood unit in Rio, built with engineer Carmen Portinho.[7] The other is Niemeyer's sinuous, mixed-use Copan Building (1962) in São Paulo, whose cantilevers and horizontal

fins act as sun-breakers, giving the body of the building a striped, stacked appearance.[8] | figs. 5–7

Niemeyer can also stack freeform cantilevers and fins; his rather rustic apartment building in Belo Horizonte (1960) seems to multiply the flat roof of his own house at Canoas Road (1952–53) and nod to Mendelsohn. Or, as in the case of his Eiffel Building (1953–56) in São Paulo, he can appropriate the *patte d'oie* scheme of Le Corbusier's "rational skyscraper." Faceted slab buildings with elaborate wooden shutters were a specialty of the Roberto brothers, such as the Guarabira (1953). At Guinle Park in Rio, Costa and structural engineer José de Azevedo Marques designed as a virtual crescent three apartment buildings, Nova Cintra (1948), Bristol (1951), and Caledonia (1954), combining the impact of a grand gesture with the advantages of repetition and orthogonality.[9]

Some of these formal ideas are really independent of function. Niemeyer's freeform slab became a huge covered plaza with serpentine borders at the Ibirapuera Park Complex (1954) in São Paulo. The same applies to his different variations of V-shaped columns, a clear case of structural organicism. Together with sinuous cutouts, they dramatize the very long and otherwise plain pavilions at that complex, one of which includes a roof supported by inverted, prestressed concrete beams designed by the engineer José Rudolff. Elsewhere, the V-shaped columns are a muscular way of clearing the ground floor in taller slab buildings, be they offices such as the Detran Building at Ibirapuera (1954), apartments such as the Niemeyerhaus in Berlin (1957), hotels such as the one planned for the Conjunto JK in Belo Horizonte (1963) or hospitals such as SulAmerica in Rio (1958). | fig. 8 At the Ibirapuera Oca Pavilion, designed with structural engineer José Carlos de Figueiredo Ferraz, arched cutouts border the cantilevers of a four-story Dom-ino-type structure contained within a 262-foot (80-meter) wide white dome. Not devoid of sci-fi overtones, the dome rises from the ground like an artificial hill, standing out against the straight pavilions nearby. In a first version of the Ibirapuera project that Niemeyer did with Cardozo as engineer, all the pavilions sported a curvilinear exoskeleton,

Reinforced Concrete and Modern Brazilian Architecture

Carlos Eduardo Comas

fig. 8 | Detran Building, by Oscar Niemeyer, São Paulo, Brazil, 1951–54

fig. 9| Brazil-Paraguay Experimental School, by Affonso Eduardo Reidy, Asunción, the Republic of Paraguay, 1952

fig. 10 | Gymnasium, Paulistano Athletic Club, by Paulo Mendes da Rocha, São Paulo, Brazil, 1958

fig. 11 | Guedes Residence, by Joaquim and Liliana Guedes, São Paulo, Brazil, 1968

fig. 12 | School of Architecture, University of São Paulo, by Vilanova Artigas, São Paulo, Brazil, 1961

like the one both men had used to distinguish the Duchen Industries Plant (1951) in the outskirts of the city.

Reidy took the exoskeleton idea to the city of Asunción in the Republic of Paraguay. Realized with straight and raw concrete frames, the Brazil-Paraguay Experimental School (1952) insinuated a new stoicism. | fig. 9 Shortly thereafter, his Museum of Modern Art in Rio (1954) had mezzanine slabs suspended from the frames by steel cables or resting over the inward-inclined branches of the outward-inclined frames. Structural engineers Portinho and Baumgart collaborated. Steel cables fixed to the ground countervail the 72-foot (22-meter) long cantilevers of prestressed concrete beams in the grandstands, designed by Uruguayan architect Román Fresnedo Siri for the Rio Grande do Sul Jockey Club racetrack in Porto Alegre (1959). A different kind of sophistication is found in the palaces and temples of Brasilia. Quasi-figurative peristyles recall caryatids and atlantes. Domes rest effortlessly over a floating platform. Spectacular exoskeletons shelter the theater and the cathedral. Niemeyer and Cardozo pursued an ethereal, anti-monumental monumentality by capitalizing on the hybrid materiality of reinforced concrete. Abhorred by rationalists that denounced these forms as concrete-clad steel, it is, rather, concerned with beauty and wonder—a thoroughly novel and indeed quite appropriate response to the exceptional programs, even if it shatters the delicate balance between the representative and constructional aspects that had been a hallmark of the Carioca style.

Niemeyer settled abroad in the mid-1960s. His French Communist Party Headquarters in Paris (1981) is elegant; the Algerian University of Constantine (1972) is pure bravado. From the start of the 1960s, São Paulo commanded, through the work of architects Artigas, Paulo Mendes da Rocha, Joaquim Guedes, and Lina Bo Bardi—who rejected lightness as frivolity and very much preferred their concrete raw and weighty. Concrete turned into a fetish. Intimately tied to rough-wood formwork, virile straight brutalism became the cutting edge. It added crude severity to the structural rationalism characterizing sports facilities, such as the Gymnasium of the Paulistano Athletic Club (1958) | fig. 10 or Serra Pelada Stadium (1967) by Mendes da Rocha, as well as the Santa Paula Yacht Club (1961) or the Morumbi Stadium for the São Paulo Football Club (1960), both by Artigas. The latter's many schools employ exoskeletons, following Reidy's example. In Mendes da Rocha's houses, such as those built for his family and for his sister's family (1966), or in the house that Guedes and his then wife Liliana built for their family (1968), where horizontal and vertical grids replaced rectilinear and curved plates, the number of point supports decreased and their shapes became more diverse or fused with walls. | fig. 11 The Dom-ino scheme was reinterpreted as a play of virtual planes, with tempered glass panes intimating a radical chic. Prefabrication of all reinforced concrete components was adopted at the Conjunto Habitacional Zezinho Magalhães Prado, the low-income housing project in Guarulhos by Artigas, Mendes da Rocha, and Fabio Penteado (1967), as well as at student and faculty housing projects in São Paulo by Eduardo Kneese de Mello (1961) and in Brasilia, by João (Lelé) Filgueras Lima (1962). Lelé integrated services, structure, and outer envelope in the Camargo Corrêa Towers (1974), exemplifying the new office buildings in the new capital. With the help of Figueiredo Ferraz, monumentality struck once again. The São Paulo Art Museum by Bardi (1968) displays two huge frames and a suspended glass box that impacts, primarily as awesome weight, a clear span of more than 262 feet (80-meters). The mostly opaque School of Architecture of the University of São Paulo by Artigas (1961) is a reinforced concrete shrine for raising thinking architects, in which the identity between inside and outside implies a conceptually transparent architecture. | fig. 12 The austerity of raw concrete within and without was endowed with antibourgeois overtones and symbolic concerns disguised as structural honesty.

New Developments, 1976–2005

An estrangement between Brazilian architects and reinforced concrete became obvious in the 1970s. From 1975 to 1990, structural diversity accompanied a multiplication of geographical bases. Uruguayan engineer Eladio Dieste was responsible for the reinforced brick shells of many central markets, the first and finest of which was built in Porto Alegre (1974), with architects Claudio Araujo, Carlos Fayet, and Carlos Eduardo Comas. Since 1979, Lelé has made extensive use of ferrocement panels in many schools and hospitals in Brasilia, Rio, and Salvador. Severiano Porto builds both his house at Manaus (1971) and the Silves Island Inn (1983) of wood. Hybrid structures of wood and brick characterize the urban equipments of the Caraíba company town in Bahia, such as the schools by Guedes and Marcos Acayaba (1976). Against this general trend, reinforced concrete was central to one of the highlights of the period, Bardi's Pompéia Leisure Center in São Paulo (1986). | fig. 13 The job included the conversion of existing industrial sheds into cultural facilities. The clean, smooth-old concrete trusses contrast with the rough edges of the new concrete towers accommodating the sports facilities. Furthermore, during these years, the prefabrication of concrete components for warehouses, industrial buildings, and shopping centers became a viable business, sometimes taking full advantage of prestressed concrete.

Modern architecture reasserted itself in the 1990s and so did the leadership of São Paulo architects. Concrete cautiously came back into favor. Neither labor nor wood was as cheap as before, but formwork alternatives were readily available. Plywood, plastic, metal, and prefabrication made smoothness a reasonable option. Imaginative realism was the call of the day. Mendes da Rocha fully explored a diversity of solutions. He revitalized cast-in-place concrete in the Keiralla Sarhan Office Building (1984) and in the Aspen Apartment House (1986), as well as in the Brazilian Museum of Sculpture (1988). | fig. 14 Off-the-peg prefabricated components make up his Gerassi House (1988). A room built of square precast panels abuts a staircase in concrete blocks at his Galeria Leme (2004). In Recife, he rented metal-sheet forms to build the waffle slabs of a multilevel garage (2000), and he inserted a cast-in-place structure in colonial ruins to turn a warehouse into a chapel (2005). Steel trusses rest on concrete walls in the São Paulo Forma Store (1987). Mendes da Rocha is not afraid of hybridization, and many houses by an emerging generation of architects are following that lead. Deliberately raw-concrete load-bearing walls next to whitewashed masonry set apart the Slice House, designed by Procter-Rihl Studio in Porto Alegre (2003). Marcelo Ferraz (a former assistant to Bardi) and Francisco Fanucci added a Brutalist-flavored Bread Museum and Bakery School to a wooden mill that they restored and recycled in Ilópolis, Rio Grande do Sul (2008). The use of prefabricated components is a given in new São Paulo State Schools, some of which have been designed by pupils of Guedes or Mendes da Rocha, in partnerships such as Angelo Bucci & Alvaro Puntoni, MMBB, Andrade & Morettin Arquitetos, UNA Arquitetos, and Núcleo de Arquitetura.

As for the centenarian Niemeyer, he is as alive as modern architecture. His recent work has, in many ways, been extravagant and quite controversial, but the Novo Museum in Curitiba (2002) deftly incorporates and recovers a white elephant that he designed in the 1970s, a high school with huge spans and relatively low ceilings. His reputation abroad has grown once again. This 1989 Pritzker Prize winner is truly Brazil's first global architect. Mendes da Rocha, the 2006 Pritzker Prize winner, who is currently designing a new university in Vigo and a museum in Lisbon, could well be the second. Niemeyer's influence can be seen at its most subtle in two major projects by European architects in Brazil. The astylar Iberê Camargo Museum in Porto Alegre by Alvaro Siza (2006) is a skillful exercise in white concrete (outside) and plaster (inside) that can seem figural as much as minimal, forbidding as much as pervious, exquisite as well as muscular. | fig. 15 Rio's still unfinished Music City by Christian de Portzamparc (2002) combines complex auditoria for the Orquestra Sinfônica Brasileira with porosity and inclined supports inside a virtual box. Indeed, allusions found in these two projects are not restricted to Niemeyer's legacy. Both projects help to reinforce awareness of the richness of Brazilian architecture and the rather high standards already set.

fig. 13 | Pompéia Leisure Center, by Lina Bo Bardi, São
Paulo, Brazil, 1986

fig. 14 | Brazilian Museum of Sculpture, by Mendes da
Rocha, São Paulo, Brazil, 1988

fig. 15 | Iberê Camargo Museum, by Alvaro Siza, Porto Alegre, Brazil, 2006

At the same time, the hope of qualifying both ordinary and exceptional construction is much less strong than it once was. The percentage of forward-looking authorial work is even smaller than in the past, notwithstanding the fact that the percentage of the urban population has grown from 41 million people in 1940 to 170 million people in 2000, an increase from 31 to 81 percent of the total population, and Brazil remains a modernizing nation. Be that as it may, opportunities have not really dried up. It does seem that modern architecture has a future in the country, and chances are that reinforced concrete will be very much a part of it.

1 | *Modern* in this text indicates a formal tradition that grew primarily out of Le Corbusier and Mies van der Rohe's work from the 1920s, in opposition to other developments that might also have pretensions of expressing modernity (such as Art Deco), or to the more general sense of modern as contemporary.

2 | Both the Ministry of Education and the Brazilian Press Association Building were designed in 1936. The former was already occupied in 1943, more than a year before the official inauguration. The latter was partially occupied by September 1938, a few months before the official inauguration in May 1939. See "Edição Especial do Centenário," *Jornal da ABI* (Associação Brasileira da Imprensa) 2 (2008): 35.

3 | On the paradigmatic nature of the Dom-ino scheme, see Paulo F. Santos, *A arquitetura da sociedade industrial* (Belo Horizonte: Escola de Arquitetura UFMG, 1961), 160–83.

4 | Lucio Costa, "Uma questão de oportunidade: Cidade Universitária do Brasil," *Revista de Engenharia da Prefeitura do Distrito Federal* 2, no. 4 (March 1937).

5 | See Arthur J. Boase, "South American Building is Challenging," *Engineering-News Record*, October 1944, 121–8; "Building Codes Explain the Slenderness of South American Structures," *Engineering-News Record*, April 1945, 68–77; and "Brazilian Concrete Building Design Compared with United States Practice," *Engineering-News Record*, June 1945, 80–88.

6 | Begun in 1956, the Jockey Club took 18 years to complete.

7 | The Conjunto Residencial Pedregulho project dates from 1946.

8 | The Copan Building project dates from 1951.

9 | The Guinle Park plan was first established in 1943.

Notes on Weight and Weightlessness

Steven Holl

In Lucretius's philosophical poem *De rerum natura* (The Nature of Things) written during the first century BCE, one finds that knowledge tends to dissolve the world's solidity. Lucretius set out to describe the state of physical matter; he warns us at the outset that matter is made up of invisible particles. He is the poet of concreteness, of physical material viewed in its permanent and immutable surfaces, but he tells us that emptiness is as tangible as solidity, and that this emptiness is found by way of concrete material.

At around the time of Lucretius's writing, the primary rim atop the Pantheon's drum was formed of concrete fused with fragments of travertine. The core meaning of this building, however, resides not in the dome or the drum that forms its primary body, but in its space and the light provided by its nine-meter oculus. Always changing, the light tells the time of year and day. It is possible to ascertain the season simply by observing the angle of the sun coming through it. When I was a student, I lived behind the Pantheon for nine months and went into it every morning to try to understand the mystery of its space.

Concrete evokes themes of solidity, but I seek its mystery. Instead of certainty, I prefer doubt. I believe that we are in a condition today wherein doubt is a positive dimension. Instead of substance, I want essence. Instead of mass, value—a reevaluation of all values. Instead of material, ideas. At the end of his life, architect Louis Sullivan is believed to have said that if they were to tear down all of his buildings, it wouldn't matter. It was the idea that counted. Instead of actuality, I look for implication. Instead of denotation, I desire connotation. Instead of being, just suggestion. And in contrast to mass or solidity, weightlessness of meaning.

I always hoped to begin an essay with the periodic table. When you look at the hierarchy of it, the two most prominent elements in the universe are helium (He) and hydrogen (H). These elements make up ninety percent of our existence.

Thinking about mass and weightlessness in a literal way and addressing the four states of matter—solid, liquid, gas, and plasma—the last appears the most interesting to me. Plasma is the state in which certain portions of electrons are freed from their atoms, bringing the state of the atom (or molecule) and its density into focus. Atoms are composed of large amounts of empty space. Imagine the interior of the Radio City Music Hall as a hydrogen atom; the nucleus would be the size of a flea inside the theater. Ninety-nine percent of the atom's mass is squeezed into one trillionth of this volume. As an architect, this comparison helps. What we see as solid is indeed quite empty. Atoms make up everything solid in the world, but they consist almost entirely of empty space.

This essay is organized around seven categories of concrete, which also serve as a way of reading my firm's projects. We have realized several works using concrete, yet when beginning a project, I never begin with concrete as an *a priori* idea. I always start with the particular site, program, and an idea that drives the design; paradoxically, I have found that it is the physical weight of concrete that channels the potential weightlessness of architectural meaning.

Continuous Pour

The first category is continuous pour, and in my work it dates back to 1989 in Fukuoka, Japan. I was terrified to work there; I was afraid of losing control of the details. I had realized a few small projects, and my reputation here in New York up to that point was built in terms of the refinement of detail and the invention of haptic dimensions. I was afraid that, in this large building, I was going to lose it all. I organized the structure around everything other than concrete. The two interlocking concepts were *hinged space*, an idea about rotating walls and an interpretation of *Fasuma* and *Shoji* screens; and *void*

fig. 1 | Void Space/Hinged Space, Fukuoka, Japan, 1989–91

fig. 2 | Spatial Retaining Bars, Phoenix, Arizona, 1989

fig. 3 | Museum of Contemporary Art
Kiasma, Helsinki, Finland, 1992

space, which introduced reflection. In this Void Space/Hinged Space housing project, empty space was key. | fig. 1

You can see in the section of the building that it is more than fifty percent void. There are thirty apartments, all with front doors facing outside. The entire structure is concrete, which was continuously poured, day and night. At a certain point, the Japanese contractors called in panic, saying, "We're up to the fourth floor, and there are thirteen apartments we can't get into." And I said, "Just keep pouring, and you're going to see that thirteen front doors are on the top walkway outside." It was a very interesting process of learning. I began to trust the contractors. The quality of their concrete work was amazing.

While the void spaces characterize the exterior geometry, hinged space is the core idea on the inside. Apartments could be inhabited with flexibility; spaces could shift. The units are still in use today, after fifteen years. We filled the exterior void spaces with shallow water on the south and gravel on the north. The ponds reflect the sunrise, the sunset, and the rain. From the apartments, you can feel the spirit of nodal lines from raindrops filling the void space of the ponds. Sunlight reflecting from the south into voids on the north animates the ceilings with water-rippled light.

A project of continuous pour for the City of Phoenix from 1990 focused on the edge of the city. The aim was to preserve the desert by containing the sprawling city. These spatial retaining bars contained living, working, and recreational areas. | fig. 2

The site's history includes the former presence of the Hohokam Indians, who lived in this desert for 1,000 years. The traces of 250 miles of 30-foot-wide canals are still present, part of the mystery of their civilization. The structure's geometry is analogous to the 30-foot width of the ancient canals. A kind of bent tube of space, they provoke an apparition of an ancient way of life living in harmony with the Earth. At the city's edge, we proposed to scrape the suburban sprawl and return the desert to its pure state by stopping the cul-de-sacs right at that line and building these spatial retaining bars that go down into the ground, and up, defining 180-foot cubic spaces. When the sun is setting or rising, light starts to glow on the bottom side of these bars like an apparition at the edge of the preserved desert.

Continuous pour was also used at the Museum of Contemporary Art Kiasma in Helsinki, Finland, which was completed in 1992. Concrete is the backbone of this building; it forms a double-warped curve. | fig. 3

The rest of the building is composed of a metal structure and trusses, Rheinzink, and channel glass. The concrete curve provides all of the lateral support, right down the center of the building. It is also the curve that you experience as forming the spaces. It is difficult to make a section of this building because it changes every meter. In a sequence moving through the building, there are twenty-five galleries, each with a different type of light. The last and largest gallery is lit from above; light seems to blow the shape open in weightlessness.

Precast

In 1997 the centerpiece north wing of the landmarked building Higgins Hall at the Pratt Institute in Brooklyn, New York, burned down. To create a new infill section, we pulled the floor levels across from the adjacent buildings, which date from the 1850s, to form a dissonant zone and define a new entrance space. We recycled bricks from the old burned-out portion so that the building would rise like a phoenix from its remains. The new structure comes down on six exposed concrete columns. We wanted precast concrete because it is similar to stone; its surfaces are pure and smooth from their metal forms. The pieces, made in Canada, were beautiful.

Inside the building, where the dissonant zone is—and where, from the exterior, the facade breaks—the adjacent floors don't meet. When you walk across the space, suddenly you encounter a ramp, where you have to turn and begin to walk in a direction perpendicular to your origin. From this new perspective, you can see into the garden or the city. The whole addition revolves around this idea of the old floor levels forming a new space. The concrete just supports the weightlessness of a thought; the dissonant zone turns the body in space.

With the addition to the Nelson-Atkins Museum of Art in Kansas City, we needed to break the competition rules. We were competing with six other architects, and the brief required us to build on the north side of the existing museum building. We were inspired, however, by an inscription carved in stone on the facade; it stated, "The soul has greater need of the ideal than of the real." The weightlessness of that thought resonated and provoked us to risk a more ideal solution.

At the completed addition to the museum, there were some dimensions of experimental concrete done with Guy Nordenson's engineering. In the parking garage, there were no beams, but what we called "wave Ts." Precast-concrete parking garages are typically structured with double Ts or a single T. We joined the bottom flanges to make a wave T, spanning 65 feet without transverse beams. These precast elements, weighing 67 tons each, create the special character of that space. The project revolves around complimentary contrast (i.e. the stone and the feather). Light is the key element of the entire project. Through sculptor Walter De Maria's *One Sun and 34 Moons*, light penetrates into the parking garage from above. | fig. 4

Because of the dynamic quality of the sun and water, you can feel the time of day. By the rippled reflections of the sun, you can see when the wind is blowing. Light penetrates even when the pond outside is frozen. The new building is fused with the landscape, emerging as blocks of light. Inside at the fluttering Ts, there is a manipulation to get a mixture of southern and northern light. If you really look at the northern light, it has a bluish tint; southern light is a warm yellow. The fluttering Ts are like musical instruments. The whole experience of the space revolves around these changes in the weightlessness of light. | fig. 5

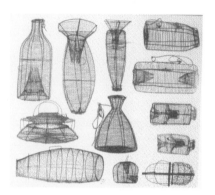

Exoskeleton

My first freestanding building, a house in Martha's Vineyard from 1984, uses an exoskeleton type of structure. At the time I was re-reading *Moby Dick*. Herman Melville describes how the Indians inhabiting the island pull a whale skeleton up on the beach, drape bark and skin on it, and inhabit it. This inspired the exoskeletal frame of the house. Its exposed wooden-frame structure literally determined the grounding of the building on this particular site, yet the analogy is weightless. | fig. 6

For MIT's Simmons Hall dormitory in Cambridge, the main idea was porosity. The original master plan was for a continuous brick wall of dormitories; instead we proposed a maximum porosity structure. The four new dormitories along Vassar Street could have different types of porosity: diagonal, all-over, vertical, and horizontal. The all-over scheme chosen for Simmons Hall was made vertically porous in the common spaces.

The social spaces of the building, the meeting rooms that connect the different houses, are trowelled concrete on ruled surfaces that open to skylights at the top. The building's porosity aims for weightless void spaces.

Notes on Weight and Weightlessness
Steven Holl

fig. 4 | Parking garage, Nelson-Atkins Museum of Art,
Kansas City, Missouri

fig. 5 | Fluttering Ts, Nelson-Atkins Museum of Art

fig. 6 | House at Martha's Vineyard, Massachusetts,
1984–88

fig. 7 | Simmons Hall at MIT, Cambridge, Massachusetts, 1999–2002

fig. 8 | Assembly of precast panels, Simmons Hall, 2000

fig. 9 | Construction view of Linked Hybrid, Beijing, China

It is a prefabricated exoskeleton frame with insulation on the outside. Engineer Ove Arup's analysis of the building showed it was an excellent passive solar wall. the winter sun comes in, but due to the depth of its concrete structural frame, the summer sun stops at the sill. There are many windows that students can open, top and bottom windows (nine total per room) that allow for natural air circulation. We are using the mass of that skeleton as an energy reserve—a kind of flywheel. | fig. 7

The building was built out of 291 pieces of precast concrete from Canada. Every piece was different. There was a single adjustable-steel mold. The rebars and the different sections were shuffled for each piece. Everything was digitally controlled from Nordenson's office and ours in New York. All 291 panels arrived in flawless condition and went into place. It took an average of thirty-five minutes to set each panel. | fig. 8

I wanted color at the microsection; specifically, for the depth between the outside of the perforated concrete frame and the exposed concrete on the inside to indicate the ten dormitory houses so that students could identify where they live. When I met with the committee of advisors and students, they said, "We don't want to be identified from the outside! We don't want people to know where we are as an individual house." I returned to the drawings and saw Nordenson's structural diagram. I thought, why don't we use this structural steel diagram? It indicates number-five bars as blue, number-six bars as green, number-seven bars as orange, number-eight bars as red, etc. By the colors in the microsection you can read the structural forces in the building.

The real porosity has to be activated by the building's use. We positioned the cafeteria on the street. It was the first time MIT built a cafeteria in a dormitory in twenty-five years. It's used by other dorms, like MacGregor, where they only have vending machines in the lobby. Now students can come and get real vegetables. There's a life in this building that I'm very proud of. The weightlessness of the people in the spaces animates the porosity. Like a slice of the city, all these connections are functioning as a social catalyst.

Linked Hybrid in Beijing is another exoskeletal construction, the largest project we've completed to date. We were initially invited to do the facades and I asked the client, "Why don't you aim at a larger vision for this project? Give us a month and a half, X amount of money, and we'll come back with imagination." We added several urban programs: bridges that connect the towers with functions, a teahouse, restaurant, spa, and swimming pool. We suggested a Montessori School kindergarten, landscape mounds with different functions, and a cinematheque floating on its own reflection in a large central pond. They decided they wanted to build it all.

Beijing is very dense. This is not a 1960s street-in-the-air idea. It's a cinematic aerial link. We also designed shops and a dense urban texture lining the whole base of the project. The sky bridges were difficult to engineer due to the city's strict earthquake requirements. They are attached to the towers (and their aperiodic movements) by structural anchors on roller mounts. | fig. 9

Color in this project was taken from the polychromic Buddhist temples of China. We used an aleatory process to organize color within the building and to bring a new mode of chance to the I Ching. For six weeks we worked to locate all the colors in the exoskeleton's deep thickness; these were applied to the window heads and jambs. The idea was for a city within a city, creating a sort of cinematic life of weightlessness and exuberance. For the northern landscape, we envisioned five mounds for the phases of life: the Mound of Childhood, the Mound of Adolescence, the Mound of Middle Age, the Mound of Old Age, and the Mound of Infinity.

A Montessori School is located in the Mound of Childhood. The Mound of Adolescence holds a basketball court and a rollerblade and skateboard area. In the Mound of Middle Age, there is a teahouse, a t'ai chi platform, and two tennis courts. The Mound of Old Age is occupied by a wine tasting bar. The most mysterious, the Mound of Infinity, was made from two incisions in the rise.

I gave the owner and contractor a drawing of a very simple stone floor with circles representing different galaxies.

The idea was to abstract the organization of a galaxy. The entry circle is the Milky Way, which is 10,000 light years across and 100,000 light years in diameter—a ratio of 1:10. There are many other galaxies and many other circles cut through the concrete; these circles of light animate this meditation space. | fig. 10

The entire project is geothermally heated and cooled, and there are 660 geothermal wells. As of the time of construction, it was the largest geothermal installation in China. All 750 apartments have two plumbing systems that form the basis of an integrated greywater treatment system that feeds all the pond and landscaping water. Water shortage is a very serious problem in Beijing. The central pond is a huge body of recycled water. There is enough water in these apartments to easily fill this pond all year round, to keep it refreshed, and to irrigate the gardens. We even had enough left over to flush the toilets with recycled water. With greywater recycling, when you have enough building mass, it really does work. As with the geothermal wells, 660 at a 100 meters deep, there's an economy of scale.

One aim of the World Design Park Complex competition was the fusing of architecture, landscape architecture, and urbanism. It's a great public park in the center of Seoul, Korea, which is a very dense city. The project is to replace a couple of underused football stadiums. Our idea was to make a park with at least two or three layers. The brief indicated that several functions had to be located in the park. I thought, nothing is worse than having a park with these function pavilions. An ancient city wall had to be indicated; we shaped it as a glass passage.

The entire project is a triaxial weave, a composite structure with post-tensioned concrete. Functions that would have become pavilions instead form an armature that fuses landscape, architecture, and urbanism into a new texture—a park with several layers and with a vertical turning that extends vertically, with exhibits about the extinct flora and fauna of Korea. | fig. 11

Shotcrete

Shotcrete is a kind of concrete that saves one side of the formwork. While we were working on the Bellevue Arts Museum in Bellevue, Washington (a suburb of Seattle), the contractor said, "We can save 250,000 dollars if you eliminate one side of the formwork and just shoot concrete on with a sliding form." At the time, this was the largest shotcrete building in Seattle. The outer structure forms a very strong backbone for the building, with just a few little columns inside. Seattle has one of the heaviest earthquake zones, but this building will easily take a level-nine earthquake (on the moment magnitude scale) via the lateral shotcrete walls on the perimeter. The concept is *tripleness*: that is, there are three kinds of functions in three layers, topped with galleries of three kinds of light. Tripleness is weightless.

Tilt-Up

An early inspiration for tilt-up is the Kings Road House by Rudolf Schindler, where the slabs were tilted by hand. With today's powerful cranes, the tilts can be much larger. A large tilt-up structure from 1997 was for the Chapel of St. Ignatius at Seattle University. The driving idea was seven bottles of light in a stone box. There are sixty different nationalities that attend the university. We wanted the central idea to have two meanings, a double entendre. These different nationalities could be represented as a gathering of different lights. The seven main liturgical programs of the Jesuits—the Procession, the Blessed Sacrament, the Choir, the Narthex, etc.—could also be represented. This led us to the notion of seven bottles of light in a stone box.

As the project developed, we couldn't afford stone. Together with the contractor we considered tilt-up on a giant scale with penetrating stain. The project involved the erection

Notes on Weight and Weightlessness

Steven Holl

fig. 10 | Construction view of the Mound of Infinity, Linked Hybrid

fig. 11 | Model view, World Design Park Complex, Seoul, Korea, 2007

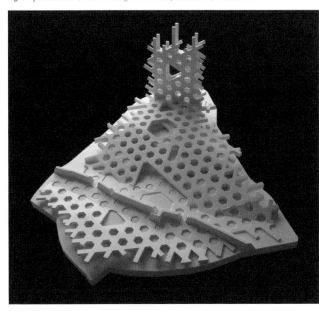

of the largest piece of tilt-up that's ever been done on a university campus— a piece that weighed 80,000 pounds. We gave expression to the nature of a large concrete tilt-up. There are pick-points on the concrete slabs, located to balance the crane as it lifts the 80,000 pounds, which are expressed afterwards on the outside of the building as bronze caps. The expression of pick-points was controversial. When I met with the campus ministry, they said, "We like those bronze caps, but can't we adjust and move them around?" I said, "No, they balance the weight. They're exactly where they have to be, otherwise we can't pick up the slabs." | fig. 12

The walls of the building went up in eighteen hours. It was like an apparition. Kids riding their bicycles across the campus would suddenly stop in amazement, looking at a chapel that wasn't there yesterday. Father Sullivan said, "That's how it should be!" During the planning, the contractors came to the table with all of these charts and schedules. Father Sullivan calmly pushed all the paper aside, and said, "I'm not looking at any of this. It shall be ready on Easter." And it was.

The tectonic essence is expressed in the windows as a result of the interlock of tilts. The notion of light is amplified by the quality of the space and the sound within it. Acoustically the curves make the space much harder. The key to the geometric section is to make the curves focus below or above earshot. The acoustical engineer said, "I have to resign. You have to use acoustical plaster on those vaults or I'm going to lose my job. I'm going to be sued." I said I would take responsibility for the acoustics. We used scratch coat plaster. The sound turned out perfect for chamber and choir music, just under two seconds reverberation time. The sound is weightless. | fig. 13

While this structure is very heavy, the main idea of seven bottles of light is weightless. The phenomenon of complementary colors is experienced when you look at a yellow light, close your eyes, then look at a white sheet; you see blue. Each one of these bottles has a lens color the opposite of the field color. A blue field has a yellow lens. A green field has a red lens. A purple field has an orange lens.

I thought the first event that would happen in the chapel would be a mass, but there was a death on the campus; a funeral was held instead. I remember reading that when you die, when life leaves your body, it weighs the same. Whatever life is, it's weightless.

The Planar House in Paradise Valley, Arizona is also a tilt-up concrete structure. The scheme had solar collectors and natural ventilation, as well as cool pools embedded in the floor slab. The concrete yields good thermal mass in the desert. Vertical light towers rise over the pools, expressing the fusion of coolness with thermal mass, wind, and light.

Form Textured

For the competition for the Swiss Embassy Residence in Washington DC, we began with a site visit and noticed a diagonal line through the site that lines up with the Washington Monument. I remember my first view of Switzerland, from a train when I was nineteen. There were charcoal mountains and white ice and snow. I wanted to capture that rough charcoal and white. We set rough, board-form charcoal concrete in contrast with channel glass in different shades of white, both transparent and translucent. A cruciform plan, set in a precinct of a very simple courtyard, is cut with a diagonal that connects to the Washington Monument.

We won a competition for the Herning Center of the Arts in Herning, Denmark. The existing building was a former shirt factory in the shape of a shirt collar. The museum houses the largest Arte Povera collection in Scandinavia, including over twenty-five works by Piero Manzoni, who worked in Herning with cloth and textiles. Our idea was to make simple rectangles out of the two treasure houses of their galleries and lay shirt-sleeve-like elements over them to form the light-gathering ceilings. | fig. 14

Notes on Weight and Weightlessness
Steven Holl

fig. 12 | Corner detail, Chapel of St. Ignatius,
Seattle, Washington, 1994–97

fig. 13 | Interior, Chapel of St. Ignatius

fig. 14 | Interior, Herning Center of the Arts, Herning, Denmark, 2005–09

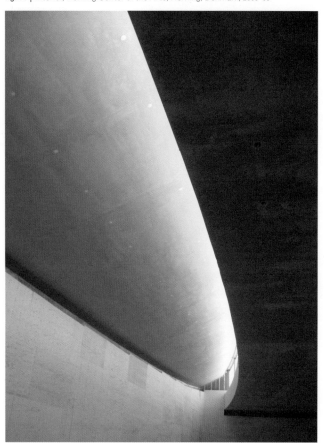

fig. 15 | Detail of concrete, Herning Center of the Arts

fig. 16 | Detail of concrete from bamboo formwork, Nanjing
Museum of Art and Architecture, Nanjing, China, 2003–10

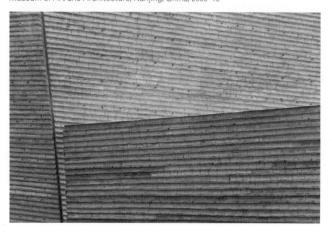

The permanent collection and the temporary exhibition space in the boxes can be closed and everything else, the cafe and auditorium, can be accessed and used after hours. At the galleries, sleeves of light fall over the top. We used truck tarps to line the exterior concrete forms in order to give the fabric texture, connecting back again to the works of Manzoni. | fig. 15 The collection contains his greatest work, *Socle Du Monde*. The weightlessness of the architecture connects to his art. He also canned his own shit as art. Very amazing, crazy, wonderful spirit. A spirit of the weightless.

The Nanjing Museum of Art and Architecture also experiments with form-lined textures that have a connection to the City of Nanjing, which was once the capital of China. It's part of an exhibition site with several buildings organized by Arata Isozaki. It was our first project in China. We began thinking about the fundamental, historic difference between Western and Chinese painting. After the thirteenth century, Western painting developed vanishing points and fixed perspectives. Chinese painters, although aware of perspectives, rejected the single-vanishing-point method. Instead, they were producing landscapes with parallel perspectives, in which the viewer travels within the painting. Shifting viewpoints, layers of space, expanses of mist and water—all characterize the deep, alternating mysteries of the composition of Chinese painting.

The first thought was that there would be a space of warped perspectives that would reach back to the City of Nanjing. Everything in the base and entry courtyard has a projected axonometric condition. A lightweight lanternlike element—the architecture model gallery—rises above and turns to look at the city in the distance.

Begun in 2005, it has been under construction now for over three years. I went to the site a number of times and I said, "Where are the builders?" And a man said, "They live over there." I saw a family of two men, one woman, two little kids, two chickens, and a dog. I was told that they were all working on the building! On the site, there was wonderful old bamboo that we had to remove. We inserted it in the

formwork, and you can see this great concrete texture that the building will have. This was the first bamboo-formed concrete building in China and was already copied before it was completed. | fig. 16

The structural frame that's coming down on two columns was the hardest thing; it's so asymmetrical. The mystery of "How is that standing up?" is a very exciting thing to achieve. Arriving from Nanjing and looking back at the building, the structure marks the entrance gate for the rest of the complex. That entire structure of white steel, with Nordenson's two columns, was installed for 300,000 dollars. (In the United States it would be three million dollars). The latitude with which you can experiment in China is really interesting because of the enormous difference in costs.

Cable Stay with Concrete Frame

In 2006 we won the competition for the Vanke Center in Shenzhen, China, the fastest growing city in planetary history. Since 1982, Shenzhen's population grew from 8,000 to 12 million. The average age is 26. Our site is on the bay looking at the South China Sea. Instead of four or five buildings, we imagined the complex program could be made into one elevated structure, embracing the horizon of the sea. The elevated structure is as long as the Empire State Building is tall.

All of the ground area below—a tropical landscape—becomes public with inhabited mounds, cafes, restaurants, and an auditorium. The building code allowed for a building up to 35 meters high on the site; at this height we get ocean views for all parts of the program.

The client had several failed competitions from a program that had proposed a hotel building, an office building, and the Vanke Center. We thought, "Why not combine everything? Then if you want to make the Vanke Center larger, move the partitions over; if you want to make the hotel larger, move the partitions." To this day, they're still moving these partition lines. They can never decide how much of this or how much of that. A microclimate is created below the building. It was 90 degrees in July when I was there. There was a cool breeze at ground level.

After we won the competition on July 29, 2006, I went during the first week of November to Shenzhen's planning department, which is one of the most progressive planning departments in the world. They have a 3-D wrap-around cinematic theater. You design a building, they plug it into the city, and show it to you. They tip the view up, and they say, "Would you like to go this way, or that way?" We received the building permit for this horizontal skyscraper in ten days. The structure was designed by Dr. Xiao Congzhen, the engineer who rose to the challenge of the 50-meter span. | fig. 17

The Vanke Center combines a cable-stay system, like the system used in cable-stay bridges, with a concrete frame. The cable-stay system maximizes the structural capacity of steel in tension, while the concrete frame maximizes compressive capacity. The photo shows Dr. Xiao Congzhen at the earthquake test bed, standing beside a scale model, where the tension rods are jacked up to a scaled tension by special sensors, and it's loaded with forty tons of lead. They shook the structure beyond an earthquake magnitude of nine. The most difficult part of designing the structure was transferring the tension to the concrete frame; we realized this when seeing the gigantic cast-iron joints, which had to be installed where the tension members connected to the concrete frame. | fig. 18

One of the main goals is to open this whole site to public programs, which are housed underneath in a tropical landscape with flowering elements. You can come out of a cafe in a mound and see this building going over you like a low-flying plane. Programs inside the mounds include a 500-seat auditorium. We also developed a Shenzhen 360 Window;

when walking along on the bottom floor, you can take a little stair down and see 360-degree views of the landscape drifting below. You're right at the edge of the underside of the soffit, and there is a glowing nighttime quality in that space of suspension and weightlessness.

I started these notes with the idea of weightlessness expressed in light. I'd like to conclude with weightlessness expressed in sound. I think Buckminster Fuller said, "There will be a time when our world will consist of thought translated into sound." A Columbia GSAPP studio I've run a number of times focuses on the exploration of a conceptual strategy derived from sound. One of the inspirations is Iannis Xenakis and Le Corbusier's Philips Pavilion, realized in Brussels, Belgium, in 1958. Xenakis composed two minutes of music for the people coming in and going out of the pavilion. Edgard Varèse composed eight minutes and five seconds of *Poème électronique*. Xenakis's music is formed from the sound of burning charcoal, electronically altered.

The weightlessness of an idea that drives the design has to find its material. In conclusion, I'm going the other way, toward the immaterial. This moment in time that we occupy, to me, is very exciting because of the doubt, not because of any certainty. Nowadays we are considering the new horizons of science, such as the CERN reactor's potential discoveries of the mysteries of mass. We still don't understand mass. Instead of solidity, consider mystery. Instead of substance, focus on essence. Instead of the weight of mass, consider value, which is weightless. Let's focus on the idea instead of the material, and the implication instead of the actuality. More important than what we are is what we suggest. It is the weightlessness of ideas that propels and drives us. I close this essay with a quote from Italian writer Italo Calvino: "Meaning is conveyed through a verbal texture that seems weightless, until the meaning itself takes on the same rarefied consistency."*

* From Italo Calvino, *Six Memos for the Next Millennium* (Cambridge: Harvard University Press, 1988), 16.

Notes on Weight and Weightlessness

Steven Holl

fig. 17 | Architect Li Hu with cast-iron joint used to connect tension members to concrete frame, Vanke Center, 2007

fig. 18 | Engineer Xiao Congzhen with concrete model of Vanke Center on earthquake test bed, 2007

Projects

89
Horizontal Skyscraper: Continuous City / Continuous Garden
Vanke Center, Shenzhen, China
Steven Holl

102
Concrete, or the Betrayal of Geometry
Nanjing University Performing Arts Center, Nanjing, China
Tel Aviv Museum of Art, Tel Aviv, Israel
Preston Scott Cohen

116
Tower and Temperament
O-14, Dubai, United Arab Emirates
Jesse Reiser + Nanako Umemoto

124
A Circular Journey
Congregation Beth Sholom, San Francisco, California
Stanley Saitowitz, Mason Walters, and Stephen Marusich

130
São Paulo: A Reinforced Context
Houses in Ribeirão Preto and Ubatuba, São Paulo, Brazil
Angelo Bucci

Horizontal Skyscraper: Continuous City / Continuous Garden
Steven Holl

Vanke Center, Shenzhen, China
Steven Holl Architects

Hovering over a newly evacuated landscape that is part garden, part extended plaza, and part earthform, the Vanke Center is a new type of horizontal skyscraper. The building itself is a hybrid form of urban landscape programmed to include apartments, a hotel, and offices for the headquarters of China Vanke Co. Ltd., in addition to a wide range of social functions and urban uses.

Appearing as if it had once been floating on a sea that has suddenly subsided, the structure of the center appears to levitate as if to form a new horizon. Seen from beneath, the building leaves the earthbound visitor firmly situated but nonetheless at a distance from a suspended urban world.

Held on 8 concrete cores measuring approximately 10 meters (32.8 feet) square, the extended, floating horizontal spans are an average of 50 meters (164 feet) in length. These distances, made possible by a never-before-implemented, hybrid structural system, gives the final mass an uncanny visual presence. The structure, set at a height of 35 meters (115 feet), conforms to the zoning envelope; a series of programs set within this volume is fused in a single, massive loop. The concept was proposed as an alternative to the anticipated placement of several smaller structures at distant intervals on the site. Instead of subdividing the site into discrete buildings programmed for specific uses, the elevated horizontality of the Vanke Center generates a large green space at grade.

The structural engineering and the building's open ground level provide a new quality of protection against tsunamis, while the porous microclimate created below it serves as a landscape for public use and everyday life. The structural systems combine steel with concrete—specifically, the mass and inertia of a concrete frame with the lightweight cable-stay technology of bridge engineering—to span tremendous distance without the anchorage typical of suspension bridges or the tension and compression of cantilevers. The building leverages its own weight; the concrete frame serves as a ballast and resists compression, enacting and maintaining the bearing and spanning capacities. An immobile yet dynamic structure, it creates and enables a form of laminar flow in urban space: the worlds above and below it become embedded within each other and are mutually supportive.

Within the structure, a public path begins at the entry lobby of a hotel—or the dragon's head. The path runs through an ensemble of programs. Hotel and apartments turn into office zones; traversing the structure the visitor is never clearly outside or inside a given program, as each anticipates the next and the distances collapse.

The underside of the floating structure forms the Vanke Center's main elevation—a sixth elevation, newly activated and revealed as the ceiling of the park below. Suspended from the Vanke Center are a set of new rooms and new windows. They provide a 360-degree view of the landscape below, bridging the two worlds and offering a vantage point that is of both and neither space.

As an urban strategy the building fuses with the landscape and attempts to integrate the two realms. This provides several new potentials for sustainability and energy management. Solar panels occupy the immense horizontal surface of the roof, which makes use of local materials such as bamboo. The glass facade is protected against heat gain and wind by a system of porous louvers. The microclimate beneath the building is further enhanced with cooling ponds fed by a system that recycles the building's greywater. In this realm, concrete returns to its more historic role: immensely shaped, solid mounds organized by program, assuming vigorous plastic shapes and revealing the imprint of their formwork.

The tropical landscape—a topological and continually changing space—migrates in relation to the horizon above and forms the basis for an experimental interchange between nature and urban life.

Phase I: Under construction

The auditorium mound: a bamboo-formed concrete shell with planted roof

91

Vanke Center, Shenzhen, China
Steven Holl Architects

Sunken window at hotel node stair

View from the top of the L-shaped courtyard, with
the marble plaza on left and Vanke headquarters in the
background. The courtyards measure approximately
7 meters (23 feet) deep.

Walking columns at Little Finger (before steel was installed), a fully cantilevered
branch of the main structure, measuring approximately 20 meters (66 feet).

Vanke Center, Shenzhen, China
Steven Holl Architects

opposite: Phase 1: Vanke headquarters. The soffit and roof
[illegible] and the intermediate floors poured. After tensioning is
complete, the scaffolding is removed and the intermediate
floors are connected to the core.

Intermediate steel tensioning knuckle at core

Steel beam at an intermediate floor before the concrete floor is poured. The tension cable is protected by steel sleeves composed of 50-millimeter (2-inch) thick cementitious fireproofing and intumescent paint to achieve a 3-hour fire rating

View of the tension cables, with threaded end in foreground and the bottom secured to bracing capitals at the soffit level

Vanke Center, Shenzhen, China
Steven Holl Architects

CAD drawing of steel-cable knuckle, approximately 2.5 meters (8 feet) wide

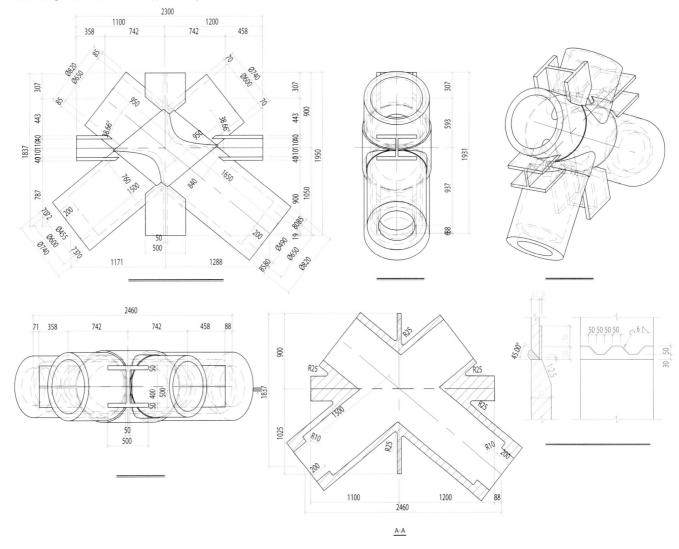

A-A

Section through Soho/condo branch, from structural set showing cable-stay system
at shear walls and cores. The longest span is approximately 50 meters (164 feet).

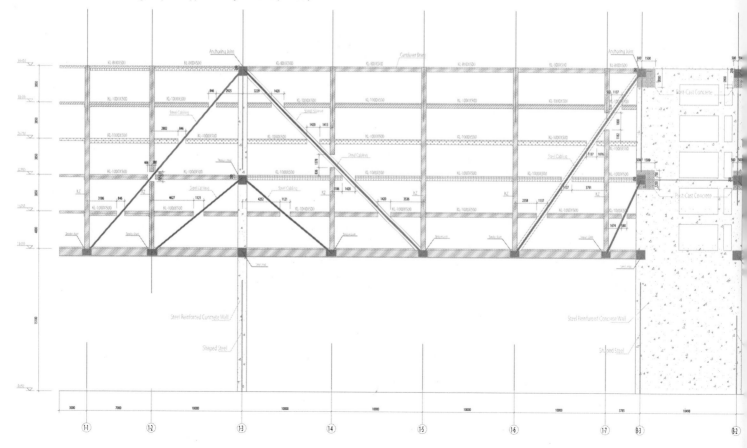

Vanke Center, Shenzhen, China
Steven Holl Architects

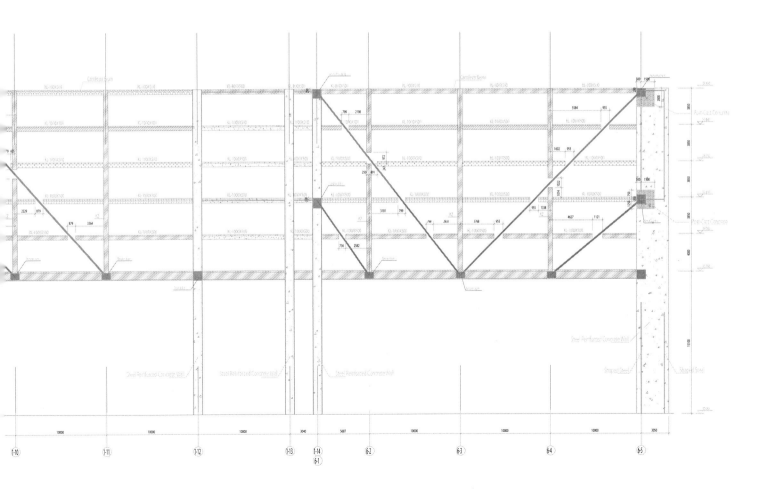

First and second floor plans

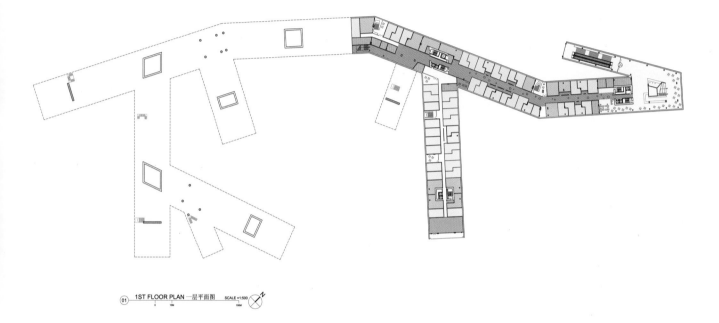

01 1ST FLOOR PLAN 一层平面图   SCALE =1:500

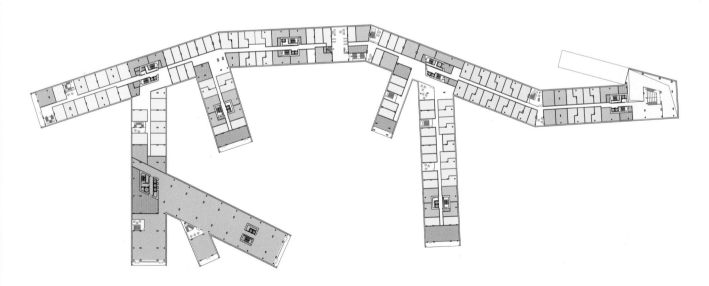

02 2ND FLOOR PLAN 二层平面图   SCALE =1:500

Vanke Center, Shenzhen, China
Steven Holl Architects

Little Finger and walking steel columns

Concrete, or the Betrayal of Geometry

Preston Scott Cohen

Nanjing University Performing Arts Center, Nanjing, China
Preston Scott Cohen

In the Tel Aviv Museum of Art and the Nanjing University Performing Arts Center, concrete becomes the battleground of the most essential forces acting on architecture—geometric, ideological, and economic. Ultimately the character of the material and a persistent professional negotiation allows it to achieve an alchemical, political settlement.

In both projects, the translation of curved surfaces to flat planes or other curves establishes a dialectic between approximation and precision, between idealized geometry and literal formwork. What is at stake in these projects is the relative coarseness or fineness, low or high resolution (to borrow terms from the realm of digital imagery), a tolerance for pixilation as opposed to a drive toward smoothness and exactitude.

More than anything, local politics and economic and material constraints established the types of construction deployed in each project. In Nanjing there was never any question that the primary structure, as well as the facades, had to be built using cast-in-place concrete, but in Tel Aviv the translation from original design to final construction followed a far less predictable path. In both cases, the ensuing impasses were unresolvable without a series of asymmetric negotiations between labor and technique, as well as between material, weight, and their antecedents in geometry.

Construction

The unfamiliar shapes designed for Nanjing were a cause of distress for the engineers at the local Chinese Architectural Institute at Nanjing University, leading them to design an excessive structural solution. As a result, the number and sizes of both the columns and beams are comparable in mass to the structures of significantly taller buildings. In plan the primary structural frame is distributed along several fragmentary grids, such that it does not conform to the linear development of the hypars. The discrepancy between the roof-surface geometry and the structural frame is seen on the interior. The roof is constituted as a second system of folded plates in conformity with the hypar surface developers. This enabled the application of a tiled surface, which was an economically feasible means to finish the large surface area in this context. Due to the planning guidelines of the campus in which it is sited and the number of exceptions that this special building had already been granted, as well as the rough quality of cast-in-place concrete in China, it was never an option to expressively expose concrete as an exterior finish material. The solution, linear ceramic tiles laid in a herringbone pattern, covers the entire building envelope. Only in China could tile be affordably and beautifully laid to cover such a vast surface area.

Nanjing University Performing Arts Center, Nanjing, China
Preston Scott Cohen

Polyjet model, Nanjing University Performing Arts Center

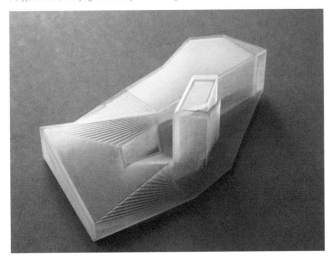

The exterior is rendered in gray tones arranged progressively to reinforce the spiral-inspired form.

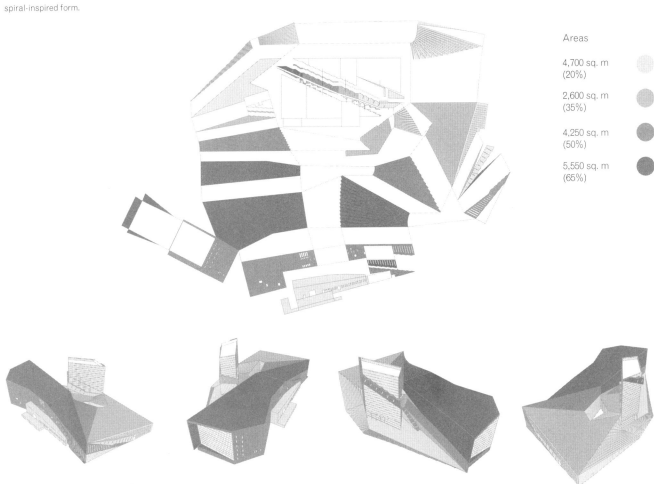

Areas

4,700 sq. m
(20%)

2,600 sq. m
(35%)

4,250 sq. m
(50%)

5,550 sq. m
(65%)

Nanjing University Performing Arts Center

Nanjing University Performing Arts Center, Nanjing, China
Preston Scott Cohen

The hyperbolic parabolas redefined as folding plates clad in tile

Tel Aviv Museum of Art, Tel Aviv, Israel
Preston Scott Cohen

To understand the material and design transactions in the Tel Aviv Museum of Art project, it is best to begin by looking at both near and far views of the building, which display an indeterminacy of scale and a monumental effect. Very close-up, the surface is remarkably smooth and precise, achieving qualities similar to polished marble; it appears impervious. Such a characteristic is impossible to achieve with cast-in-place concrete, and it is very different from exposed concrete buildings in Israel, most of which are in a midcentury brutalist style.

This smooth type of surface is a departure from the initial competition design for the project, in which curved forms were to be cast-in-place concrete. The idea at the outset was to produce a form that would resist the popular tendency to import the postmodern stone facades of Jerusalem. Historically Tel Aviv's buildings have been composed of concrete and stucco. In an attempt to reaffirm the International Style of the city, the new museum was designed to have curved shapes that would be prohibitively expensive to build in stone. In this way, the building was designed to preclude the possibility of the stone aesthetic that has contributed to the discontinuation of Tel Aviv's remarkable architectural heritage.

Within the context of Israel, cast-in-place concrete as a finish is, for all intents and purposes, taboo. For many, it recalls a bygone era of provincialism and undignified pragmatism; or worse, it signifies the uglier, present-day military infrastructure. If the museum were to be built in concrete, it would have to be of the architectural, precast variety. So began the long research into how to bring about a geometry that could be built, using structural concrete that would then be clad in architectural concrete. The hypars were translated into a quad-panelized system that would enable simpler formwork construction of the structural wall.

The trouble began with the estimated cost of introducing the steel tracks needed to guide the planarity of the panels, which were to be attached to the structural wall from the exterior. Making matters more difficult, a considerable portion of the exterior is composed of surface areas for which cladding panels would need to be suspended upside down. The panels were too small to accommodate integral steel-reinforcement bars; without these, architectural concrete would not be structurally feasible.

More daunting still was the task of persuading Museum Director and Chief Curator Motti Omer, as well as the office of the city architect, to approve architectural concrete in the first place. Why accept the cost of cladding in concrete, as opposed to stone, which was perceived to be the more substantial material? There was mounting pressure to concede to stone. After all, having translated the curves to planar panels we had inadvertently created a building that would lend itself to being built in stone more easily than in concrete.

Translating the hypars into panels had brought us right back to where we began: facing the seemingly intractable imperative to import the historicism of Jerusalem to the heart of its modern counterpart: Tel Aviv. In order to work with the dreaded stone cladding, we forced ourselves to muster up excitement about a new idea; that is, to overcome the nostalgia represented by stone and arrive at an unprecedented aesthetic solution. Converting the hypars to panels, we now argued, introduced implicit distortions and anamorphoses that would transform the stone into something completely unexpected. The building's form would allow stone to be used in a manner that could provide a wholly new understanding of the material.

This strategy of artful self-persuasion would come to pass, but not until a year was spent designing the intricate stone pattern. The design allowed for the nearly horizontal rows of stone to run continuously from one oblique panel to the next, with the vertical divisions within each row being equidistant; a standard dimension was produced for all of the stones, saving substantial costs at the quarry.

The stone became a less attractive solution, however, once it became clear that pieces needing to be hung upside down would have to be proportionally very small, creating an excessive and laborious mosaic pattern riddled with numerous installation-related problems. The ideal solution was lightweight stone laminated to honeycomb reinforcement board, which would allow for larger and thus fewer pieces, but this was not an option because the laminate product had not yet been certified for use in Israel.

The breakthrough solution arrived when the builder, Hezkelevitch Engineering, having secured the contract to build the museum, suggested that we do away with the structurally reinforced wall and make a curtain wall of precast-concrete panels attached to steel ribs. The architectural concrete panels would be far thicker and thus could include steel reinforcement rods. The proposal was met with skepticism when first proposed to the city and to Omer; architect and client had arrived at an impasse. The parties agreed to allow the builder to produce comparative mock-ups in stone and concrete.

Upon comparing the mock-ups, the advantages of the concrete panels couldn't have been clearer. The stone was small and its subdivision pattern distracting. In contrast, the concrete curtain wall allowed the panelized geometry to be realized without subdivisions. The sheer size and smoothness of the panels was overwhelmingly impressive.

Also, hidden was the reality that the concrete solution was less expensive than the stone. Thus there was something built into the concrete, an economic advantage—a powerful force, indifferent to all who wished to control the outcome.

The concrete panels are cast on large, smooth steel tables, with an easy-to-control vibration mechanism. Magnetic steel dams were used to define the many different shapes and angles of the panel edges. Cast in two stages, the concrete is high quality (B-40) with a high percentage of cement in the mix, relative to sand and aggregate. Anticipating the leverage and cantilever rations of assembly, the panel sizes and weights varied. Panels designed to be located closest to the center of the crane's reach weigh 8 tons and measure 24 square meters (approximately 250 square feet), while those

at the greatest distance weigh 6 tons. Without the need for a cast-in-place concrete structural wall, the panels could be maneuvered from behind the envelope during installation, making it possible to precisely control the relationships between panels.

Concerns remained about wear and tear due to the salty moist air, in particular the possibility that mold would grow in the panels and cause discoloration. More importantly, the curtain wall needed to deal with water resistance. Research showed that the density of the material made the panels waterproof, and a sprayed-on backing was added to guarantee that there would be no penetration.

Until the moment the mock-ups were produced, the anamorphic geometry of the panels and the patterns of growth and change were emphasized or de-emphasized, accelerated or decelerated willfully during the course of the design process in order to alter perceptions of the building from different positions along the perambulatory promenade surrounding the building. Ultimately, however, limitations imposed by assembly determined the final pattern. The distribution of the panels corresponds to the distance of each panel from the center of the cranes, either reinforcing or countermanding the anamorphic perspectives. Meanwhile, there were the minimum allowable angles between the sides of the panels and the maximum dimensions allowable on the casting tables. Ultimately, what is most compelling about the facades is not the monumental scale and size of the panels, nor the forms they cumulatively build; rather, the way in which their relative sizes and amplitudes are determined simultaneously by laws of geometry inherent in the hypar's panels, as well as the anamorphic progressions and the limitations of materials as defined by the locations of the cranes.

Lightfall Construction
The final proposal for the museum project is constructed as three independent structural systems: a steel structural frame dominated by Vierendeel trusses; the curtain wall composed of reinforced architectural precast concrete; and,

at the heart of the building, a cast-in-place structure aptly named the Lightfall by Omer. The Lightfall is not clad directly. Conceptually it can be argued that the building's facade is its cladding system, offset and expanded to form a shell containing the volumes between it and the Lightfall.

The surfaces of the Lightfall presented their own set of problems due to the inability of the formwork boards to conform directly to the hyperbolic geometry. They are too large for the boards to progressively taper along the linear developers of the hypars. Therefore the boards run parallel to one another in sets that are clipped by the edges of other sets and by the edges of the limits of the hypar surfaces, thus creating a patchwork of independently defined curved surface areas, a faceting that approximates the curvatures of the geometric substrates of the overall hypars. Though the final constructed geometry of the Lightfall deviates from the absolute geometry of its surfaces, it will be perceived to represent the hypars more closely than the facade panels do. Ironically, the panels are actually closer to the surface geometry, given that their vertices lay in the surface developers. In this sense, the building teaches us that the most effective visual and tangible expression of geometry in architecture does not necessarily correspond to the most lawfully truthful rendition of it.

In architecture, concrete construction not only signifies or materializes geometry, but can also be understood relative to a utopian horizon—a drive toward exactitude. Technical perfection appears to involve the ultimate concealment of means: cardboard, laser cut, or stone cut, as opposed to the contingencies of a liquid pour.

Conclusion

In Nanjing and Tel Aviv, the processes are brought about by negotiations that are never counterintuitive or divergent from geometric ideals; they are based in variables of material, production, and, ultimately, historically inherited perceptions. In this equation, architecture's realization necessitates the betrayal of geometry, according to techniques that have yet to achieve perfection. To the extent that it misses its goal,

architecture implies technological obsolescence. Each case exemplifies the limitations of its time and cultural heritage. The valor assigned to that which remains and survives—the architecture itself—puts into question the deep role that negotiation and betrayal play in what is ultimately valued.

Yet the dialectical relationship between geometric and construction-based constraints is among the most important. The refinement of concrete is not only technical and disciplinary. Descaling and rescaling, dematerialization and rematerialization, the implicit representation of one material by another, the aestheticization of the industrial, and the production of new forms of monumentality are among the most important effects of large-scale concrete construction in architecture. This is when the terms of each variable are caught in an upheaval and the negotiations between surface and support, mass and weight, become embedded in the historicism of not only monumentality but the modern movement itself and the material techniques it valorizes. In the end, it is the networked balance of demands that produces a renewed possibility of material integrity and thus of culturally grounded monumentality.

Tel Aviv Museum of Art, Tel Aviv, Israel
Preston Scott Cohen

Plan, Herta and Paul Amir Building, Tel Aviv Museum of Art, by Preston Scott Cohen, Tel Aviv, Israel, 2010

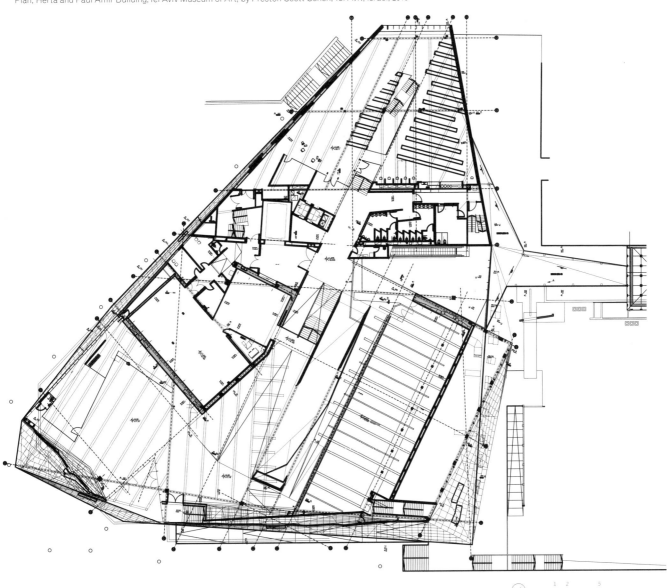

Tel Aviv Museum of Art, under construction, August 2009

Tel Aviv Museum of Art, under construction, 2009

Tel Aviv Museum of Art, Tel Aviv, Israel
Preston Scott Cohen

Steel-structured ribs clad in reinforced, precast-concrete panels, 2009

Precast-concrete facade panels

The 900-square-meter (2,953-square-foot) gallery is used as a factory for the fabrication of precast-concrete facade panels. The panels are lifted through an opening created by the skewed position of the gallery relative to the rooms above.

Panel sizes and weights were varied according to the anticipated leverage of the cranes. Panels located closest to the center of the crane's reach weigh 8 tons and measure 24 square meters (approximately 250 square feet), while those at the greatest distance weigh 6 tons. In total there are 460 uniquely shaped facade panels.

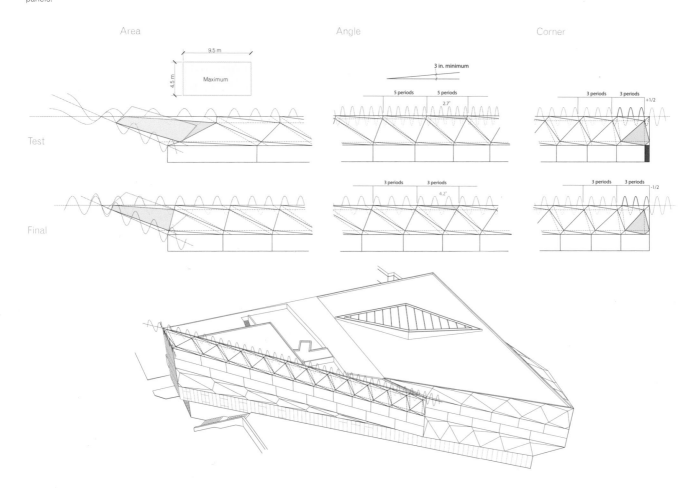

Tel Aviv Museum of Art, Tel Aviv, Israel
Preston Scott Cohen

Under construction, 2009

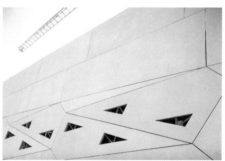

Precast-concrete facade panels

View of site during construction

Section through galleries and Lightfall

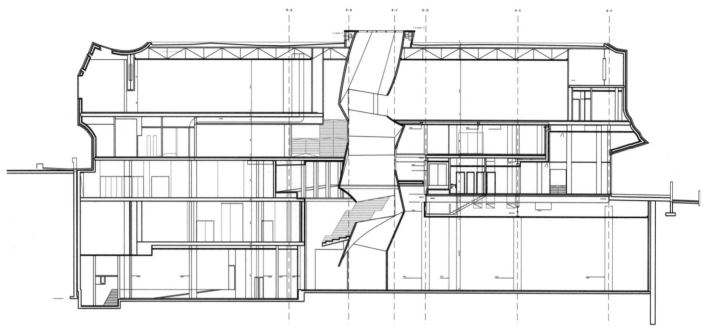

Lightfall working drawings

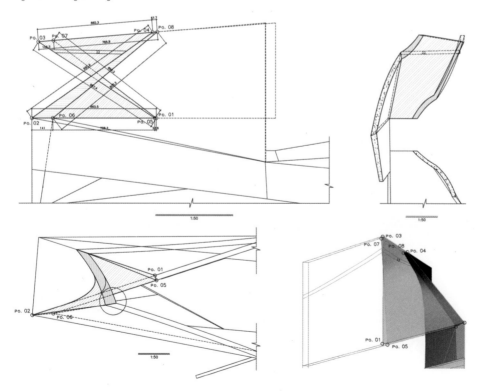

Tel Aviv Museum of Art, Tel Aviv, Israel
Preston Scott Cohen

Lightfall concrete cast unveiled, May 2009

The structural supports for the formwork are arranged according to the ruling lines of the hyperbolic parabolas.

Tower and Temperament

Jesse Reiser + Nanako Umemoto

O-14, Dubai, United Arab Emirates
Reiser + Umemoto

Dubai is going through an unprecedented phase of urbanization and growth. Its reliance on imported models of urban design and its excessive variety of architecture has resulted in a sea of meaningless variety and a luxe skyline composed of towers that hysterically demand our attention. The city's efforts to create a sense of place are in vain, for such skylines are ubiquitous. Themed developments and environments are typical responses to perceptions of the generic, often resulting only in superficial specificity. Within a sea of the new generic, the question remains as to how to proceed, how to address what has come to be the typical building block of such an emerging city, and how to create a singular address within this riot of sameness posing as difference.

Dubai's example can be considered relevant for many emerging global cities. The cliché of the iconic office tower expresses a diluted version of the ideals of expansion and transparency; in fact, with the common office tower, we see ubiquitous transparency and unconstrained expansion. The ideologically driven towers of Mies and Wright are ancient ancestors of Dubai's relentless stacks of chrome and mirrored glass, appearing as the pragmatic end of a once utopian ideal. Developers have efficiently codified the language and styles required to produce "iconic" buildings; as a result, these typical developer buildings are overlaid with retrograde techniques that reinforce derivative classical motifs or generic tripartite organizations: typical arcade, base, middle, and top. What may be expressed in one case as the high-tech style could just as well be historical or contextual—style of system doesn't matter. In moving away from the postmodern notion of iconic to the new iconic, consider the difference between a monument and a memorial. Wherein a monument imposes effect without context, a memorial is completely contextual,

tied to history of place or narrative. Normative towers, with their profound lack of innovation, are in such ways tied to "narratives of iconicity," rather than actually being iconic.

We are not advocating a return to vernacular building, nostalgic historical motifs, or a proliferation of homogeneous modernism, but rather a thorough reformulation of the tower type through an examination of local conditions and materials that yield a formally intelligent and environmentally responsive design strategy, more so than the current standard. The result is that "type" has been turned inside out. Structure and skin have been flipped, offering a new economy of tectonics and space. Systematic inversion, however, does not lead simply to glazing an exterior structure; nor does this mean the transposition of the curtain wall behind it, because the simple transposition of structure and skin provides a limited range of organizational and visual effects. The limitation lies in the nature of the slick, single-surface wrapper of the typical curtain-wall tower, which merely combines environmental enclosure with whatever semiotic the wrapper was designed to carry.

This organizational shift affords many tangible benefits. In O-14, the enclosure is not simply a single skin but a deep, layered zone in section, composed of an exoskeleton sunscreen, a one-meter air gap, and an inexpensive window wall mounted between floor slabs. In addition to an enhanced sense of depth, as compared to the single-surface enclosure, the layered enclosure performs an environmental function: first by substantially blocking light and heat before it is transmitted to the glazing; and second by inducing a chimney effect that pulls cool air up the glazing wall, reducing cooling costs by an estimated 30 percent.

The exoskeleton shell of O-14 becomes the primary vertical and lateral structure of the building, allowing the column-free office slabs to span between it and the minimal core. By moving the lateral bracing of the building to the perimeter, the core, which is traditionally enlarged to receive lateral loading in most curtain-wall office towers, can be minimized for only vertical loading, utilities, and transportation.

Additionally, the typical curtain-wall tower configuration results in floor plates that must be thicker to carry lateral loads to the core; yet in O-14, these can be minimized to only respond to span and vibration.

The Toad and the Pyramid

The skin of a toad is a symphony of disruption. Graphically the skin is mottled with markings that are intended to blur, confuse, and obfuscate. The skin is also textured with small bumps, which have no organizational relationship with the pattern, and serve only to confuse legibility, often preventing the need for evasion of predators. Furthermore, the overall form of the toad itself—sometimes taut, sometimes loose—blends the two systems into a coordinated but inseparable whole.

In opposition to biological pattern and geometry, typical Cartesian structural and spatial arrangements operate in part-to-whole subdivisions that merely scale down the overall organizational matrix. Modernist adjustments of such subdivisions—to reinforce the human scale, or, more prosaically, the floor-to-floor dimensions—have become so ingrained in the tectonics of skins as to excite no effect at all. Even the mannerist distortions of postmodernism reinforce this norm by flaunting its deviations from it. If it can be agreed that we must find a way to achieve a monumental or more truly iconic geometry, then the simple grandeur of building big is not sufficient for the contemporary building, as it was in the time of Cheops. Like the toad, overt design agility precludes physical agility.

In a typical office building, the subdivision of the building mass would locate program in a predictable way, incorporating larger windows and offices at corners; however, in O-14, the fenestration (or perforation) is independent of mass. In its joining of two divergent design models—simple volume and variegated pattern—O-14 frustrates any easy reading of scale or height. Externally the pattern seeks to attenuate the monotony while still preserving the sense of the sublime and monumentality. Like the pyramid, its simple silhouette seen from a distance provides no stable reference of scale. In the near view, its disruptive patterning defeats any clear scalar reading, which is reinforced by the deliberate lack of correspondence between the floor levels and diagrid. The change in pattern induces a move away from a hierarchical subdivision of fenestration and in so doing reorganizes the hierarchical occupation of office space. The tower plan is thus liberated from typical programmatic determinations through a unique distribution of fenestration on each floor.

Much like the toad, the pattern changes as its relationship to the viewer changes, and in conjunction with additional patterns of light and shadow it produces a virtual form that is more complex than the actual built form. Because of this, the building can be simplified yet still display a level of formal richness while incorporating the logics of efficient production methods and structural economies.

The alloys that make up the structural grid of the former World Trade Center in Manhattan were intricately modulated to achieve variable strength areas in an effort to maintain the relentless uniformity of its elevations. This accommodated the variable stresses in the tower while also allowing the apertures to be larger and uniformly sized; yet in the end, it was governed by the rules of prefabrication and economy. With O-14, the strength of the shell is modulated based on a mediation between materiality and aperture. Variable stresses are accommodated by increasing and decreasing the material at different locations in the structure so that a uniform-strength concrete can be used, thus simplifying the material preparation. Changes in overall opacity are accommodated by changing the strength of the concrete mix. The mix is a balance between strength and fluidity, as extreme fluidity is necessary for larger contiguous-pour segments, utilizing self-consolidating concrete and slip-forming technology. Herein lies the economy of the system: within its constraints, a wide spectrum of forms can be possible without unduly impacting the overall cost or production time.

Additionally, a set of significant yet unforeseen effects is produced when viewed from the floor plates looking out from within. The axes of the punched openings extend the user's vertical and horizontal vision, unnaturally exposing the slabs underneath and extending peripheral views to create an odd sense of disturbed ground. Similarly, a sense of disjointed connectivity is given when one looks beyond the shell, through several smaller holes at once, as portions of the view are whited out by the shell. These blurred readings of closeness and distance throw into sharp relief the overproliferation of Cartesian geometry and its habitual use in vertical and horizontal orientations. Its reflexive application has made a cliché of the perforated window and has dulled its drama and expansion, limiting the effects of the perceived extension from building into context.

The Generic and the Accidental

The period of high modernism can be characterized by a dialectical tension between the generic (classical and impersonal) and the accidental (the unique).* Rather than seek the accidental or the accumulation of disparate elements, our process of design produces a singularity, which through its systematic nature produces unique yet systematic conditions. Difference is produced by similarity, resulting in ubiquitous difference or continuous variation.

The design of O-14 compounds these ideas, foregrounding the uses and functions of the office spaces within, yet also emphasizing the appearance, porosity, and effects generated by the facade. Since the program will locally reorganize itself in relationship to the apertures, this combination rejects the pure separation and codification of parts and components, as in structural rationalism or structural expressionism, in favor of a matter-force arrangement wherein matter and force are viewed as one. Like the combination of toad and pyramid, the building endeavors paradoxically to have a monumental agility—a shift in perception that allows it to be read as mass, logic, and system.

As an analogue, consider the muscle tone of an athletic body compared to that of an overweight body. The former can be thought of as explicit, overpowered, and hyper-rational; and the latter as having formlessness and a lack of material

hierarchy. The beauty of a well-toned body, like the actress Audrey Hepburn, lies not in an average between the two extremes but in the singular material memory of an extreme state (starvation) that is latent yet palpably expressed in a body ostensibly associated with the norm.† In an architectural context, this is expressed neither in terms of an account of the histories of designing, nor in the traces of process, but rather as a pregnant materiality. Just as the overall appearance of O-14 cannot be reduced to its component logics, the trickle-down of forces, generating expression in the building, are not reducible to structure alone. Instead, the building takes on what might be called a well-tempered expression, allowing it to function and perform in several modes at the same time without any individual feature becoming overtly expressed.

* Colin Rowe, "Mannerism and Modern Architecture," in *The Mathematics of the Ideal Villa and Other Essays* (Cambridge, MA: MIT Press, 1976), 29-57.
† The Hepburn analogy was brought to our attention by Jeffrey Kipnis.

Unrolled shell drawing, O-14, by Reiser + Umemoto, Dubai, United Arab Emirates

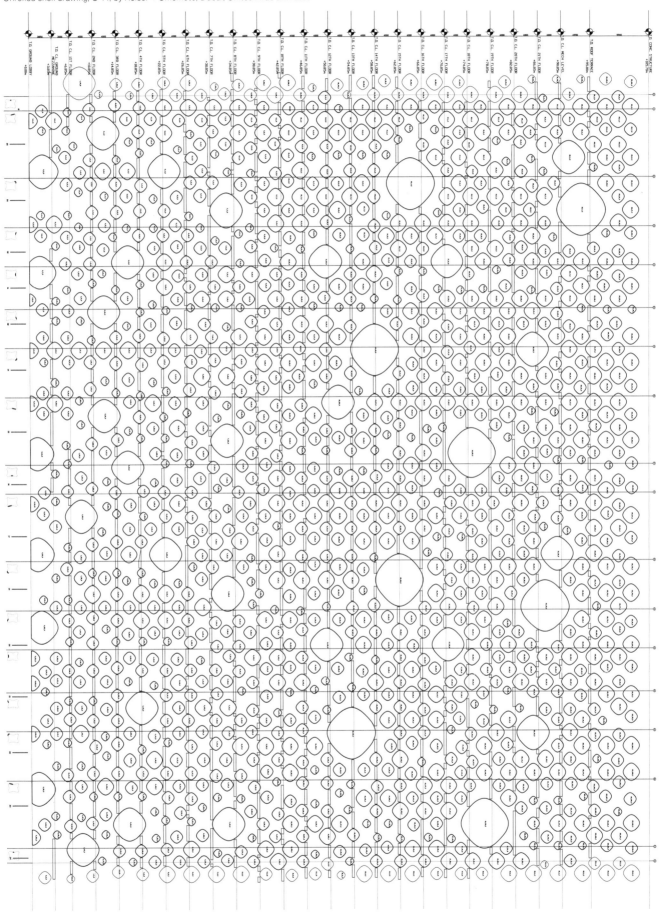

Night view during construction, 2010

Aerial view during construction

Shell pattern variations

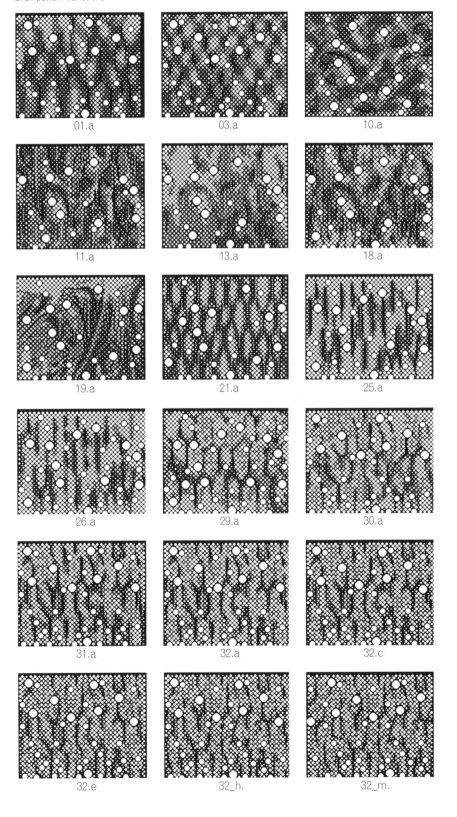

01.a   03.a   10.a

11.a   13.a   18.a

19.a   21.a   25.a

26.a   29.a   30.a

31.a   32.a   32.c

32.e   32_h.   32_m.

Shell construction, showing rebar matrix and foam void forms

Interior view, showing transition detail from 400 to 600 millimeter (1.3 to 2 foot) shell

Interior during construction, 2009

View of bridge between podium and tower

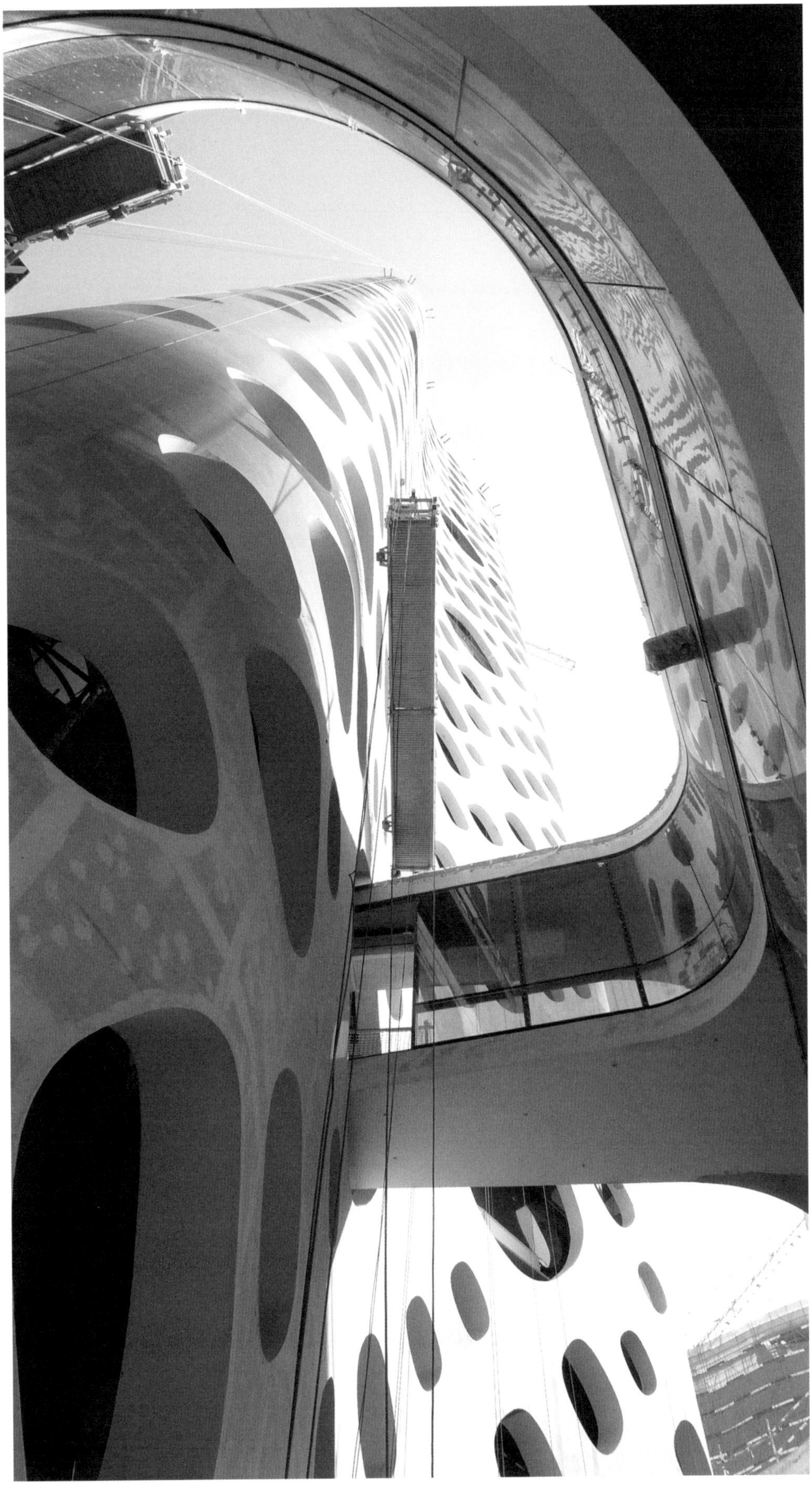

A Circular Journey

Stanley Saitowitz, Mason Walters, and Stephen Marusich

Congregation Beth Sholom, San Francisco, California
Stanley Saitowitz / Natoma Architects Inc.

The Congregation Beth Sholom synagogue is sited in the relatively flat Richmond district of San Francisco, at the intersection of Park Presidio and Clement Street.

A plinth is established where all of the nonreligious programs of the campus are contained. Two buildings are placed on the plinth, forming a courtyard in between. The first, the social hall, is a reflective cube; the second, the sanctuary, is a concrete structure clad in masonry.

At Congregation Beth Sholom the entry sequence establishes the distinction of a sacred place in the city, reached by way of passage—a circular journey of turning and rising and turning. The first point of arrival is the lower court, from which a stair ascends to the courtyard. Here the three elements of the complex—sanctuary, social hall, and existing school—are connected. This circular route enables the sanctuary to be entered from the west, facing the Ark of Torahs in the east (an important liturgical requirement).

The design for the sanctuary begins from the inside, with the creation of a sacred room—a space in the round—focused on the center, where services are conducted. The format of two facing tiers of seating is in the shape of the remains of the earliest synagogue at the fortress of Masada in modern-day Israel.

An essential aspect of Conservative Judaism is egalitarianism; women and men participate equally in the liturgy. The Orthodox Jewish tradition of separating women in a balcony or by a curtain is eliminated. The form of the room engages gravity as an ally. Entering at the lowest point, the room fills like a cup, maintaining an intimate density even when not packed. Its walls are people. The room, a vessel, focuses all worshipers in a single community centered on the bimah.

Jewish tradition equates iconography with idolatry, therefore all figurative images are forbidden. The space is abstract, without figuration. The only window in the synagogue is a slice of sky in the ceiling. All light enters the room from above, with views of the sky creating a sense of sanctity in the midst of the noise and bustle of the city. The first religious structure of the Jews was the Tabernacle, described by Moses in the book of Exodus, and carried in the wanderings through the desert. The text often focuses on the means of connection of the parts, rather than what is connected, as if the building itself is a metaphor for the community it joins.

Here the roof floats over the cup and is connected with light. The ceiling is sliced by the sky. By night, it is lit with stars of light.

Structure

Early interaction between the architect and structural engineer took place to determine how the sanctuary bowl structure should be designed to be self-supporting, given that the shape includes both flat and curved surfaces (unlike a typical shell of revolution, such as a dome). The upward-curving floorplate morphs from level, at the low point, to nearly vertical at the top. This transition suggested a change from a flat plate in the lower areas to a deep-wall beam, both in the same curved element. The intersecting vertical sidewalls behave as deep, cantilevered beams supporting the curved slab. Essentially the curved slab is hung like a catenary from its own upper edge, which in turn is supported by the outer ends of the sidewalls. The sidewalls carry the majority of the gravitational loads symmetrically to the central pedestal below. In order to limit cracking and deflection of the shell, a three-dimensional network of post-tensioned tendons were used to reinforce the slabs and walls in a way that would allow the structure to behave as described above: the curved slab tendons become "hangers" as they transition to a vertical profile; transverse tendons at the top of the curved slab counteract the shell's tensile stress caused by the hanging slab; and longitudinal tendons at the tops of the vertical sidewalls resist cantilever

125

Congregation Beth Sholom, San Francisco, California
Stanley Saitowitz / Natoma Architects Inc.

tension, allowing the walls to span to the pedestals. Virtually all of the gravitational loads are thus balanced by the action of the tendons, essentially eliminating any tendency to deflect or crack.

Another interesting structural challenge was the substantial seismic-lateral forces generated by the mass of the bowl atop the pedestal and foundation. The high center of mass resulted in large overturning forces, which would require a deep foundation. Piles or piers would have been very costly and disruptive to install; anchoring the mass of the structure rigidly to the earth would exacerbate the effects of ground shaking. Instead the pedestal was placed on a large, 4-foot (1.2-meter) thick concrete mat. To verify the seismic stability of the resulting design, the structure and soil were modeled using structural analysis software and evaluated dynamically using nonlinear-response-history analysis. The results indicated that a beneficial rocking action would take place in a major seismic event, during which the corners of the mat foundation would actually lift slightly as the bowl and pedestal sway back and forth together. Such rocking, while not acknowledged by building codes, is widely recognized as a beneficial mode of behavior that lessens the lateral forces experienced by the structure, slightly increasing the lateral displacements.

Section diagram, Congregation Beth Sholom Synagogue, by Stanley Saitowitz / Natoma Architects

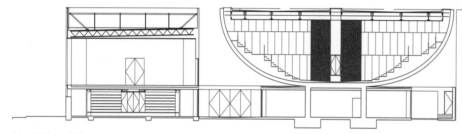

0'   10'   20'

Sanctuary under construction

Interior of sanctuary during construction

Congregation Beth Sholom, San Francisco, California
Stanley Saitowitz / Natoma Architects Inc.

Exterior view of the sanctuary

View of the interior

Sanctuary side view

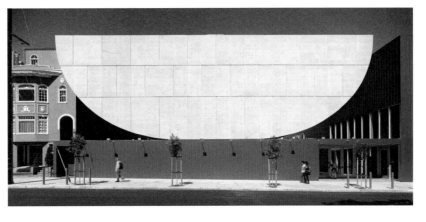

Entry courtyard

Congregation Beth Sholom, San Francisco, California
Stanley Saitowitz / Natoma Architects Inc.

Meditation room

São Paulo: A Reinforced Context

Angelo Bucci

Houses in Ribeirão Preto and Ubatuba, São Paulo, Brazil
SPBR

From a single picture of São Paulo, Brazil, a viewer can infer that the entire city was cast into forms.

In this context, concrete has spread everywhere, as a material that has overcome insurmountable social, geographical, and economic barriers. From the urban core to the outskirts of the city, from luxury houses to slum dwellings, everything has been shaped in concrete to support the twenty million people living together in the same place. Concrete can be seen as a gray, inert, and hard support, but it can also be seen as a raw material full of possibilities. Recognizing the numerous possibilities of this material, it is as if concrete refused to cure and solidify, remaining a fluid potential, always ready to be poured into another shape.

Vilanova Artigas designed the University of São Paulo School of Architecture out of this same raw material. Walking through the building, we can listen to his lessons as if taught by the concrete itself; sometimes these are whispered kindly, sometimes spoken clearly, and at other times incisively, in a loud voice. One can also experience the reality of Artigas's thoughts when the building is so crowded that it looks as if it has been converted into the whole city; or rather, as if the city had been converted into a building and São Paulo itself were our architecture school. The work is at once a building, a person, a city, and a multitude. In São Paulo, reinforced concrete is not only a material; it is a landscape. I mean it is not a matter of choice. It is just natural. The structure of this context strongly imprints the way a *Paulista* architect approaches the subject and object of his or her work.

House in Ribeirão Preto
Visiting the project site for the first time, it was a disaster. Its naturally sloped topography had been undone, creating a flat platform located a half meter above street level. It posed a risk to the neighbors' houses for no reason other than that the previous owner believed that a flat site would fetch a higher price.

To understand that unmade topography as a nonground in this case proved to be a productive hypothesis. By refusing to accept that situation as a given, it was possible to rearrange it in an unusual way. The topography was understood as a potential volume·of soil that could be shaped differently: 225 cubic meters of material, with its own aesthetic properties that could be formally recycled. Three boxes were constructed and filled with that volume of earth, becoming three huge garden stones and defining three different levels or plateaus. In order to be placed on such a groundless site, the house had to float over it.

The Shortest Vertical Distance
To achieve the intended relationship between street level, the new plateaus, and the floating slabs, it was essential that we reduce the vertical distances in order to constrain the distance between them to just a half level. This goal was achieved by inverting the structural order: a pair of beams, each sitting on two columns, was placed and the slabs were hung from them. The simplicity of the structural scheme is apparent in section. From ground level, however, the structure appears less clear: the columns are oddly displayed, the slabs seemingly not thick enough, and the beams unattached to the slabs. Yet when grasped from multiple points of view and considered as a whole, the clarity and simplicity of the structural elements become apparent.

Inverted Construction Process as Possibility
The casting sequence of the structural elements presented a significant challenge. While it was built from bottom to top, the order of the beams and slabs was inverted. The first slab was cast with no supporting structure, as was the second. It was only after both slabs were already in place and completely supported by scaffolds that the pair of beams could be

cast into the roof slab. Even though I was working with a great structural engineer, Ibsen Puleo Uvo, the construction process was considered a risky plan at the time. It makes sense to call this house a precedent; if the risk had not been taken, I would not have been able to move forward.

House in Ubatuba

Placed exactly on the latitude line of the Tropic of Capricorn, Ubatuba is one of the most important cities on the São Paulo coast. The site for this house borders the beach on one side and reaches up 28 meters (92 feet) to street level. Protected by environmental laws, the trees on the site as well as the hard slope (with 50 percent grade) inspired the entire design strategy.

The Strategies

Three columns in reinforced concrete support the house. The casting of these columns was easily achieved using sliding formwork. The house touches the ground only at those three points. From street level, four steel beams (from which the slabs were hung) were assembled on top of those columns. The slabs would be cast from top to bottom in order to avoid the use of scaffolding. As such, the construction process could (in theory) be faster, more rational, and more affordable.

In practice, however, the cost of placing the four steel beams on the columns made it unfeasible when compared with a similar structure cast in reinforced concrete. The reason was simple: while steel structure is not widespread in Brazil, concrete technology is quite developed. Surprisingly, in a comparative ranking, concrete performed better in several ways; in this specific case, it was mostly due to the rented formwork and the possibilities for using scaffolding. In a consensus between everyone involved, we opted to stay with the mainstream technology of reinforced concrete.

Architecture and Construction Process

In both strategies the resulting architecture would be quite similar, but the construction process would be completely inverted, with the slabs now cast from bottom to top. If the risks associated with such a process were to be accounted for in the construction budget, for insurance proposes, this construction possibility couldn't exist. Actually, it is likely that such a process will not exist for some time in Brazil. The risks were much greater than those described in the House in Ribeirão Preto. The scenario in Ubatuba included the additional challenge of pouring three levels of slabs without any support structure at all—the entire construction process contending with a significantly steep site, located in a very rainy area.

Several components of the structure appear displaced from their usual locations, as if they were the result of an exploded structure: the beams are placed on the rooftop; one column is displaced from the beam; and there is no column supporting the largest slab, which floats among the trees. Learning from the context of São Paulo and from the works of Mendes da Rocha, these two houses explore a particular kind of design operation: disassembling existing arrangements into separate potential elements in order to combine these elements into new fragmentary arrangements.

While designing the hung slabs, at times they appeared as light as the elements of a mobile. I calculated their weights to balance the whole exactly as one would for a mobile. Of course, this kind of moving structure could not be achieved. In any case, I still think about those components and their meanings, imagining that they are not fixed but remain dynamic, dancing like one of Alexander Calder's mobiles; they are always ready for a different arrangement.

Downtown São Paulo, looking east

Faculty of Architecture and Urbanism, University of São Paulo, the House Like the City

Ribeirão Preto House, by SPBR, São Paulo, Brazil, 2002

Houses in Ribeirão Preto and Ubatuba, São Paulo, Brazil

Cross section with site, House in Ubatuba, São Paulo, Brazil, 2009

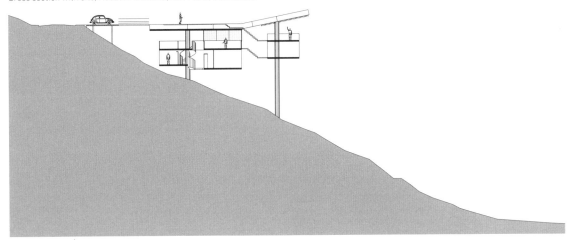

Exterior view

Interior view, 2009

Under construction by Bremenkamp, House in Ubatuba, 2007

Swimming pool resting on a single column, 2009

Interior during construction, 2009

Houses in Ribeirão Preto and Ubatuba, São Paulo, Brazil

SPBR

Exterior view, 2009

Structural Engineering + Material Science

137

Exposed Concrete: Design, Engineering, and Performance

Werner Sobek + Heiko Trumpf

143

Magical Structuralism

Guy Nordenson

147

From Wire Mesh to 3-D Textiles: Progress in New Reinforcements for Ferrocement and Thin-Cement Composites

Antoine E. Naaman

158

Engineering in Cuba

Ysrael A. Seinuk

168

Nanotechnology in Concrete

Surendra P. Shah

175

Ultra-High-Performance Concrete in Highway Transportation Infrastructure

Benjamin A. Graybeal

177

Form Over Mass: Light-Concrete Structures

Hans Schober

Exposed Concrete: Design, Engineering, and Performance

Werner Sobek + Heiko Trumpf

Introduction

Our perception of a structure is determined by its shape, surface qualities, and color. The perception of exposed concrete surfaces in particular depends on the quality of these surfaces at both the macro- and microscopic levels. The formwork, as well as the additives and aggregates, crucially influence these qualities.

Concrete is the only building material that can be brought into any shape while at the same time being cost-effective and having high load-bearing capacity. Ultra-High-Performance Concrete (UHPC), new composites such as Fiber-Reinforced Concrete (FRC), gradient concrete, highly perforated members, and high-precision prefabricated units enable architects and engineers to realize a wide range of complex, geometrical structures. These new materials and construction techniques also help to minimize the quantity of material used, thus reducing cost. The Mercedes-Benz Museum in Stuttgart, designed by UNStudio, is a very good example of an integrated realization process for a complex building structure; the project demanded a great deal of technical design requirements with respect to the concrete surfaces and formwork. Shaping concrete in an innovative way also means solving the formwork problem; with a few exceptions, there is no reason at all to pour concrete into a formwork in order to produce plain surfaces. The surface of exposed concrete can be used to show a wide range of sophisticated designs, from printing, texturing, and painting to surfaces that reflect the positive shape of the formwork itself. It is essential to treat the surface of concrete in a way that is worthy of the many opportunities offered by the material.

Mercedes-Benz Museum, Stuttgart, Germany

The entrance has been raised in order to elevate the museum's use above that of its industrial surroundings.

Conceived as a landscape of mobility, an evenly ascending mound guides visitors to the entrance. Lifts in the atrium take visitors to the top floor, where the tour descends through the building from the top down. | figs. 1–3

The vertical structure of the automobile museum condenses the museum's program into a relatively small area. The physical design of the building is a double-helix structure. The intersecting rotational arrangement of the different levels span across the symmetrical cloverleaf floor plan. The leaves of the cloverleaf progress around a triangular atrium, forming five horizontal levels, each consisting of a single and a two-story component that houses the collections and stages the settings for the automaker's legendary vehicles. All of the technical elements are gathered together in large structures that double as hollow-box girders arranged alternately in the atrium and the facade; at the same time, they provide sufficient strength to allow the roofing in all levels to be built without supporting columns.

It was only possible to implement the demanding geometrical design by using cast-on-site concrete. The formwork for the double-curved structural elements represented a particularly interesting challenge. The entire work was generated as a parametric computer model, encompassing double-curved structural elements. The construction of the preformed, moulded blanks was automated using three-dimensional data. A new process was developed to simplify fabrication of the formwork for the double-curved surfaces; this made it possible to create the curvature using custom-built planar elements with elastic properties, which allowed them to be pressed into the desired shape. This process, for example, was how 150 different two-dimensional, sectional shapes of formwork facing were generated. Together they describe the complete double-curved surface, making it possible to fabricate the formwork for twist components. | figs. 4–6

Samples and 1:1 mock-ups were used to test the castings in order to examine and evaluate the final condition of the concrete elements with regard to their optical and haptic qualities. It was only possible to achieve the highest-quality result—as well as develop an approach to solving existing problems—with formwork of nonplanar surfaces, thanks to the precisely organized and extremely close-knit cooperation between architects, engineers, experts in geometry, and all of the professional planners and companies involved from the very beginning of the planning process.

Guidelines and Engineering Standards

The quality of the exposed concrete surfaces in Germany is essentially guaranteed by guidelines and standards, such as those contained in the *Guidelines for Exposed Concrete* published by the German Society for Concrete and Construction Technology (Deutscher Beton- und Bautechnik-Verein e. V.). These guidelines divide the requirements that exposed surfaces must fulfill into four so-called exposed concrete categories (SBs), ranging from SB1, with low optical demands; through to SB4, which covers concrete surfaces of particularly high design significance. The texture and uniformity of the color tone, as well as the porosity and evenness of the surfaces, are divided into requirement classes, providing a guideline to assist the planning engineer as well as the company carrying out the work in order to achieve optimal results with regard to the aspects outlined above.

Furthermore, as part of the planning process, the intended quality level of the exposed surfaces is already specified precisely at the tender specification phase. Included in the planning phase are exact details regarding formwork facing, the texture of the formwork elements, and the formwork placement with regard to foundation bolt holes and joints of structural elements. Reference components intended to demonstrate the expected future result—making it possible to monitor deviations from the desired end result—are fabricated at a 1:1 scale before the beginning of the execution phase.

The most crucial prerequisite for obtaining exposed concrete surfaces of the highest quality is close cooperation between the specialist professions involved in the construction from the very start of the initial planning phases. Only an integrated planning process can achieve exposed concrete surfaces of such a quality, as can be seen from the example of the Mercedes-Benz Museum. | figs. 7–8

Conclusion

Designing a building as a part of the built environment means taking into consideration more than simply the primary functions, such as load-bearing qualities. People do, can, and must expect the quality of the built environment to go beyond technical correctness or even perfectionism. Architects and engineers should consider that a building—regardless of whether it is a bridge, a high-rise, an industrial construction, or a retaining wall—must fulfill a wide range of aesthetic demands. These demands necessitate education, in our design teams and at our universities, which is far from the usual. It necessitates an understanding and a mastery of the connection and the interrelation between material, shape, structure, sustainability, surface, color, and light. In our work with concrete, this understanding and mastery must be the next step.

Exposed Concrete

Werner Sobek + Heiko Trumpf

fig. 1 | Mercedes-Benz Museum, night view, by UNStudio, Stuttgart, Germany, 2006

fig. 3 | 3-D exploded diagram of the building structure

fig. 2 | Facade detail

fig. 4 | Parametric computer model of double-curved surface

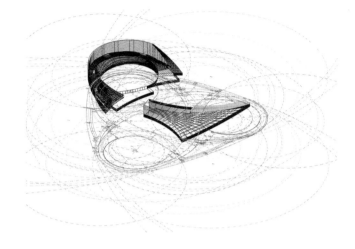

fig. 5 | Shutter patterns and formwork for the double-curved surface

fig. 6 | Final view of the double-curved concrete surface

fig. 7 | View of the interior

fig. 8 | View of the interior

Magical Structuralism

Guy Nordenson

It is not surprising that the latent ideology behind the theme of the Solid States: Changing Time for Concrete conference was the standby Corbusian case for technological revolution and historical necessity, as demanded by the march of new materials, new products, and new frontiers. Contemporary architecture loves this myth. As an engineer, I, too, am congenitally excited by new materials and methods, but I am also cautious, having seen too many exciting new ideas, ideals, and inventions end in disaster. The world's ongoing economic meltdown—thanks to the financial "engineering" of exotic products—is only the most topical case of the magical post-structuralism that has affected not only the finance industry but much of our global culture in the prolonged Reagan Era that has dominated the past quarter century. So it may be soothing—in this enervated context—to offer up a few cases and paradoxes, under the rubric of "magical structuralism," that reconsider this ideology of technological progress.

Dreaming Engineering

My first cue is from Dreamland: Architectural Experiments Since the 1970s, the exhilarating exhibition curated by Andres Lepik at the Museum of Modern Art in the fall of 2008. The exhibit of drawings and models of once unrealized and unrealizable architectures demonstrated just how far the current practice of architecture has crossed over to the surreal. What once excited the realm of fantasy is now the grim reality of Dubai, Abu Dhabi, Shenzhen, and Beijing.

Consider the case of the 1958 Philips Pavilion by Le Corbusier and Iannis Xenakis, a project full of paradox and conflict. Starting from Le Corbusier's sketch of the exhibition pavilion as a stomach that digests visitors, Xenakis and Le Corbusier conceived a completely illogical tensile structure that slowly evolved through many false starts, dead ends, and stumped contractors, and was finally built of concrete tiles cast on sand dunes in Holland and then assembled on-site in Brussels. | fig. 1 Both as a project and a completed work, it was delirious, contentious, ephemeral, and not least of all, influential. It can be regarded as a precedent for the epic narrative structure, be it Jørn Utzon's Sydney Opera House (1973), Norman Foster's Hongkong and Shanghai Bank (1986), or Frank Gehry's Guggenheim Bilbao (1997).

Closer to home, the Jubilee Church, formally known as Dio Padre Misericordioso, in Rome (2003), on which I consulted for Richard Meier, used a similar construction of stacking, curved prefabricated blocks while referring to the local Roman stone and to ferrocement precedents. The use of the exposed monolithic blocks heightens the spatial energy of the church, yet their construction posed significant challenges, which led to the invention of a giant robot, "La Macchina," that delighted the local children for over two years; in the end, it even created a structure from a new form of self-cleaning, smog-eating, superwhite concrete manufactured using titanium oxide by Italcementi. | fig. 2

These are not realizations of teleological necessity—of a material, computational, or even social invention; rather, these are cases of a compulsive and irrational drive toward abstraction that somehow has led to idiosyncratic and even useful inventions.

Surreal Production

The surreal madness of some of the products of the last boom in construction—from Dubai to Tribeca—is at least partially the responsibility of designers and their critics. For one thing, we seldom discuss labor conditions or even the economic conditions of projects. What are the daily lives of the workers like? What are they paid and how do they live? Where do they live? Clearly in the boomtowns of China and the United Arab Emirates, the disparity of income between the migrant workers and the new middle or upper classes has provided the "window" for the developers of exuberant architecture.

During the construction of Linked Hybrid, a project that we collaborated on with Steven Holl Architects in Beijing, the workers were briefly allowed to occupy the hotel portion of

the complex. | fig. 3 This was the better moment of the process. For the most part, the workers lived in poor conditions on-site. They were paid about $100 a month, while the apartments were for sale for upwards of $5,000 per square meter. For me, the conflict in this project was between the radical social ambitions, which I think are integral to the success of Steven Holl's design—such as the bridges, the school, the cinematheque—and the stark economic inequality that provides the "window" for their realization. The crass corruption of the commercial process was what I could not resolve for myself. At least, unlike some other projects that pretended to greater nationalist purposes, Linked Hybrid's paradoxes were up front.

Experimental Empiricism

Of all the experiences of magical structuralism, the most extreme have been those I've had at the World Trade Center (WTC) site. For seven years I have been in and out of work on and around the site, including for the original World Trade Center Tower 1 of 2003, the Goldman Sachs Headquarters in 2004, and, more recently, the exposed slurry wall of the World Trade Center Memorial Museum. | figs. 4–5

The slurry wall began as a very sentimental idea, a celebration of the symbolic quality that this "bulwark of democracy" had stood through the trials of 9/11—a crude overstatement and simplification. Yet, as the only visible structure at the current WTC site during the interminable saga of mediocrity, the wall became a de facto monument and symbol of post-9/11 endurance. With the help of consulting engineers Simpson Gumpertz & Heger, and working for architects Davis Brody Bond Aedas, we designed an invisible structure that would hold a section of the wall—in the end, measuring only 60 feet (18 meters) wide—and fought against numerous obstacles, both ideological and gravitational, to keep the ruin visible. The challenge was to keep the chaos of debris behind the wall stable and also to confront the overriding opinion that behind the wall was a hallowed space filled with dangers. By building a system of counterfort walls using

slurry construction behind the wall, we arrived at a solution and braved the superstitions. Again, the odyssey of the project took unexpected turns but will and wiles overcame the apparent necessities.

Magical Structuralism

The tyrant and great architecture patron Sigismondo Malatesta had as his motto "tempus loquendi, tempus tacendi," which translates as "a time to speak, a time to be silent." A related Quaker saying advises that we "say as much as necessary and as little as possible." Technology does not drive history; rather, it is the entanglements of human desire for power, for beauty, and for immortality, and the opportunities and obstacles of reality, that give true magic to our work. Technology in the service of desire is, at its best, doing as much as necessary and as little as possible.

fig. 3 | Linked Hybrid, hotel occupation by workers, by Steven Holl Architects, Beijing, China, 2007

fig. 4 | World Trade Center Tower 1 model, by Guy Nordenson and Associates, 2003

fig. 5 | World Trade Center Memorial Museum, section of slurry wall, photograph by Guy Nordenson and Associates, 2006

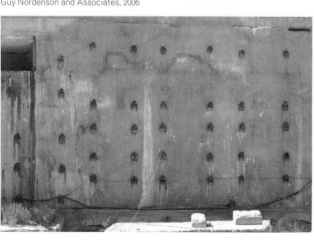

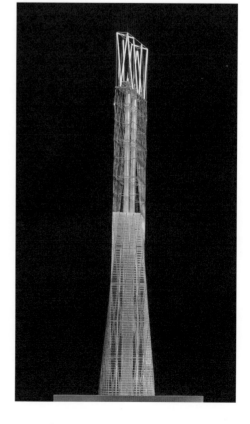

From Wire Mesh to 3-D Textiles: Progress in New Reinforcements for Ferrocement and Thin-Cement Composites

Antoine E. Naaman

Background/Definition

This essay focuses on the evolution of reinforcements for thin, cement-based composites, defined here as products having less than about 50 millimeters (approximately 2 inches) in thickness. Such composites are composed of two main components: a cement-based matrix and reinforcement. The reinforcement may be made of different materials, which can be continuous, discontinuous, or a hybrid combination of both. Related products include cement boards, corrugated cement sheets, pipes, cladding, shells, water tanks, boats, housing elements, and the like. While conventional reinforcements for these products are steel-wire meshes or laths, new forms of reinforcements have emerged over the years with the objective of improving performance and minimizing total product cost. These include Fiber-Reinforced-Polymer (FRP) reinforcements, textiles, or fabrics, which use high-performance fibers such as carbon, Kevlar, Spectra, and the like; new steel-unidirectional-reinforcing mats made with extremely high-strength wires or strands; 3-D textiles or fabrics using polymer fibers; 3-D textiles using a combination of polymer fibers and steel; and reinforcement that uses shape-memory materials to induce self-stressing or internal prestressing.

The first thin-reinforced-cement material was invented by Joseph-Louis Lambot and patented in France as *Ferciment* in 1855. It can be considered the first patent on reinforced concrete. Today the commonly used English term is *ferrocement*. While ferrocement implies the use of cement and, initially, steel reinforcement (from the French *fer*), other reinforcements have been used in thin-cement products. The main difference between ferrocement and reinforced concrete relates mostly to scale. Reinforced concrete uses larger reinforcing bars instead of wires or meshes, and a concrete binder, which, unlike cement paste and mortar, contains large-size

aggregates. Moreover, reinforcement in ferrocement is distributed throughout the thickness, while in reinforced concrete it is localized. The American Concrete Institute (ACI) provides the following definition: "Ferrocement is a type of thin-wall reinforced concrete commonly constructed of hydraulic-cement mortar reinforced with closely spaced layers of continuous and relatively small-size wire mesh. The mesh may be made of metallic or other suitable materials."[1] This last sentence opens the field to the use of polymer reinforcements such as high-performance carbon or aramid fibers, and also encompasses some modern applications such as textile-reinforced concrete (TRC). In a classic book on the subject of ferrocement and laminate-cementitious composites written by me in 2000, I suggested extending the definition by adding the two following sentences: "The fineness of the mortar matrix and its composition should be compatible with the mesh and armature systems it is meant to encapsulate. The matrix may contain discontinuous fibers."[2] These sentences were added to ascertain the compatibility of the matrix with the reinforcement in order to build a sound composite and to accommodate the use of discontinuous fibers or microfibers to improve performance in hybrid composites when desirable. Figure 1 shows a typical cross section of ferrocement and should be distinguished from what is generally defined as reinforced stucco. | figs. 1–2 While hundreds of references can be found to address these materials, a select number of recent reports and books is given at the end of this paper and should be considered a good starting point for further inquiry.[3–12]

Reference Materials of the 1960s and 1970s

In simple terms, a cement composite consists of two main components (as I mentioned earlier), the cementitious matrix and reinforcement, both of which have evolved enormously since Lambot's first patent. The evolution of the matrix—a colossal subject in its own right—will not be dealt with here. It is sufficient to say that the matrix, which in the time of Lambot may have achieved only 10 megapascals (MPa) compressive strength, today can be obtained with strengths of up

fig. 1 | Typical section of ferrocement, showing several layers of distributed welded wire-mesh reinforcement in a relatively thin section

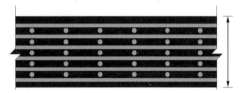

fig. 2 | Typical section of stucco, where one layer of metal lath or wire mesh is used in a matrix about 7/8-inch (22 millimeter) thick

fig. 3 | Examples of steel meshes used as reinforcement for ferrocement and thin-cement composites

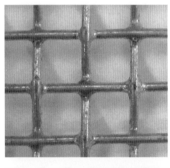

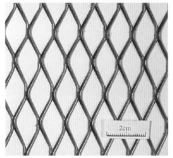
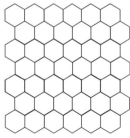

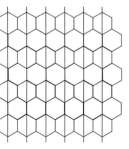

Hexagonal wire mesh   Improved hexagonal mesh

fig. 4 | Examples of high-performance 2-D polymeric meshes, textiles, or fabrics

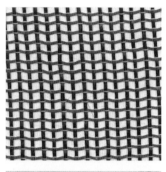

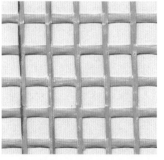

to 20 times that value. The tensile-yield strength of the steel wires used by Lambot may not have been much more than about 240 MPa. Today, steel wires with a tensile strength of 15 times that or higher are available. Moreover, reinforcement materials include not only steel but also other high-performance polymer fibers such as glass, carbon, aramid, Kevlar, Spectra fibers, and others.

Since the initial idea of ferrocement quickly led to a thicker form that became conventional reinforced concrete, the use of ferrocement and related research fell relatively dormant shortly after the mid-1850s. Only about a century later, in the 1940s and '50s did the Italian engineer and architect Pier Luigi Nervi recognize the possible advantages of ferrocement, not only for boat building but for terrestrial applications as well, and he carried out some engineering-based experiments on its mechanical properties. What is considered modern ferrocement, however, was reborn in the 1960s, driven by interest from many amateur boat builders and small fisheries. Serious research on the subject followed in the mid-1970s, with the establishment of the ACI Committee on Ferrocement, as well as the International Ferrocement Information Center at the Asian Institute of Technology in Bangkok, Thailand.

Reviewing what was available in the 1960s and '70s in terms of reinforcement and the relative ability to produce a ferrocement-type product, one would find steel-wire meshes of different forms, such as woven- or welded-square mesh, hexagonal (chicken-wire mesh), and diamond shape (expanded metal used in stucco applications). | fig. 3   Other potential reinforcements were also available, including meshes made of natural fibers such as jute or sisal; and polymer meshes, textiles, or fabrics of various forms such as nylon, polypropylene, and polyester. These were considered of low performance because of their low elastic modulus in comparison to that of steel and concrete and their relatively low tensile strength in comparison to advanced synthetic fibers such as glass and carbon. The elastic modulus represents the stress needed to induce a unit deformation in a material. Thus, everything else being equal, the stress needed to extend a rubber band by 1

inch (2.5 centimeters), for example, is much smaller than the stress needed to extend a steel wire of the same length and cross section by 1 inch. From this example, it can be intuitively concluded that the elastic modulus of rubber is much smaller than that of steel. The yield strength of most widely available steel meshes ranges from about 240 MPa to about 600 MPa. While the elastic modulus of steel does not depend on its strength—that is, it remains almost constant at about 200 GPa—steel meshes may show an equivalent elastic modulus of lower value than that of steel because of the weaving or other manufacturing process. Thus, a woven-square steel-wire mesh could be considered to act as if its equivalent elastic modulus is half to two-thirds that of the steel from which it is made. A chicken-wire or aviary mesh would have an even lower equivalent modulus.

For all reinforced concrete and cement composites, there is a simple rule based on mechanics that can be followed to design a composite with higher performance: increase both the ratio of tensile strength of the reinforcement to the compressive strength of the matrix, and the ratio of elastic modulus of the reinforcement to that of the matrix. This requirement, related to the moduli ratio, may explain why low-end polymer meshes made of polypropylene, for instance, were not widely or successfully used, although polypropylene fibers had strengths comparable to that of conventional steel-wire meshes; however, based on the above simple rule, it can be concluded that polypropylene fibers may be compatible with very lightweight cementitious matrices, which show both low compressive strength and low elastic modulus.

Going back to the steel-wire meshes on the market in the 1970s, high-yield strengths were not available and could not be obtained beyond a certain strength. Indeed, in the production of woven-wire meshes, the use of high-strength wires leads to very "springy" wires that do not deform very much during alternate bending, making the weaving process difficult to control. In the case of welded meshes, the welds at the joints weakened the wires and thus again led to reduced strength. Thus in the 1970s, most available wire meshes on the market showed tensile strengths less than 700 MPa, while tensile strengths close to 1,000 MPa could be obtained only exceptionally, such as in research experiments.

The volume fraction of steel-mesh reinforcement in ferrocement generally ranges from about 2 to 8 percent; the 8 percent threshold is exceeded only with difficulty.[2-3] Typically such a value may be obtained by packing together as many layers of mesh as possible within the composite; both the tensile and bending resistance of the composite increase with respect to the volume fraction of reinforcement. In particular, analysis of the section suggests that the bending resistance increases almost proportionately to the volume fraction of reinforcement (or the number of layers of mesh) primarily because the steel mesh has extensive yielding behavior. Under these conditions, modulus rupture values—that is, the equivalent elastic bending resistance in the cracked state— could reach about 50 MPa with 7 percent reinforcement content.[2] Until the 1990s, this was considered the mechanical limit of the material.

Advanced FRP Meshes, Textiles, or Fabrics—2-D Systems
During the mid-1980s and early '90s, polymer meshes, textiles, or fabrics made with high-performance fibers such as carbon, glass, Kevlar, or Spectra were tested for ferrocement applications. | fig. 4 Since they exhibited high tensile strength in comparison to the conventional low yield strength of steel-wire meshes on the market, they were immediately viewed as a way to increase the performance of ferrocement composites.

Both analytical and experimental studies, however, show that adding FRP meshes, textiles, or fabrics in excess to the two extreme layers, with the goal of improving bending resistance, does not lead to a sufficient improvement to justify the additional cost of the intermediate layers. This is because, unlike steel meshes, FRP meshes using high-performance fibers such as carbon, Kevlar, or glass show a linear-elastic stress-strain response in tension up to failure, with no yielding. Thus the addition of intermediate layers of mesh for bending may lead to successive failures of the mesh layers at

ultimate resistance, instead of allowing for the simultaneous combination of forces from different layers of mesh, as is the case with yielding steel-wire mesh.

Using only two extreme layers of reinforcement, however, FRP meshes demonstrated that their higher tensile strength could be an asset, and this led to composite moduli of rupture (equivalent elastic-bending resistance) of close to 25 MPa with less than 1.5 percent total volume fraction of reinforcing mesh. Furthermore, to remedy the absence of intermediate layers of FRP meshes and to improve shear resistance, discontinuous fibers were added to the mortar matrix, leading to hybrid combinations of reinforcement. The fibers were primarily needed to improve shear resistance, both vertical and interlaminar, and to help utilize the tensile strength of the mesh as much as possible by increasing the strain capacity of the mortar matrix in compression. Such an increase would allow for an increase in the compressive force within the compression zone, permitting the tensile force to maintain equilibrium and thus increasing the bending resistance. Moduli of rupture close to 40 MPa were thus obtained using only 2.26 percent total volume fraction of reinforcement, with two extreme layers of carbon mesh (1.26 percent reinforcement) and 1 percent discontinuous polyvinyl alcohol (PVA) microfibers.[11-12] Thus, comparing the maximum modulus of rupture of ferrocement with that of conventional steel meshes (50 MPa with 7 percent reinforcement) to that of hybrid ferrocement containing high-performance carbon meshes and fibers (40 MPa with 2.26 percent reinforcement), one can conclude that the hybrid combination offers a better overall efficiency of 250 percent in terms of volume of reinforcement used. Even with this improved efficiency, equivalent elastic-bending strengths (or moduli of rupture) in excess of 50 MPa could not be easily achieved with high-performance polymer reinforcements. Cost-related issues are not discussed here but should also be taken into consideration for real applications. In summary, the most efficient model for thin-cement composites reinforced with 2-D polymer meshes would have only two extreme layers of mesh reinforcement and a matrix reinforced with microfibers. | figs. 5–6

Advanced Steel Reinforcements for Thin-Cement Products—
2-D Systems

Producing steel-wire mesh with high-strength wires, whether woven or welded, was not practical from the viewpoint of manufacturing, as explained earlier; however, pseudomeshes were developed for other purposes. Belgian manufacturer Bekaert S.A. marketed a meshlike product called *Fleximat* in the early 1990s, made in one direction from high-strength fine-steel strands, and in the other direction from low-end polymer yarns in a leno-weave process. Fleximat was used as reinforcement for conveyor belts used in quarries, mines, and similar applications. Fleximat fabric offered very high tensile strength in only one direction; one would have to place two layers of Fleximat, normal to each other, to obtain equally high strengths in two directions with a layout similar to a square-steel mesh. | fig. 7

In this decade, a high-strength steel-based product similar in purpose to the Fleximat mesh was introduced to the U.S. market with the trade name HardWire. It was initially marketed as a substitute to adhesively bonded FRP sheets, or plates such as carbon or Kevlar, used to repair reinforced-concrete members, where bonding is achieved through an epoxy resin. Hardwire is similar to a 2-D mesh. In the primary direction, it is composed of parallel steel strands spaced at approximately 6.25 millimeters (0.2 inches), although different spacing is also available; the strands are adhesively bonded by a square mesh made from glass fibers. Thus the product looks like a wire mesh. | fig. 8 The glass-fiber mesh, however, is neither strong nor significant, being used only as support to the steel strands. The strands are made each from five steel wires with an approximate diameter of 0.3 millimeters (0.01 inches) each. The wires have very high tensile strength of the order of 3,150 MPa and are typically used to fabricate tire cord for high-performance tires. Two layers of HardWire placed normal to each other can be used to simulate a 2-D square mesh similar to conventional steel-wire meshes used in ferrocement.

Tests carried out by the author on 12.5-millimeter (0.5-inch) thick ferrocement plates, reinforced only with two extreme layers of HardWire mesh and fibers, led to moduli of

rupture in bending close to 105 MPa, with only 1.76 percent HardWire reinforcement (two layers) and 1 percent PVA fiber. [2, 11, and 13] If we adjust the reinforcement to include equal bending strength in two directions, it would lead to a total volume fraction of reinforcement of 4.52 percent, including the fibers. Similar tests using Fleximat fabric led to a modulus of rupture of 127 MPa, with an equivalent total volume of reinforcement of 3.7 percent. Adjusted to two directions, the total volume would become 6.4 percent. Thus, comparing the maximum modulus of rupture of ferrocement with conventional steel meshes (50 MPa with 7 percent reinforcement) with the above results (105 MPa at 4.52 percent reinforcement), one can almost achieve a double in modulus of rupture at about two-thirds the total volume of reinforcement. This is almost three times more efficiency. More importantly, this shows that a modulus of rupture of 125 MPa in thin cementitious products can be achieved, and it currently represents a record high-performance limit to exceed in the future.

Tri-Dimensional (3-D) Reinforcement—Cost Issues

It is important to keep common cost issues encountered in the manufacturing of ferrocement and thin-concrete products in perspective. There are three main sources of cost for a typical product: cost of the cementitious matrix, cost of the reinforcement, and cost of labor. Typically the cost of the cementitious matrix is less than 10 percent of the total cost, even when several additives enhance the matrix. Most likely, the matrix cost is less than 5 percent. The combined cost of reinforcement and labor thus amounts to more than 90 percent of total cost. [2 and 13] In developing countries the cost of reinforcement and labor are almost equally divided. Placing several layers of mesh reinforcement and possibly spacing them according to design is labor intensive and thus costly. While some industrial processes were developed to handle the use of synthetic-mesh reinforcements, no such process exists to handle steel-wire meshes.

It becomes clear from the above that improvements in the efficiency of the reinforcement—for instance, by

fig. 7 | Fleximat fabric with unidirectional strength

fig. 5 | Typical section of thin-cement composite with several layers of FRP mesh

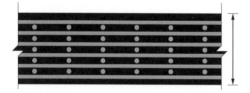

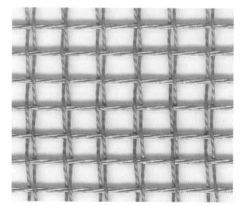

fig. 6 | Typical section of efficient, fiber-reinforced polymer hybrid composite with only two extreme layers of mesh and fibers to replace intermediate layers of mesh

fig. 8 | HardWire reinforcement with unidirectional strength

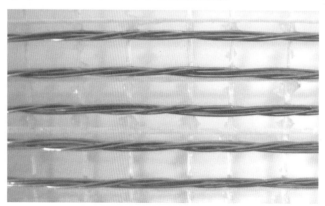

reducing the number of mesh layers needed in the design—and improvements in the production process to reduce labor cost will have the most significant effect on the final cost of the product.

The first improvement, reducing the number of layers of mesh, can be resolved by using only two layers of high-performance steel-wire meshes or advanced FRP meshes and adding microfibers to the matrix, as described above. The second improvement, reducing labor cost, can be resolved by the use of 3-D instead of 2-D reinforcements. The idea behind the design of a 3-D reinforcement is to develop a single-armature system that, when placed in a mold and infiltrated by a cement matrix, will lead to the desired product. Three-dimensional reinforcement systems can also be designed and tailored to satisfy particular performance requirements.

3-D Reinforcement Systems Using Steel

Many users of ferrocement, wishing to simplify the construction process, have thought about 3-D reinforcement systems for ferrocement applications. This became particularly pressing in the late 1980s, as asbestos fibers were banned from use in cement boards and sheets due to health concerns. Tri-dimensional reinforcement systems in the form of 3-D meshes (Watson's mesh) were tried, as well as 3-D meshes made by simply connecting two parallel steel meshes (using welded links or coil spacers). | fig. 9 These methods turned out to be costly and their use was limited. Watson's mesh was discontinued in the 1980s.

Another idea suitable for both steel- and fiber-reinforced polymer meshes was to use an armature system made out of a fiber mat sandwiched between two layers of reinforcing mesh. | fig. 10 The sandwich is placed in a mold and infiltrated by a fine cement-based matrix. Besides the advantage of ease of construction, the system produces a composite with reinforcement spaced exactly as needed (with minimum labor), and the fiber mat improves the shear and bending resistance of the composite.

3-D Reinforcement Systems Using Polymer Fibers

It is only in the late 1990s and early 2000s that 3-D meshes—also described as 3-D fabrics or textiles—derived from the technology of textiles and fabrics became available for research studies in ferrocement-type products. In particular, the Institute of Textile Technology (ITA) at RWTH, Aachen University in collaboration with the Technical University of Dresden Germany, pioneered a number of 3-D textiles for applications in cement and concrete composites, which they have termed Textile-Reinforced Concrete (TRC).[9 and 12] The 3-D fabrics have the advantage of placing the reinforcement exactly where it is needed and tailoring its properties to particular applications. They also offer tremendous advantages in simplifying construction and saving on labor cost. Such 3-D meshes can be readily produced in thicknesses ranging from approximately 10 to 50 millimeters (0.4 to 2 inches), which is perfectly suitable for ferrocement and thin-cement composite applications. Moreover, textile technology offers the advantage of placing as much reinforcement as needed by design (generally less than 4 percent by volume) exactly where it is needed, and tailoring the fabric properties and shell volume for particular applications. | figs. 11–12 The 3-D textiles allow for the production of composites with holes or cavities, thus leading to a reduction in weight for the final product. Analytical modeling suggests that bending resistance close to 30 MPa can be achieved with these 3-D systems using current FRP materials.

Thus, these 3-D systems, while definitely reducing production labor, have not demonstrated high performance such as high bending resistance, as expected. This is because, as a group, bundles of fibers, strands, or yarns made from high-performance polymer fibers do not show the same tensile strength as the individual fibers from which they are made. Typically a glass fiber may have a tensile strength of 3,500 MPa. Textiles, fabrics, or meshes use strands containing a large number of fibers, typically ranging from 200 to 12,000 fibers. A glass fabric made with strands containing approximately 200 fibers per strand and used in cement composite may show an equivalent tensile strength of only 800 MPa. This

fig. 9 | Examples of 3-D mesh systems with steel reinforcement: **a:** Watson's mesh (discontinued production), **b:** two square steel meshes joined by welded link, **c:** two square steel meshes joined by coiled links

a.
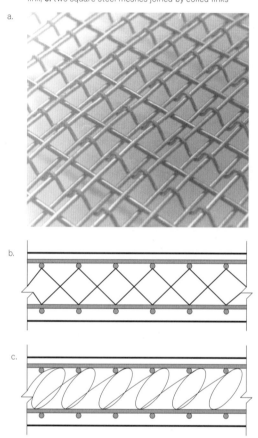

fig. 10 | Typical sandwich-type reinforcing system using a fiber mat core between two extreme layers of mesh: **a:** concept, **b:** example with steel mesh and PVA fiber mat

a.
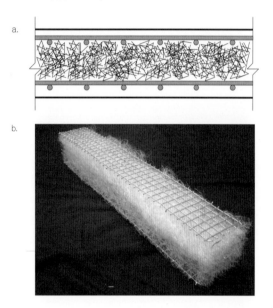

b.

c.

fig. 11 | Examples of 3-D mesh systems with FRP textile reinforcements fabricated at the ITA in Aachen, Germany, **a:** 3-D spacer textile, **b:** 3-D spacer stiff textile, both approximately 15 millimeters (0.6 inches) thick

a.

b.
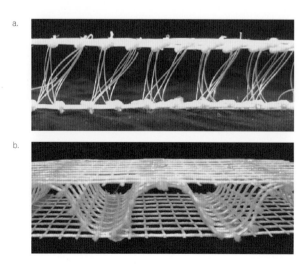

155

From Wire Mesh to 3-D Textiles

Antoine E. Naaman

fig. 12 | **a:** 3-D ribbed textile sketch and sample produced by ITA in Aachen, Germany, for preliminary testing, **b:** The resulting thin-cement composite can be either solid or with cavities that can be filled with Styrofoam to reduce its weight (the panel can be made to float)

a.

b.

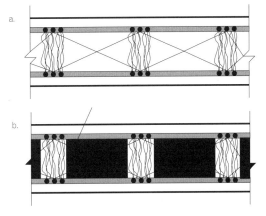

fig. 13 | New 3-D textile incorporating steel strands produced by ITA in Aachen, Germany (note the steel strands showing at the left end of the textile)

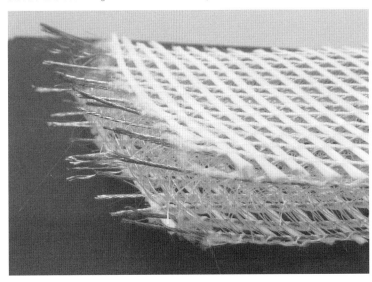

is because, under tensile loading, the fibers are not loaded simultaneously at the same level, and progressive fiber fracture occurs. If the strand is made with fibers embedded in a polymer resin, it is likely that the equivalent strength would increase to 1,200 MPa. On the other hand, if the fibers are perfectly aligned and embedded in a resin—leading to a rigid and perfectly straight strand structure—a much higher tensile strength can be achieved similar to a conventional FRP bar. One can get roughly 60 to 70 percent of the strength of the fiber; however, in such a case the 3-D fabric will be extremely costly and very difficult to manufacture.

This prompted the investigators at the D\ITA in Aachen and at the University of Michigan to look at introducing high-strength steel cord into the textile to replace some of the glass yarns, in order to take advantage of the strength and toughness of steel, while preserving the inherent constructional advantages offered by the 3-D textile. Recently the research team at ITA was able to produce such a 3-D textile, a world first in the integration of steel and FRP reinforcements. The textile uses glass fibers for the fill (transverse direction), polypropylene fibers for the vertical spacing (acting as spacers and shear reinforcement), and high-strength steel strands inserted in the weft (longitudinal direction). The vertical polypropylene fibers can be made to protrude beyond the plane of the main longitudinal reinforcing wires, thus allowing for the desired net cover of cement matrix desired over the main reinforcement. Such a textile offers the best possible performance by taking advantage of the strength and ductility of steel while using conventional polymer fibers and permitting a 3-D textile machine to fabricate the textile. The contribution of the polymer fibers remains effective and provides the support armature for the steel reinforcement and the shell of the armature. A typical 3-D FRP steel-hybrid textile is shown in figure 13. | fig. 13

Looking Ahead: Passive and Active Reinforcements
It is evident that cement composites with higher performance—qualified here as high strength and high ductility—necessitate the use of high-performance cement matrices on the one hand and high-performance reinforcement characterized by both a high tensile strength and a high-tensile elastic modulus on the other hand. Such criteria favor high-strength steel products and high-performance polymer fibers such as carbon, Kevlar, Spectra, and the like. Since manufacturing and labor cost consume a large portion of the cost of these composites, the use of 3-D reinforcing systems may play a key role in future expansion and developments.[13]

In comparing high-performance FRP meshes, textiles, or fabrics with steel meshes, it is likely that the competition will be very close and that the advantages of one over the other will depend on criteria other than strength or moduli of rupture. For instance, the fact that FRP materials can (at the present time) be made into 3-D textiles that form the armature system and can be simply placed into a mold and infiltrated by a mortar matrix gives FRPS a significant advantage in terms of savings on labor cost. FRPS are also significantly lighter in weight than steel, and thus easier to handle in the field. The bottom line, however, is total cost, and steel remains very competitive not only in terms of performance, such as equivalent bending strength, but also in terms of total cost of the product. Manufactured 3-D steel meshes or hybrid-combination steel and textile 3-D meshes may offer optimized solutions in the future. Clearly the ability to manufacture a particular 3-D textile at reasonable cost will provide a key advantage.

In most of the above discussion, it was assumed that the reinforcement remains relatively passive; that is, the reinforcement is stressed only when the structure is stressed. It is possible, however, to make the reinforcement more active by creating self-stressing thin-cement composites. Self-stressing in cement composites can be obtained by either an expansion of the matrix, a contraction of the reinforcement, or both. Bond and/or anchorage between the two components is assumed to be perfect. The advantages of prestressing are similar to those of conventional prestressed concrete and include a higher resistance to cracking and thus improved corrosion resistance, impermeability, and durability. Smart reinforcing materials currently available include shape-memory alloys (SMAS) and some special polymer fibers that possess the unique property of being able to be frozen temporarily in a particular state and then, with proper heat or radiation treatment, reverted to their previous equilibrium condition. For instance, an SMA wire mesh is first stretched to a certain strain level and stabilized in that state; then it is used in a cement-based matrix. Once the matrix has hardened, the reinforcement is relaxed from its induced deformation by heat or radiation; in attempting to shrink back to its previous state, it provides, through bond and or anchorage, the needed stress in the matrix. In some tests carried out on thin-cement sheets, an initial prestress of about 7 MPa was achieved.[14] The challenge, of course, is to go much higher.

Concluding Remarks

This paper has presented some of the progress in the reinforcement of ferrocement and thin-cement composites since their inception; one hopes that the results will inspire new researchers to take up the challenge and introduce improvements in the future, raising the limits achieved thus far. We need to exceed a modulus of rupture of about 125 MPa to minimize the cost-performance ratio; to produce optimized 3-D reinforcements at minimal cost; to take advantage of self-stressing reinforcement by inducing internal prestress levels exceeding 7 MPa; and to inform and educate the public and the profession about the advantages and potential applications of these composites. We need to keep dreaming at least slightly beyond the borders of reality.

Acknowledgments
The developments described in this essay, as related to 3-D textiles and fabrics with polymer fibers, were carried out primarily at the RWTH, Aachen University in Germany, with Thomas Gries and Andreas Roye from the Institute of Textile Technology, Wolfgang Brameshuber from the Institute of Building Materials, and Josef Hegger from the Structural Engineering Institute. Their collaboration is gratefully acknowledged.

References
The potential list of references would be too long and would still not do justice to all those who contributed ideas and advances in the development of ferrocement, laminated cement composites, and thin-cement composite products. The following endnotes contain a large number of further references within their pages, and should be consulted for further inquiry.

1 | "ACI Committee 549 (1997) State-of-the-Art Report on Ferrocement," *Concrete International* 4, no.8 (August 1982): 13–38. Reinstated as ACI 549-R97 in *Manual of Concrete Practice* (Farmington Hills, Michigan: American Concrete Institute, 2002), 549R-1–549R-26.

2 | Antoine E. Naaman, *Ferrocement and Laminated Cementitious Composites* (Ann Arbor, Michigan: Techno Press 3000, 2000).

3 | "ACI Committee 549, Guide for the Design, Construction, and Repair of Ferrocement, ACI 549.1R -88," *ACI Structural Journal* 85, no.3 (May/June 1988): 325–51. Also reinstated as 548.1R-93 and published in ACI *Manual of Concrete Practice* (Farmington Hills, Michigan: American Concrete Institute, 2007), 549.1R-1–549.1R-30.

4 | "ACI Committee 549 (2004) Report on Thin Reinforced Cementitious Products," *Manual of Concrete Practice* (Farmington Hills, Michigan: American Concrete Institute, 2007), 549.2R-1–549.2R-28.

5 | P. Balaguru, ed., *Thin Reinforced Concrete Products and Systems* (Farmington Hills, Michigan: American Concrete Institute, 1994), SP-146.

6 | J. I. Daniel and S.P. Shah, eds., *Thin-Section Fiber Reinforced Concrete and Ferrocement*, (Detroit, Michigan: American Concrete Institute, 1990), SP-124.

7 | A. Dubey, ed., *Thin Reinforced Cement-Based Products and Construction Systems*, Special Publication SP-224, (Farmington Hills, Michigan: American Concrete Institute, 2004).

8 | *Ferrocement Model Code*, by IFS Committee 10-01 (Bangkok, Thailand: International Ferrocement Society, Asian Institute of Technology, 2001), 95.

9 | W. Brameshuber, ed., "Textile Reinforced Concrete," *State-of the-Art Report of RILEM Technical Committee 201-TRC*, Report 36, Bagneux, France: RILEM Publications, 2006).

10 | Antoine E. Naaman, "Ferrocement: Four Decades of Progress," *Journal of Ferrocement* 36, no. 1 (January 2006): 741–56.

11 | Antoine E. Naaman, "Progress in Ferrocement and Hybrid Textile Composites," in *Proceeding of the 2nd Colloquium on Textile Reinforced Structures—CTRC2*, ed. M. Curbach (Dresden, Germany: Dresden University, 2003), 325-46.

12 | M. Curbach, ed., *Proceeding of the 2nd Colloquium on Textile Reinforced Structures—CTRC2* (Dresden, Germany: Dresden University, 2003).

13 | Antoine E. Naaman, "Thin Cement Composites: Performance Comparison between Steel and Textile Reinforcments," in *Composites in Construction*, ed. P. Hamelin, D. Bigaud, E. Ferrier, and E. Jacquelin (Lyon, France: University of Lyon, July 2005), 1155–64.

14 | Krstulovic-Opara and Atoine E. Naaman, "Self-Stressing Fiber Composites," *ACI Structural Journal* 97, no. 2 (March/April 2000): 335–44.

Engineering in Cuba

Ysrael A. Seinuk

Change can elicit two kinds of reactions: there is change that people are enthusiastic about and there is resistance to change. This resistance can come in the form of timidity, perhaps, but it could also be political; in some situations, change affects our designs but is beyond our control. We have heard a great deal about experiments with new materials in concrete and there are many new materials being tried all over the world, but there are just as many that you don't see that are being used here in the United States. Indeed, resistance to new materials within the building industry in the United States has its own history, a situation that only becomes fully visible when compared with similar situations in other nations.

The Habana Riviera by Igor B. Polevitzky, built in 1957, is a sixteen-story casino hotel in Havana, Cuba, which already in the mid-1950s was using very high-strength concrete. | **fig. 1** At that time in the United States and particularly outside of New York, which was a dominant construction center, this type of material was not being used. Very early, in 1937, engineers in New York, such as C. S. Whitney, proposed a completely different design system for concrete. It was a phenomenal proposal, and the whole world adopted it. It was called the ultimate-strength design method of reinforced concrete.* Buildings in the 1950s, such as the Habana Riviera, were designed using this method. When I came to the United States in 1960, this method was not in use, and it was not until 1964 that the American Concrete Institute (ACI) code was adopted, in which there were a few pages in the back mentioning that system.

Elsewhere, however, tall buildings in concrete were being realized, such as the Edificio FOCSA (1956), which at 35 stories was the tallest building in Havana. | **fig. 2** Even at the time, one could find statements by engineers or engineering associations to the effect that concrete buildings could not be taller than 20 stories. Nor was the Edificio FOCSA the tallest concrete building in the world; in Brazil, there was a building

that was about 5 or 6 meters (16 to 20 feet) taller. Edificio FOCSA already used 8,000-psi concrete, but the manuals that we had in the United States listed concrete with strengths of 2,500 or 3,000 psi, and there was a very interesting new development that might have reached 3,750 psi. There were even more ambitious plans in Cuba, including a design by the architect Martin Dominguez for the 50-story Edificio Libertad in 1959, using 8,000 psi concrete. | **fig. 3** Unfortunately, it was not built because a change in Cuba that year paralyzed everything.

The realm of bridge construction provides some of the most vivid comparative references. The Walnut Lane Memorial Bridge in Philadelphia (1950) designed by Belgian engineer Gustave Magnel was the first prestressed bridge to be built in the United States. | **fig. 4** The first prestressed concrete bridge had been realized over a decade earlier in 1937—the bridge in Aue, Germany, designed by Franz Dischinger. The problem was not the American engineers, who were willing to use prestressed concrete but were unable to do so; rather, the building codes did not include the prestressed system. The Walnut Lane Memorial Bridge, which is very elegant, has a central span of about 160 feet (48.8 meters). The central span of this bridge as well as the bridge in Arimao, Cuba, which was designed and engineered by Luis Saenz of roughly the same period and which happens to be a few miles from the Bay of Pigs, measures 248 feet (75.6 meters). | **fig. 5** Another example of a post-tension bridge, the Cuyaguateje River Bridge in the province of Pinar del Rio, also designed and engineered by Saenz-Martin, has a central span of 330 feet (100.6 meters) and was built using American technology: Roebling cables. The jacks also came from the United States. | **fig. 6** Almost the same span was achieved at the Bacunayagua Bridge (1959) on the border between the provinces of Havana and Matanzas, designed and engineered by Saenz-Cancio-Martín; its arch spans roughly 300 meters (984 feet). You can clearly see the use of high-strength concrete in the slenderness of the columns on the piers. Another bridge, the Tuinicu River Bridge, also designed and engineered by Saenz-Cancio-Martín, was built to replace a bridge that was blown up during the

Engineering in Cuba

Ysrael A. Seinuk

fig. 1 | Habana Riviera, by Igor B. Polevitzky, Havana, Cuba, 1957

fig. 2 | Edificio FOCSA, El Vedado, Cuba, constructed 1956, photographed in 2000

fig. 3 | Model of Edificio Liberdad, by Martin Dominguez, 1959

fig. 4 | Walnut Lane Memorial Bridge, engineered
by Gustave Magnel, Philadelphia, Pennsylvania, 1950

fig. 5 | Arimao River Bridge, engineered by Luis Saenz, Cuba, 1950s

fig. 6 | Cuyaguateje River Bridge, engineered by Saenz-Martín, Pinar del Rio, Cuba, 1956–57

fig. 7 | Tuinicu River Bridge, engineered by Saenz-Cancio-Martín, Cuba, 1956–57

fig. 8 | Zaza River Bridge, designed and engineered by Mario G. Suárez and Arango
Y. Salas, Cuba, 1959

Cuban Revolution. | fig. 7 Constructed in only seventy-two days, it is also a post-tension construction, whose shape follows the bending pattern of the bridge.

An example of prefabrication and assembly in concrete can be found in the Zaza River Bridge, designed and engineered by Mario G. Suárez and Arango Y. Salas; it was constructed entirely in pieces. | fig. 8 Each triangular segment was produced on the ground and put in place using American Stressteel cables. The bridge was to replace another bridge that had been destroyed. Construction began from each side, with the central span being completed last. The two cantilevers that approached the central span allowed the cranes to advance and continue placing the subsequent parts. Another example of precast-concrete technology is the Villanova University in Havana, designed by the architect Manuel Rodriguez. The beams are 60 feet (9 meters) long, and the triangular sun-breakers on the facade are also precast, while the folding plate at the top is not. In this case, formwork was used not in the construction but in the factory, which made the project much more economical.

This series of examples shows something of the uneven way in which technological developments were incorporated into different building industries due to the highly different regulations effective in different places at the time. Cuba, during the 1950s, was using concrete technology that was far in advance of what was available to engineers working in the United States. When I came to work as an engineer in New York during the 1960s, I brought with me what I had learned from working on the designs of those bridges.

In an early project realized for the Long Island Rail Road in Forest Hills, we created a deck over the railway tracks, with a span of 60 feet (18.3 meters) that was to carry a 16-story building. | fig. 9 To build the deck, we used prestressed, precast box beams. To anchor it, we used a wall laced with multiple post-tension strands, with each jack pulling 15 strands. The project was the first time in New York that multiple post-tension strands were used in a building. | figs. 10–12 The technique was far from new; it had been used already by Magnel,

as well as by Fritz Leonhardt in Germany around twenty-five years earlier. Much later, we used post-tension at the Trump Tower (1982) in New York. In order to accommodate the shopping mall in the base of the tower, we used large columns that opened up like an A-frame, which eventually had to carry fifty stories. Post-tension was used to take the tension in the bottom. | fig. 13 Post-tension walls were also important to another project at the time, the Helmsely Palace Hotel (1980), which was the first building in New York to be built at the rate of one floor every two days, or what was called the two-day cycle. | fig. 14 In the lower floors, post-tension walls carry columns that are fifty stories high in order to create a ballroom. The technology was fully available at the time; it is simply a question of knowing how to use the concrete and what to use it with.

Concrete was also used in a structure we engineered for the entrance to Philip Johnson's estate, albeit at a very different scale and using a very different technology. The building was supposed to be the reception building for visitors to the estate. Its remarkable curves were created by bending a particular kind of panel that was produced in Italy. | fig. 15 The panels contain a three-dimensional mesh, connected by small steel elements and with polyurethane in the center. The panels are available in standard widths of 1.2 meters (3.9 feet) in any length and are extremely rigid. The rigidity of the panels allowed me to realize the first building in my life that I did without ever making any structural drawings.

During construction, Johnson was standing on-site. He made himself a little platform and would say, "I want more curve over here, less curve over there." Once he was satisfied, he said, "I'm satisfied." I told him, "Philip, once we spray the concrete—not shotcrete, but concrete—you cannot change this." And he said, "It's okay." Photographs cannot quite convey how sharp the edges are, and how smooth the curves are. Philip baptized the building as *The Monsta* because he says that he felt as if it were alive. | fig. 16 Every day when he came out of his glass house, he used to go to the building and pet it.

It has been said that working with concrete is like the job of a good chef, which is perhaps another way of saying that a good chef is a combination of architect and engineer. One of the biggest mistakes that can be made on any project is for the project to be designed and then handed over to an engineer to create a structure. It costs the same amount if the architect begins talking to the engineer in the initial design stages of a building. In the end, it is neither the architect nor the engineer alone but the thinking processes between them that can create an economical structure.

For the O-14 tower by Jesse Reiser and Nanako Umemoto, in discussing the building, we took advantage of its shape, which is like a folded plate, to be able to create a three-dimensional Vierendeel truss in the perimeter of the building, a structure that will handle the building's seismic and wind loads and eliminate the need for shear walls in the interior. Shear walls are a nuisance—a nuisance that is necessary sometimes—but a nuisance nonetheless. | figs. 17–18

Another eighty-story tower in Dubai is by the architect Chad Oppenheim. When you see a building today with this high degree of structural and formal irregularity, you can almost bet that it is in the Persian Gulf, because such buildings are very expensive. The issue with this building, however, is that the irregularity is such that its columns keep moving from a group of floors, to another group of floors, and finally to another place altogether. In the ends the columns are no longer vertical. This is where concrete, because of its plasticity, is a phenomenal material. We have been able to design all of the columns' movements without the use of a single-transfer girder, which is another anathema in terms of cost.

The ability of engineers to use cutting-edge techniques depends on the regulations that they are working under, and, despite the fact that half a century has passed since I began working in the United States, things have not changed drastically. There has been much discussion, for instance, regarding innovations in formwork, but there is a great deal of construction that can be done without formwork. In Atlantic City, New Jersey, buildings of fifty stories are built without formwork. This is because builders are able to use a product that cannot be used in New York, and it makes the building

much more economical. This is yet another example of resistance to change from the political side. There is resistance, for instance, to the use of certain types of techniques in New York, not from the Department of Buildings, not from the engineers, nor from the architects—but from the unions. And the situation is not simply local.

Traveling around the world, one can find examples of many techniques that are not used here that save an enormous amount of money in concrete buildings. The engineer has to help the architect create whatever they want to create. But the engineer also has to have the strength of character to tell the architect, "You should change that. That doesn't make sense." Over the years, I have worked with many architects. In most cases, when I'm working with a great architect, he or she will listen.

* C. S. Whitney, "Design of Reinforced Concrete Members Under Flexure or Combined Flexure and Direct Compression," *Journal ACI* 33, no. 3 (March/April 1937): 483–98; and C. S. Whitney and E. Cohen, "Guide for Ultimate Strength Design of Reinforced Concrete," *Journal ACI* 53, no. 5 (November 1956): 455–90.

fig. 9 | Long Island Rail Road (LIRR),
engineered by Hertzberg and Cantor
(engineer in charge: Ysrael Seinuk),
Forest Hills, New York, 1965

figs. 10–11 | Deck of the railway, under construction, Forest Hills, New York, 1959

fig. 12 | Cable ends, LIRR, Forest Hills, New York

fig. 13 | Cables with tension jacks

fig. 14 | Helmsely Palace Hotel, engineered by the Office of Irwin G. Cantor (partner in charge: Ysrael A. Seinuk), New York, New York, 1980

fig. 15 | Diagram of concrete panels for the entrance to Philip Johnson's estate

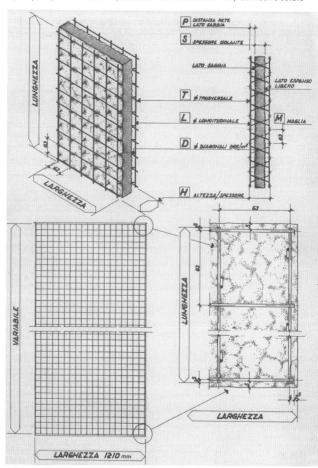

fig. 16 | *The Monsta*, Philip Johnson estate, 1995

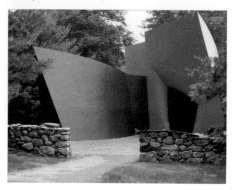

figs. **17–18** | O-14 tower, by Reiser + Umemoto, Dubai, United Arab Emirates, 2008–10

Nanotechnology in Concrete

Surendra P. Shah

I teach a course in materials to engineering students at Northwestern University, and I begin my class by bringing in three objects. The first is a perfume bottle that is a few millimeters thick and made from a high-performance cement-based material. Next is a credit card made with extruded cement, whose tensile strength is 200 MPa. Finally I bring a third item and ask my students to guess what the material is made of. Most students guess that it's made of rubber. In fact, it is an example of an extruded, fiber-reinforced cement-based composite. Its enormous ductility comes from micro-fiber reinforcement.[1]

Many exciting new developments in concrete have been made possible by taking advantage of the current emphasis on nanotechnology. Looking at the history of recent developments in concrete technology, it is clear that great emphasis has been placed on increasing the strength of concrete, which has led to new forms of high-strength concrete. The development of high-compressive-strength concrete was architecturally motivated and started with high-rise construction in Chicago. My involvement was with the Water Tower Place building (1976) designed by Skidmore, Owings & Merrill. High-strength concrete was tested, at that time, to around 9,000 psi. When tested in the lab, it felt very brittle, but I pointed out that this brittle failure was due to the type of testing machine that was used. A smooth failure is attainable if the right testing system is utilized (so–called closed-loop testing).[2] In fact, we have tested 200-MPa concrete and shown that the failure is gradual. The use of high-strength concrete began in Chicago and is now in use worldwide. The world's tallest building to be made with high-strength concrete will be in Dubai. In fact, all of the super-tall buildings (more than fifty stories) are now made with high-strength concrete.

Next we realized that strength is not the only important factor. Durability is also important, particularly for problems related to the corrosion of reinforcing steel. Attempts to improve long-term performance led to high-performance concrete. Its use is especially important for transportation structures.

These developments were made possible by our ability to manipulate the microstructure of cement hydration. When cement is mixed in water, it forms floccules and hardens; this leaves big holes. | fig. 1 When concrete is super-plasticized, cement particles are dispersed so that the voids get smaller, but they are still there. If the voids are filled with submicron particles, such as silica fume, as with Ultra-High-Performance Concrete (UHPC), then a very strong concrete is produced. In addition to manipulating the microstructure, we have learned how to predict the microstructure of hydrating cement and how to relate microstructure to properties such as diffusion and permeability.

Now, where does research go from here? The approach we are using is a classical approach of materials science, one that examines how concrete is made and how it is processed. By analyzing these processes and comprehending how structure develops at various levels, specific material properties can be related, most commonly strength, durability, and ductility. Currently there is quite a bit of emphasis on a property called *rheology,* the ability to manipulate concrete as a liquid. One example is self-consolidating concrete, which eliminates the need for vibration thus reducing noise and dust pollution.[3] Another example of manipulating concrete in the fresh state is extrusion.

I will give three examples of advantages that can be gained from current developments in nanotechnology: characterization, sensors, and new materials. In characterization, researchers are using a variety of tools such as soft X-rays and neutron scattering. One example that we are doing uses atomic force microscopy. A nanolevel-cantilever probe goes over the surface, using a photodiode detector to capture the morphology of the material at the nanoscale. | figs. 2–4 Viewed at this scale, the material is essentially spheres, or nanospheres. What we have currently developed in UHPC by using submicron particles can be pushed a step further

Nanotechnology in Concrete

Surendra P. Shah

fig. 1 | a: Cement mixed with water forms floccules and hardens; **b:** cement particles are dispersed; **c:** the voids are filled with submicron particles

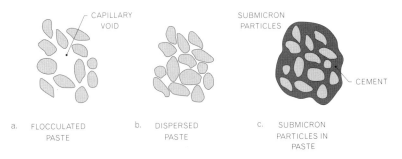

CAPILLARY VOID

SUBMICRON PARTICLES

CEMENT

a. FLOCCULATED PASTE

b. DISPERSED PASTE

c. SUBMICRON PARTICLES IN PASTE

fig. 3 | Atomic force microscopy image of calcium silicate hydrate (CSH); image size: 1.5 × 1.5 micrometers, spherical particles of the order of 40 nanometers; maximum height difference between different points: ~ 0.3 micrometers

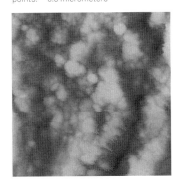

fig. 2 | Atomic force microscopy

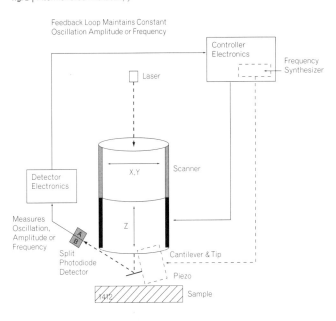

Feedback Loop Maintains Constant Oscillation Amplitude or Frequency

Controller Electronics

Frequency Synthesizer

Laser

Detector Electronics

X,Y   Scanner

Z

Measures Oscillation, Amplitude or Frequency

A
B

Split Photodiode Detector

Cantilever & Tip

Piezo

Sample

fig. 4 | Nano-indentation on six-month-old cement paste: w/c 0.5; image size: 60 × 60 micrometers; **a:** indent locations, **b:** Young's Modulus in GPa

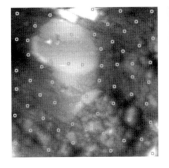

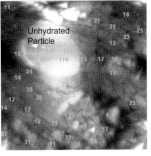

Unhydrated Particle

using nanoparticles to fill in these voids. In fact, we have a project with researchers in Bilbao to use colloidal nanosilica to take that next step.

What are the properties of these spheres at the nanoscale? To find out, we are using a Hysitron Triboindenter, an instrument that not only indents the material at the nanoscale, but also allows researchers to see where they are indenting. | fig. 5 In one result of the study, one can see unhydrated cement grain (in white) surrounded by calcium silicate hydrate (CSH). The image on the left shows the position of the indentation, and the one on the right gives the values of modulus of elasticity in units of gigapascals (GPa). It can be seen that an unhydrated cement particle has a modulus one order of magnitude higher than a hydrated particle. The process of hydration makes material more porous and weaker. That means, to make very strong concrete, one needs to use as many unhydrated particles (or as few hydrated particles) as possible, provided that hydration percolates in three-dimensions. This is the trick with UHPC. | fig. 6

The second application of nanotechnology deals with sensors for monitoring the construction process. Currently there are no nondestructive tools available to monitor if freshly cast concrete is gaining strength as rapidly as it was designed to do. There is a lot of interest worldwide in developing noninvasive monitoring tools. Researchers in Germany, for example, are using nuclear magnetic resonance spectroscopy (NMR), which is the same as magnetic resonance imaging (MRI) used in hospitals. At Delft University of Technology in the Netherlands, researchers are using gigahertz frequency to measure dielectric constants. We are using ultrasonic waves to detect in situ compressive strength. How do we do it? The waves generated by sound are called *P-waves* (pressure waves). We are using what are known as *shear waves* or *transverse waves*. When concrete is in liquid form, immediately after it is cast, all of the waves come back because liquid cannot transmit shear waves. As the concrete continues to change from liquid to solid, some of the shear waves are transmitted and some are reflected.

The ultrasonic frequency we are using is 2.25 megahertz. As the concrete hardens, the wavelength, which begins in the 100-nanometer scale, changes. | fig. 7 Five compositions were cast and cured at different temperatures. Regardless of the temperature, we get a unique relationship between this nondestructive wave reflection and compressive strength. Monitoring concrete so that it has the same quality control, let's say, as an aerospace composite, is the next step that people are looking for.

The last advantage is reinforcing concrete at the nanoscale. If you pull a concrete sample and plot the tensile force against elongation, a curve is attained such as the one labeled "matrix" in figure 9. Concrete is poor in tension, with a tensile strength of around 3 MPa. But more importantly, because of heterogeneity, even after the crack is formed, concrete continues to resist tension. This makes concrete a quasibrittle material.[4] When one uses macro-reinforcement, such as rebar, prestressing strands, or conventional fiber reinforcement, there is no increase in modulus of elasticity or tensile strength. | fig. 8 But once the crack is formed, the reinforcement constrains cracks from opening. This is exactly what rebar and prestressing strands do. What happens, however, if fibers are used at the microscale? The image in figure nine shows the results of some work that we have done with microfibers that are 14 microns in diameter and 2 millimeters long. When using these microfibers, the tensile strength increases substantially. In addition, the response is very ductile. | fig. 9 The research community calls this: Ultra-High-Performance Fiber-Reinforced Concrete (UHPFRC).

The next obvious step is to go a scale further and use nanofibers so that the cement itself, which is the most brittle component of concrete (and contains nanocracks), becomes ductile. My group has just started working on this; the fibers we are using are called *carbon nanotubes*. There are two issues with carbon nanotubes. First, they are very difficult to disperse; and second, they are very expensive. In an effort to solve both problems, we have found a method that combines surfactants and ultrasonic energy to disperse the fibers. | fig. 10

171

Nanotechnology in Concrete
Surendra P. Shah

fig. 5 | Ultrasonic sensing, experimental setup

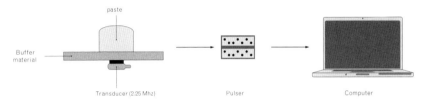

Wavelength: ~ 0.1-1 micron
at early ages

fig. 6 | Compressive strength correlation with reflection loss

Portland cement mortars, w:c:s=0.5:1:2

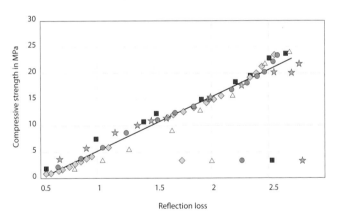

fig. 7 | Nanotechnology and fiber-reinforced concrete

Can we achieve superplasticity by modifying at nanoscale?

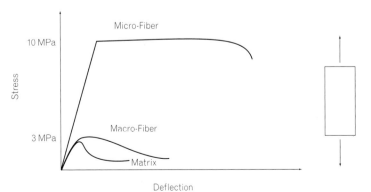

fig. 8 | sem images of poorly dispersed carbon nanotubes forming bundles in eighteen-hours-old cement paste

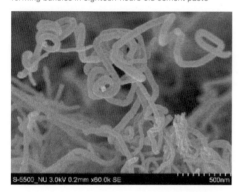

fig. 9 | Tensile strength comparison of carbon nanotubes (in gigapascals)

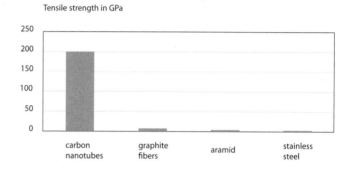

Tensile strength in GPa

fig. 10 | Effective dispersion of carbon nanotubes; **a:** without surfactant and **b:** sonication with surfactant; sem images at 500-nanometer scale

Requires ultrasonicenergy and the use of surfactant

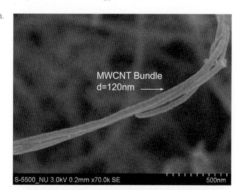

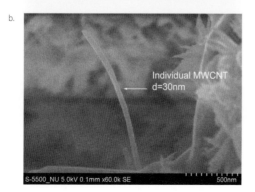

fig. 11 | Comparative cost study with various methods of reinforcement

Material	Cost per Kg ($)	Dosage (kg/m3)	Cost per m3 of of Concrete ($)
CNTs	150–2000	0.3–4	45–8000
Carbon Fibers, 10–14µm diameter	8–20	2	16–40
Carbon Fibers, 7µm diameter	55	2	110
Carbon Nanofibers	350–700	2	700–1400
Graphite Nanofibers	1730	2	3460
Steel Fibers	1.7–5	30–160	51–800
PVA Fibers	10–13	15	150–195
Polypropylene Fibers	5–9	0.6–19	3–171

fig. 12 | Transmission electron microscopy image showing carbon nanotubes from a Damascus sabre: multiwalled tubes with the characteristic layer distance 0.34 nanometers.

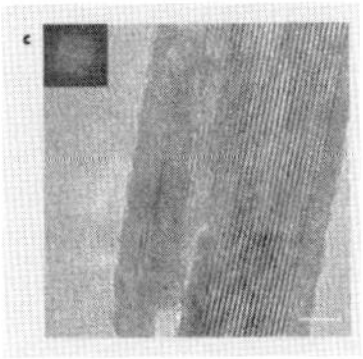

A typical result with well-dispersed, carbon nano-tube–reinforced materials is shown in figure 12. Two things are worth noting: one, the amount of fiber used is very small, 0.08 percent; two, in spite of the small amount of fibers, there is a substantial increase in modulus of elasticity and tensile strength. How is that possible? One answer is that the carbon nanotubes alter the nanostructure of CSH. We were able to confirm this when we examined the composites made with carbon nanotubes using our nano-indentation technique. We found that in the presence of carbon nanotubes, the modulus of CSH is higher than without them. Using such a small amount makes it economically possible to use carbon nanotubes as reinforcement for concrete. | fig. 11

Regarding carbon nanotubes, there is an example that is quite intriguing: the so–called *Damascus sword*, which dates from the Middle Ages, was renowned for being extremely tough and strong. Recently a professor from Germany examined it using several techniques, including a transmission electron microscope. He found that this sword was reinforced with carbon nanotubes. | fig. 12 The way that the iron was brought from India, combined with the way it was made into steel, transformed the carbon into carbon nanotubes. If they could do it in the Middle Ages, we can certainly do it now.

1 | P. Balaguru and S.P. Shah, *Fiber Reinforced Cement Composites* (New York: McGraw Hill, 1992).

2 | S.P. Shah and S.H. Ahmad, *High Performance Concrete and Applications* (London: Edward Arnold, 1993).

3 | SCC 2005, *Proceedings of the Second North American Conference on the Design and Use of Self-Consolidating Concrete* (Washington DC: Hanley Wood Publication, 2005).

4 | S.P. Shah, S.E. Swartz, and C. Ouyang, *Fracture Mechanics of Concrete: Applications of Fracture Mechanics to Concrete, Rock, and Other Quasi-Brittle Materials* (New York: Wiley, 1995).

Ultra-High-Performance Concrete in Highway Transportation Infrastructure

Benjamin A. Graybeal

As in most of the developed world, highway infrastructure in the United States is greatly dependent on concrete and steel. Following the infrastructure construction that occurred in this country in the mid-twentieth century, decades of wear and tear have in recent years begun to focus attention on the need for durable, long-lasting structures.

Innovative materials with enhanced mechanical and durability properties make it possible to construct new infrastructure and rebuild aging highways and bridges with structures that last longer. Over the past two decades, significant advances in research on cementitious materials have led to the development of a new class of market-ready materials with many times the strength and durability of conventional concretes. One emerging technology, known as UHPC, has the potential to significantly affect the U.S. highway system.

Challenges remain, however, that continue to limit the widespread implementation of projects using this new technology. Among them are the lack of design-code provisions, inadequate industry familiarity with the product, and high initial costs. Addressing these issues will require significant knowledge transfer, support, and buy-in within the industry, as well as greater reliance on life-cycle costing.

The Federal Highway Administration (FHWA) has been investigating the use of UHPC in transportation infrastructure since 2001 and has made major strides in introducing the concrete and transportation industries to this next generation of concrete technology. As of early 2009, three UHPC superstructure bridges were opened to traffic in the United States, and a number of other UHPC transportation projects were in the design and preconstruction phases. | figs. 1–3

There is a strong desire on the part of the Department of Transportation (DOT) within a number of states, as well as among other transportation-structure owners, to implement proven solutions that perform better than existing practices.

UHPC opens avenues to new solutions that were heretofore not possible. Significant efforts have been placed on developing these new solutions, which can lead to dramatically better performance of engineered structures over the long term. One focus of the FHWA's UHPC program has been the development of modular UHPC components to meet the goals set forth in its Bridge of the Future Initiative. The goals of this initiative, which began in 2002, include the abilities to accelerate construction in order to mitigate construction-related congestion and to present durable structures requiring little maintenance over a significantly extended design life of 100 years. UHPC's unique properties have allowed for the FHWA-led development of a new modular-bridge component, known as the pi-girder, from which testing indicates these goals can be met. | fig. 4

This 0.84-meter (2.75-foot) deep, 2.5-meter (8.3-foot) wide component designed for spans in the range of 20 to 27 meters (65 to 88 feet) is just one example of an innovation made possible by the advanced properties of UHPC.

The use of UHPC in the highway industry is progressing in the United States, just as it is around the world. Other state DOTs—including Iowa, Virginia, Florida, Georgia, and New York—are investigating the use of UHPC on their highways. Superstructures with both longer and lighter prestressed girders are a possibility. Georgia, Iowa, and New York are contemplating using UHPC for precast modular-deck components and as cast-in-place cementitious material in joints. Some DOTs, such as Iowa's, are also considering using UHPC in specific areas where high durability is required, such as for bridge-approach slabs between pavement and decks.

Advanced cementitious materials exhibiting greater strength and durability clearly have a role to play in the construction and reconstruction of bridges and other critical highway structures. The need for durable, long-lasting infrastructure has never been more evident.

Ultra-High-Performance Concrete in Highway Transportation Infrastructure

Benjamin A. Graybeal

fig. 2 | The second UHPC bridge in the United States, Cat Point Creek Bridge, Warsaw, Virginia, 2008

fig. 1 | The first UHPC bridge in the United States, Mars Hill Bridge, near Ottumwa, Iowa, 2006

fig. 3 | The first UHPC pi-girder roadway bridge in the United States, Jakway Forest County Park Bridge, Aurora, Iowa, 2008

fig. 4 | UHPC pi-girder, a solution proposed by the FHWA as part of the Bridge of the Future Initiative

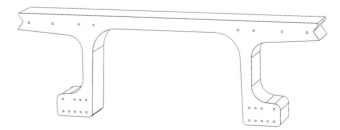

Form Over Mass: Light Concrete Structures

Hans Schober

Lightness Through Efficiency

Concrete shells make optimal use of the possibilities offered by concrete as a plastic material and are therefore outstanding examples of building in accordance with the inherent characteristics of materials. The shells designed by Pier Luigi Nervi, Félix Candela, Eduardo Torroja, and Heinz Isler are all impressive examples. | fig. 1

In opposition to the structural efficiency of concrete shell construction, however, stands the difficulty of manufacturing double-curvature shapes.

Regarded as being too expensive, the construction of new concrete shells has almost disappeared; the key, therefore, to a revival of concrete shell construction is to lower the cost of manufacturing the formwork.

Absolutely minimizing the cost of formwork, however, does not create an optimal solution. A sustainable structure requires an equilibrium to be found between cost and quality, where quality does not only stand for safety, durability, and functionality, but represents an expanded conception of quality that includes aesthetics, efficiency, responsiveness to the site, human scale, and minimal use of materials.

Figure 3 depicts two examples of an ideal equilibrium between cost and quality. | fig. 2 The form of each bridge reflects the moment diagram used to develop the structure. The flow of forces is cast in concrete, and the structure explains itself. With little additional effort, formwork was created for an efficient structure, which blends pleasantly into its environment.

Another example of privileging form over mass is the Auerbach Bridge in Stuttgart, Germany (2004). Bent in plan, it is a memorable arch bridge in which the plastic characteristics of concrete, as well as its ductility, were used to create a light and efficient concrete structure without bearings or joints. The lightness and efficiency of the structure was achieved by replacing bulky beams with struts and ties, in addition to form-finding calculations that were made through the use of an inverted hanging model. The interior edge of the arch, also bent in plan, follows the curvature of the road, whereas the exterior edge of the arch is straight in plan, communicating stability. Here, the complex formwork is counterbalanced by its high quality. | figs. 3–5

Techniques for Reducing Formwork Cost

Inflated formwork

Inflated fabric solves the conflict of efficient double-curvature structures and the difficulty of manufacturing the double-curved formwork. We used inflated-fabric formwork for a stormwater storage basin that we designed in 1983. | fig. 6 Due to high soil pressure, radial cables were implemented to create a membrane, which acts as stiffening ribs within the concrete shell. The reinforcement was installed and the concrete cast on top of this formwork. Architect Dante Bini had already invented inflatable concrete domed structures in the 1960s. He placed the reinforcing steel and concrete onto the flattened fabric prior to inflation, and inflated the entire structure within one hour. A constant-pressure control is maintained while the concrete cures.

Shape repetition

In 1977 we designed a glass-fiber-reinforced concrete shell for a temporary garden exhibition in Stuttgart. The eight prefabricated sections were constructed on-site using the same wooden formwork for each section. A mixture of glass fibers and concrete was sprayed onto the stationary formwork, with a thickness of only 12 millimeters (0.5 inches) and lifted into position by a building crane. | figs. 7–10

Special geometry

The roof of an indoor swimming center in Hamburg, Germany (1967), measuring approximately 95 by 76 meters (311 by 249 feet), was constructed out of two hypar shells—joined in opposing directions—made of prestressed concrete and supported

fig. 1 | Concrete shell designed by Swiss engineer Heinz Isler, Deitingen, Switzerland, 1968

fig. 2 | The bridge's form is a reflection of the moment diagram used to create it; **a:** A railway bridge in Leipzig, Germany, 2004; **b:** An overpass near Kirchheim, Germany, 1993; both bridges, structural design by Schlaich Bergermann und Partner.

a.

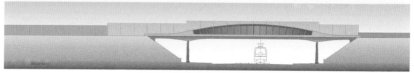

b.

fig. 3 | Auerbach Bridge, Stuttgart, Germany, 2004; **a:** The arch is straight on the convex side and **b:** curved in plan on the concave side.

a.

b.

fig. 4 | Section, Auerbach Bridge

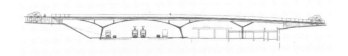

fig. 5 | Formwork for Auerbach Bridge

fig. 6 | Inflated-fabric formwork with radial cables for a stormwater storage basin, structural design by Schlaich Bergermann und Partner, 1983; **a:** before and **b:** after inflation.

a.

b.

Form Over Mass
Hans Schober

fig. 7 | Temporary garden pavilion made from glass-fiber concrete, structural design by Schlaich Bergermann und Partner, Stuttgart, Germany, 1977

fig. 8 | Spraying a mixture of glass fibers and concrete onto the formwork

fig. 9 | On-site construction of formwork

fig. 10 | Eight identical sections were constructed using the same piece of formwork

fig. 11 | The roof of an indoor swimming center consists of two joined hypars,
structural design by Schlaich Bergermann und Partner, Hamburg, Germany, 1967

fig. 12 | The hyperbolic paraboloid consists of
two families of skewed straight lines

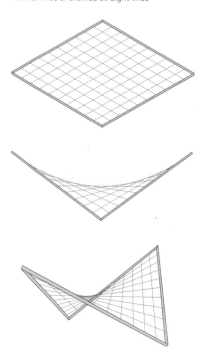

at only three points. | fig. 11 Even though the span length is quite large, the concrete shell is only 8 centimeters (3 inches) thick. The hyperbolic paraboloid proves particularly useful for concrete shells, as each hypar can be modeled using two families of skewed straight lines. | fig. 12 This allows for easy construction of the double-curved formwork using straight formwork boards, an essential cost-reducing characteristic.

Almost all of Candela's shells are based on the hypar form, and the direction of the straight lines created by the formwork boards can be read by the imprint on the concrete structure. | fig. 13

The translational surfaces also present advantageous conditions for simplified formwork. Translational surfaces permit a vast multitude of double-curved shapes consisting of flat quadrangles, where all of the quadrangles have identical side lengths but different mesh angles.* | fig. 14 This allows the formwork of a double-curved shell to be fabricated from flat quadrangles with identical side lengths. Furthermore, all formwork elements could even be manufactured from a single rectangular module that has the ability to easily change shape, like a sliding lattice grate. Structural engineers Schlaich Bergermann und Partner applied for a patent for this concept in 2008.

Prefabricated elements

Prefabrication of repetitive elements in the workshop allows for the use of complex and costly formworks. In 2005 we designed a factory cafeteria with so-called light columns supporting a green roof. All of the light columns are identical and consist of a conical shaft and four identical branches made of facing concrete. Due to this repetition, the complexity of the shape of a single element was of no relevance.

To create branches that are as light and elegant as possible, a form-finding calculation was performed to find a moment-free shape under permanent load. The optimized shape of the branch was double-curved with a thickness of 15 centimeters (6 inches) on top and 35 centimeters (14 inches) on bottom.

The wooden formwork consisted of upper and lower parts, and it was milled from solid wooden blocks using computer-numerical-controlled (CNC) machines. The upright formwork was filled from the bottom with self-compacting, high-strength concrete under high pressure to ensure a perfect surface. | figs. 15–16

* Hans Schober, "Die Masche mit der Glaskuppel: Netztragwerke mit ebenen Maschen," *Deutsche Bauzeitung* 128 (1994): p 152–163; and "Geometrie-Prinzipien für wirtschaftliche und effiziente Schalentragwerke," *Bautechnik* 79 (2002): 16–24.

fig. 14 | A translational surface can be covered with
flat quadrangles of identical side-length.

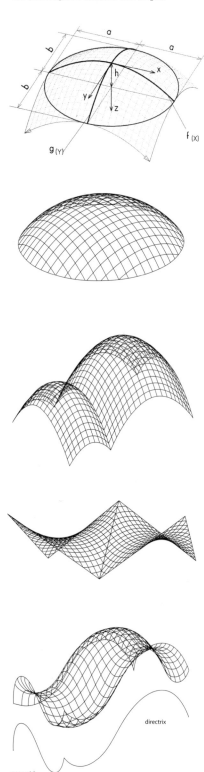

fig. 13 | Chapel Lomas de Cuernavaca, designed by Guillermo Rosell and Manuel
Larrosa, engineered by Félix Candela, Morelos, Mexico, circa 1958

fig. 15 | Factory cafeteria with identical light columns, photo taken during construction, structural design by Schlaich Bergermann und Partner, Boehringer Ingelheim, 2000

fig. 16 | Prefabricated elements on-site

Energy + Sustainability

187

Concrete and Sustainable Development

Christian Meyer

193

**An Integrated Energy and Comfort Concept: Zollverein School of Management
and Design, Essen, Germany**

Matthias Schuler

200

Green Concrete and Sustainable Construction: A Multiscale Approach

Paulo Monteiro

202

The Hypergreen Path

Jacques Ferrier

Concrete and Sustainable Development

Christian Meyer

We tend to think of sustainable development as a very contemporary buzzword, yet it is a fairly old concept. Probably the first person to formulate it was Hans Carl von Carlowitz (1645–1714), a mining administrator and son of a forester in Saxony, Germany, who called for the sparing use of trees in order to give the King's forest a chance to regenerate and sustain itself.[1] The principle of sustainable development can be considered to be self-evident; it is something that does not need to be scientifically proven.[2] Yet gross violations of this principle can probably be found everywhere throughout the ages.

By far the most important building material globally, concrete faces considerable challenges in terms of sustainable development. Worldwide more than 10 billion tons are produced each year. The 500 million tons produced in the United States represent about 2 tons each year for every man, woman, and child. There are good reasons why concrete has become such a popular building material. Consider first the general advantages. It has superb mechanical properties. If produced properly, it has excellent durability. The Romans made concrete that lasted 2,000 years, and it is still doing just fine. Concrete can be molded into basically any shape or form and adapted to many different climates and applications. It has excellent fire resistance, is generally available in just about every country on Earth, and is very affordable. Because of its heavy mass, it has good sound-insulating properties. But probably the most important advantage is the fact that we can engineer it to meet almost any set of reasonable performance specifications, more so than any other building material currently available.

As for the disadvantages, I prefer the word "challenges," which indicates that this is a problem that we can do something about, given adequate resources for research and development. Consider, for example, its low tensile strength, which is of the order of 10 percent of its compressive strength. That is the reason why ever since French gardener Joseph Monier (1823–1906) reinforced his concrete planters with steel-wire mesh, we have added steel reinforcement to concrete wherever it is subjected to large tensile stresses. Brittleness or lack of ductility can be corrected. In fact, contemporary techniques for reinforcing concrete can make it very ductile. In earthquake-prone areas such as California, where ductile materials are called for, concrete buildings can be built to the same height as steel buildings. Also, the weight-to-strength ratio of concrete, often considered a liability since it increases foundation costs, can be improved. It is now possible to produce concrete that is almost as strong as steel.[3] Thus with about a third of the specific weight, concrete can almost match the weight-to-strength ratio of steel without resorting to lightweight aggregate.

Considering the challenges in terms of sustainability, concrete's reputation is worse than it deserves, as it is assumed to have a huge environmental footprint. It is well known, for example, that the production of each ton of Portland cement releases almost 1 ton of carbon dioxide into the atmosphere. Worldwide the cement industry is estimated to be responsible for about 7 percent of all generated carbon dioxide. The production of Portland cement is also very energy intensive. Although North American plants have improved their energy efficiency considerably in recent decades, it is technically next to impossible to increase the energy efficiency of ordinary Portland cement production much further.

Apart from these improvements, there is one aspect we cannot do much about: the concrete industry has become a victim of its own success. The production of 10 billion tons of concrete requires 10 billion tons of materials. Because of the vast amount of natural resources needed, the industry leaves a large environmental footprint, which is indeed a major challenge to overcome.

The demolition and disposal of concrete structures and pavements constitutes another environmental burden. Construction debris contributes a large fraction to our solid waste disposal problem, with concrete being the largest single component. And then there are the enormous water requirements that are particularly burdensome in regions not blessed with an abundance of fresh water. The concrete industry uses more than one trillion liters of water each year worldwide, not including wash water and curing water.

Not everything about concrete is environmentally bad. For the most part, concrete is produced using local materials, thereby reducing the energy needed to transport it. And through a process known as *carbonation*, it also consumes carbon dioxide, thereby partially offsetting some of the negative aspects of cement production. The reinforcing steel is almost 100 percent recycled, and because of its hardness and stiffness, a concrete pavement offers less rolling resistance than asphalt, thereby increasing the fuel efficiency of motor vehicles. In addition, concrete has excellent thermal properties, due mostly to its thermal mass, which is an advantage both in summer and winter. In urban centers, the reflectivity of concrete reduces the heat island effect.

Sustainability Challenges and Opportunities for the
Concrete Industry
Many of the environmental challenges are not associated with concrete per se, but rather with cement production. One can summarize these challenges using this simple formula: produce concrete with as little Portland cement as possible, and do so by using the maximum amount of supplementary cementitious materials, especially those that are byproducts of industrial processes. We can also search for ways to reduce the amount of carbon dioxide that is released during the production of Portland cement and continue to reduce the energy demand per ton of cement produced.

Likewise, we can also reduce water consumption, for example, by recycling wash water, which is readily achieved in practice and already required by law in some countries. An improvement of concrete's durability can also have major impacts. For example, by doubling the service life of our structures, we can cut in half the amount of materials needed for their replacement. Similarly, an increase in mechanical strength, as well as other properties, can lead to

a reduction of materials needed. For example, doubling the concrete strength for strength-controlled members also cuts the required amount of material in half.

The use of recycled materials in place of natural resources is an obvious step. Since aggregate constitutes the bulk of concrete, the most effective recycling strategy will have to incorporate the substitution of recycled for virgin materials. The single largest source of such recycled material is concrete itself, namely the concrete rubble or debris obtained from the demolition of buildings and highway pavement renewals.

Probably the most exciting prospects for sustainable forms of concrete can be realized by studying various waste streams of our modern, technologically developed society to identify inherent properties that would add value and thereby counter the dreaded phenomenon of downcycling. This is the underlying philosophy of several of our past and present projects at Columbia University.

Supplementary Cementitious Materials
Since the first goal is a reduction in the use of Portland cement, let me start with fly ash, a byproduct of coal combustion, which is an excellent cementitious material that has a number of advantages. Theoretically it is possible to replace 100 percent of Portland cement with fly ash, provided that a chemical activator is present. The traditional optimal replacement level is around 30 percent, but so-called high-volume fly ash mixes have already been used with success, especially in Canada.[4]

The greatest advantage of fly ash is the fact that it is a byproduct of coal combustion, a waste product that would have to be disposed of at great cost, if it were not captured and reused. Moreover, concrete produced with fly ash can have better properties than concrete produced without it. In other words, there is true value in fly ash. By recognizing its cementitious properties, we beneficiate it and thus add value to it. Fly ash also generates less heat of hydration, which makes it very useful for massive concrete applications. It is also widely available and less expensive than Portland cement.

Challenges remain, however, such as the widely varying quality and chemical composition of fly ash, which typically changes from source to source. For this reason, it is difficult to maintain good quality control. But the coal ash industry has been working on this problem and has made progress in recent years. Then there is the relatively slow rate of strength development in concrete containing fly ash. This only has relevance in applications where high, early strength is required, and in such cases there are accelerators available to speed up the hydration process.

Slag—or more specifically, ground granulated blast furnace slag (GGBFS), a byproduct of the steel-making industry—is a second excellent cementitious material. Like fly ash, it generally improves many mechanical and durability properties of concrete and generates less heat of hydration. The optimal cement replacement level can be somewhere between 70 and 80 percent. In many situations, it is now recommended to use a blend of Portland cement, fly ash, and GGBFS, as was done, for example, to cast a 12-foot (3.7-meter) thick foundation slab for the Newtown Creek Wastewater Treatment Plant in Queens, New York. Because of its excellent properties, GGBFS costs about as much as the cement it replaces.

A third successful case of the beneficiation of an industrial material is condensed silica fume, a byproduct of the semiconductor industry. This siliceous material improves both the strength and durability of concrete to such an extent that modern, high-performance concrete mixes, as a rule, call for the addition of silica fume. Even though the material is difficult to handle because of its extreme fineness, its benefits are so obvious that the demand is considerable, which drives the price well above that of cement.

Finally, we can literally use garbage to produce concrete with waste-to-energy facilities or solid-waste incinerators. New York City has a serious solid-waste disposal problem, with a price tag of about one billion dollars a year. The current "solution" of shipping the waste out of the state to the lowest bidder is not exactly environmentally satisfactory. By using the bottom ash and fly ash produced in solid waste incinerators for concrete production, it is possible to add value to this waste material. While such ash has been shown to be a suitable substitute for Portland cement, it may contain unacceptably high levels of toxic elements. We have worked on encapsulating the heavy metals in the ash so that they cannot leach out, but additional research is needed to find a practical solution that is politically acceptable, including the problem of siting such plants.

Use of Recycled Materials

Recycled Concrete

As mentioned earlier, the concrete industry consumes staggering amounts of natural resources as aggregate. On the other hand, there is an ongoing need to dispose of large quantities of construction debris, much of it concrete. Whereas in Europe and Japan such debris is already being recycled on a large scale, the situation in the United States is comparably modest.[5] The disposal of demolished concrete costs money, and those charges are likely to increase. Opening new sources of virgin material, as old quarries and gravel pits are depleted, will also get more difficult. Since the cost of transportation is an important component of the cost of bulk materials such as sand and gravel, it may not take much of a shift for the economics to tip the balance in favor of recycling and reuse.

The technical challenges of turning recycled concrete into useful or even high-quality aggregate cannot be ignored. There are contaminants, large variations in quality, as well as high porosity and grading requirements. High-strength concrete is not always required, however, and most recycled concrete aggregate may be just fine for typical applications. And in many cases, it may make economic and technical sense to blend new and recycled aggregate.

Recycled Glass

Some ten years ago at Columbia University we started to study the use of waste glass or postconsumer glass as aggregate for concrete. The main technical challenge, the Alkali-

Silica Reaction problem, can be solved and does not warrant further discussion.[6]

Postconsumer glass constitutes about 6 percent of New York City's solid waste, and recycling it as aggregate for concrete is a classic example of beneficiation. The city pays recyclers dearly to remove it; that is, we accrue a considerable negative value from the outset. Yet glass has a number of advantages as an aggregate for concrete. It has basically zero water absorption, which is a plus in concrete mix design, and it increases the flowability of fresh concrete. The high hardness and abrasion resistance are advantages that can be utilized for paving stones, floor tiles, etc. The excellent durability and chemical resistance of the glass are additional advantages. Perhaps the most intriguing advantage is the aesthetic potential of colored glass, which ought to be of great interest to architects. In addition to all of these advantages, finely ground glass powder has pozzolanic properties, which means it is suitable as a partial replacement for Portland cement. As a result, the cost of recycled glass, especially if graded and sorted by color, can be several times that of natural aggregate. Terrazzo tiles with 100 percent glass aggregate have been produced commercially by the Wausau Tile Company in Wausau, Wisconsin, under license from Columbia University.

Plastics

Only a small fraction of plastic waste is recycled at present, and most of it is still downcycled. Among the reasons for this downcycling are the many different kinds of plastics currently recycled. We at Columbia are currently exploring ways of forming recycled plastic containers to be used as an ingredient in concrete, which we expect to have superb thermal insulation properties.

Dredged Material

The Port Authority of New York and New Jersey has to dredge some 4 million cubic yards each year to both deepen shipping lanes and to keep them open, to meet the requirements of newer, larger vessels. Since the Port Authority is no longer permitted to dump this material in the open ocean, it has to deposit it in engineered landfills, which is quite costly because much of it is contaminated. If the Port Authority does not find inexpensive alternatives to its current disposal method soon, it is likely to run into serious financial difficulties—a problem shared by many of the world's major ports.

We have developed a treatment method, which makes the material suitable for concrete production, because we learned how to encapsulate the heavy metals chemically to prevent them from leaching out. The economics of our treatment method remains challenging because of numerous factors that seem beyond anyone's control.[7]

Rock Spoils

Some of the material excavated during tunnel construction is suitable for concrete production, for example, for tunnel liners. Because of the low surface-to-volume ratio of a tunnel tube, only a small percentage of material is needed; we can therefore afford to be selective and chose only the most suitable material. The technical issues are again the least worrisome. A major challenge is scheduling, because we want to use the material when it is needed, not when it is excavated. This and related problems require close cooperation between the owner, engineer, construction manager, contractor, and aggregate supplier to find an optimal and environmentally sound solution.

Tires

The 300 million scrap tires generated in the United States each year pose their own significant disposal problem. Such stockpiles are not only unsightly but are fire hazards, and pose significant health hazards, specifically as breeding grounds for mosquitoes. Probably the most meaningful method of recycling scrap tires is to reuse them after retreading. Yet the most common disposal method seems to be to burn them in order to produce steam and electricity or heat. The use of tires as an alternative fuel in cement kilns is widespread throughout the United States and Europe. But their value as fuel is considerably less than that of the original material, so that such a use constitutes another example of downcycling. A different use of scrap tires is in hot mix asphalt or as crumb rubber for modifying binders in asphalt pavements.

Employing tire rubber as an ingredient in concrete production is a viable alternative to these uses. Unless specific properties of the rubber—properties lacking in natural sand, gravel, or crushed stone—can be exploited, a simple replacement of fine or coarse aggregate constitutes another example of downcycling from a strictly economic viewpoint. We have also looked into the possibility of using tire-derived steel as fiber reinforcement in concrete, but this needs more research before it can be offered as a valid solution.

Other Recycled Materials

The carpet industry often has to take back old carpets and recycle them as fiber. Much of this fiber is composed of nylon, and our research has shown that such recycled carpet fibers can serve as reinforcement for concrete. Rice husk ash has been shown to have valuable cementitious properties and therefore has been proposed as a supplementary cementitious material; rice-producing countries generate it in large quantities. The combustion of wood results in about 6 to 10 percent ash, the characteristics of which vary widely with the type of wood, its cleanliness, the combustion temperature, etc. Typical wood, when burnt for fuel at pulp and paper mills and within the wood-products industries, may consist of sawdust, wood chips, bark, and saw mill scraps. The suitability of the ash as a cementitious material has been demonstrated. Even agricultural wastes have been considered for concrete production, for example, the use of mushroom substrate as partial replacement for sand.

Economics of Recycling

Concluding with a few comments on the economics of recycling, it is worth recognizing that in a free market economy the price of a service or commodity is determined, in theory, by supply and demand. Government can and regularly does intervene with incentives—often, in the form of tax write-offs or disincentives such as fees, penalties, or outright prohibition, if it thinks such measures are in the best interest of the public. Over the last few decades, environmental awareness among the public at large has also been growing; true environmentalists do not hesitate to pay more for a commodity if it is "recycled" or "environmentally friendly."

Recycling is obviously associated with a number of cost items, such as collection, processing, transporting, and required capital investments. But there are also considerable costs associated with disposal in landfills if the discarded bottles, tires, or concrete debris are not reused or recycled. An important factor is the cost of the material being replaced. For example, there is a difference between replacing sand, which is literally dirt-cheap, and replacing imported marble chips. This point is closely related to the value added to the material through beneficiation. Here at Columbia we have developed a keen interest in identifying special properties inherent in recycled materials. By exploiting these properties, a considerable value can be added to improve the economics of recycling.

Finally, there is the most important driver in a free market economy: competition or the lack thereof. Currently, for example, only a few recyclers in the United States specialize in processing postconsumer glass. As a result, these firms are paid by municipalities to take the glass off their hands and then sell the processed glass for hundreds of dollars per ton. Increased competition should bring down the price of such recycled glass in the near future.

To conclude, the economic feasibility of recycling depends largely on the application. Virgin materials have, in general, a quality control advantage over recycled materials. But the economic feasibility of recycling will increase in time, as virgin materials become increasingly scarce and the disposal costs of solid waste, such as construction debris, keep increasing. Moreover, the exponential growth of the green building community is already changing the economic landscape. Only a few years ago, developers showed no interest in the principles of green building. But now they are realizing that building green can be good for the bottom line as well. Therefore, it is not a question of whether but when the use of recycled materials in construction becomes a routine matter. A retooled concrete industry can make a large contribution toward sustainable development.

1 | U. Grober, "The Inventor of Sustainability," *Die Zeit* 54, no. 48 (November 25, 1999): 98 (in German).

2 | The most widely quoted definition of sustainable development was coined in the well-known report of the United Nations' Brundtland Commission, published as *Our Common Future: The World Commission on Environment and Development* (Oxford: Oxford University Press, 1987).

3 | Pierre Rossi, "Ultra-High Performance Concretes," *Concrete International* (February 2008), 31–34; William Semioli, "The New Concrete Technology," *Concrete International* (November 2001), 75–78.

4 | V. M. Malhotra, "Role of Supplementary Cementing Materials in Reducing Greenhouse Gas Emissions," in *Concrete Technology for a Sustainable Development in the 21st Century*, Odd E. Gjorv and Koji Sakai, eds. (London: E & FN Spon, 2000), 226–35; V. M. Malhotra, "Making Concrete Greener with Fly Ash," *Concrete International*, May 1999, 61-66.

5 | T.C. Hansen, ed., "Recycling of Demolished Concrete and Masonry," *RILEM Report 6* (London: Chapman and Hall, 1992).

6 | C. Meyer, W. Jin, and S. Baxter, "Glascrete—Concrete with Glass Aggregate," *ACI Materials Journal* Vol. 97, no. 2 (March/April 2000): 208–13.

7 | K. Millrath, S. Kozlova, S. Shimanovich, and C. Meyer, "Beneficial Use of Dredge Material," *Progress Report* prepared for Echo Environmental, Inc., Columbia University in the City of New York (February 2001).

An Integrated Energy and Comfort Concept: Zollverein School of Management and Design, Essen, Germany

Matthias Schuler

Boundary Conditions

As a base for the integrated energy and comfort concept for any project, we research local boundary conditions such as macro- and microclimates, noise, and air quality, as well as soil conditions and available energy sources. The climate in the city of Essen is very moderate, seldom reaching temperatures below freezing and rarely exceeding maximum temperatures of 30 degrees Celsius (86 degrees Fahrenheit).

Near the school, the former coal mine Zeche Zollverein stopped actively digging in 1986, but the existing mine shafts and tunnels, measuring some 1,000 meters (3,280 feet) deep, have been kept accessible for possible future uses. As a consequence, the public owner of the mines, Deutsche Steinkohle AG, has to permanently pump water up from this depth to keep the mines from flooding.

Energy Concept

In order to make use of the mine water as a natural heat source, a heating system was required that would be capable of accepting an inlet temperature in the range of 27 to 30 degrees Celsius (80 to 86 degrees Fahrenheit). Therefore a radiant heating system within the exposed concrete ceilings was chosen; it can be reversed during the summer for nighttime activation of the thermal mass by an evaporative cooling tower. The mine water can also be used for preheating the intake air.

Building Envelope

SANAA's design concept called for an exposed external and internal concrete wall without any expansion joints. | fig. 1 Taking into account the heat conservation regulations in Germany, an insulated double-shell concrete wall would have been more than 0.5 meters (1.6 feet) thick. Such a wall would not only reduce the daylight supply, it would make the smaller windows appear more as holes than windows. The problem could not be solved simply by reducing the level of insulation in the double-shell concrete by several centimeters.

Rethinking the mine water as a free energy source available in the vicinity of the Zollverein School initiated a completely new approach to the external concrete wall: active insulation. | figs. 2–3

The system uses a monolithic, concrete-wall construction with a thickness of 0.3 meters (approximately 1 foot) and contains plastic pipes for heating the wall using the mine water. | fig. 4 "Active" insulation must ensure that the surface temperature of the inner wall is above 18 degrees Celsius (64 degrees Fahrenheit) or the comfort range for a heated environment. Long and very engaged discussions among the design team finally led to an agreement about this system, with an awareness that the noninsulated external wall surface would lose roughly 80 percent of heat to the surrounding environment, yet would significantly reduce the energy flow from inside the structure to outside. | figs. 5–6 Paradoxically the mine water, as a free, carbon dioxide–independent source of energy, allowed for this waste.

Detailed analyses of the steady state conducted by the design team, as well transient behavior of the wall temperatures during the whole year, determined a distance between pipes of 0.4 meters (1.3 feet). Intensive discussion with the structural engineers ensured that the piping system would be integrated with the reinforcement used in the wall construction. | figs. 7–11

By tempering the wall through the active insulation system, the crack dimensions could be limited to below the visual level without increased reinforcement. Where necessary, such as around the windows, distances of the piping system are made denser in order to avoid the need for T-pieces and different pipe sizes. To prevent the piping system in the walls from freezing in the case of a failure of the system's pumps, a self-draining concept was developed, which is activated when a critical temperature is reached in the wall. The mass flow and control parameters were determined through

fig. 1 | Zollverein School of Management and Design, under
construction by SANAA, Essen, Germany, 2006

fig. 2 | Diagram of piping in monolithic concrete wall

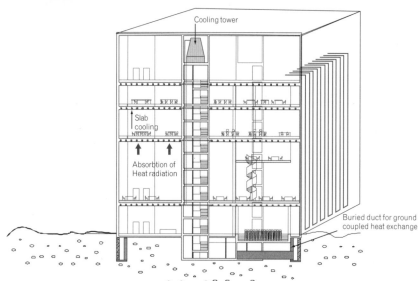

fig. 3 | Geothermal heat source

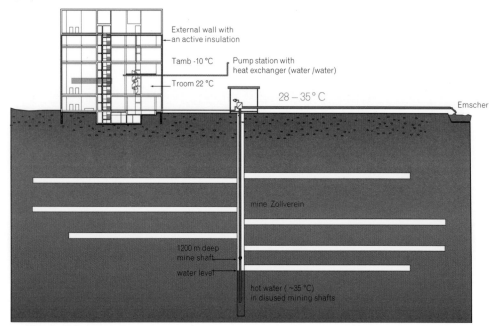

An Integrated Energy and Comfort Concept

Matthias Schuler

fig. 4 | East elevation

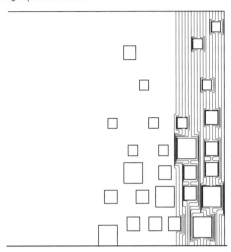

fig. 5 | Direct use of geothermal heat source as active insulation

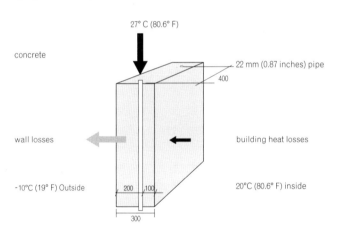

fig. 6 | Three-dimensional heat conduction diagram by Horstmann Berger

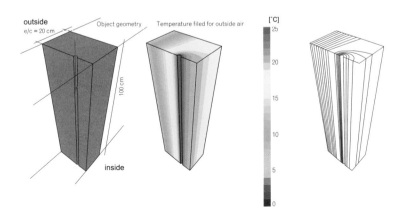

fig. 7 | Active insulation under construction

fig. 8 | Slab cooling system

An Integrated Energy and Comfort Concept

Matthias Schuler

fig. 9 | Development of activated bubble-deck slabs

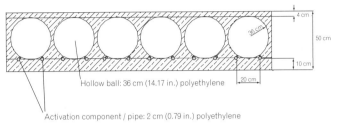

Hollow ball: 36 cm (14.17 in.) polyethylene

Activation component / pipe: 2 cm (0.79 in.) polyethylene

fig. 10 | Cross-section of bubble deck

fig. 11 | Cavity slab to reduce the dead weight by 35 percent

dynamic building and system simulations, using the Transient Energy System Simulation Tool (TRNSYS).

Even with the added costs of an integrated piping system, the monolithic wall construction was remarkably cheaper than the double-shell concrete wall, by an amount that exceeded what the project spent for the mine water system. This is the main reason why a geothermal system could be realized for the Zollverein School. Geothermal heating, for instance, was rejected at a neighboring building; without an integrated system, there would be no savings to cover the increased investment costs, and the economic balance of the approach, based on cheap energy costs, could not support the system.

Conclusion

The energy supply concept for the Zollverein School is based on mine water as a carbon dioxide–free heat source. This very strong local reference allowed for the development of a unique and outstanding energy concept. Active insulation allows for a simpler and cheaper monolithic wall construction, supporting the idea of the building envelope developed by the architects. The design solution and energy concept are based on a local resource available at the Zollverein School and, in this sense, cannot be generically replicated. Yet the close collaboration between climate engineer, mechanical engineer, structural engineer, building physicist, contractor, and architect enabled the development of an efficient energy strategy that could realize the architect's concept for the envelope and also create enough savings to make the locally available resource economically viable. | figs. 12–13 In this sense, it is an example of how close collaboration by the design team can efficiently integrate the architectural concept, specific material properties, and the local energy resources in a range of different situations.

An Integrated Energy and Comfort Concept

Matthias Schuler

figs. **12–13** | Zollverein School of Management and Design, by SANAA, 2006

Green Concrete and Sustainable Construction: A Multiscale Approach

Paulo Monteiro

Typical concrete contains about 12 percent cement, 8 percent mixing water, and 80 percent aggregate by mass. This means that worldwide 1.5 billion tons of cement are required yearly for the production of concrete. Currently, the production of Portland cement is responsible for 7 percent of the carbon dioxide emissions globally. In addition to cement, the concrete industry consumes 9 billion tons of sand and rock as aggregate annually. The consumption of materials by the world's population at this rate is only exceeded by our use of water. In addition to the 1.5 billion tons of cement and the 9 billion tons of sand and rock consumed, the production of concrete requires 1 billion tons of mixing water. To provide some comparison, the use of 1 billion tons of potable water corresponds to 110,000 times the volume of water in the San Francisco Bay. Such a rate of consumption obviously creates huge strains in regions where fresh water is scarce.

In addition, the ever-increasing need to enlarge the built environment is compounded by the bleak future facing our aging civil infrastructure. Corrosion, frost action, sulfate attack, and cracking due to the Alkali-Silica Reaction have all significantly reduced the life cycles of buildings, bridges, dams, roads, and marine structures. To provide one example, of the 597,340 bridges in the United States, 73,784 (about 12.4 percent) are currently considered structurally deficient.

Neither the current rate of clinker use in the production of cement nor the decay of civil infrastructure is sustainable. In the Department of Civil and Environmental Engineering at the University of California Berkeley, we are developing four lines of research in order to develop green construction. The first is to improve the nanostructure of the hydration products used in concrete production; the second is to develop dedicated membranes that allow for the use of both recycled water and seawater in the production of concrete; the third is the development of geopolymers from waste products, with the goal of replacing the use of Portland cement; and the fourth is integrated research on the mechanisms of concrete deterioration in order to develop innovative repair strategies.

The optimization of the nanostructure of the reaction products used in concrete is a key component of this research program. Research has begun at Argonne National Laboratory using total X-ray scattering to analyze the pair distribution function of the amorphous phase. At Los Alamos National Lab, work has begun using filtered difference spectroscopy and Small Angle Neutron Scattering (SANS) to characterize the water in the nanocavities of the porous amorphous phases in concrete. The bulk of nanostructure characterization, however, will occur at Advanced Light Source (a division of Berkeley Lab), where an intensive investigation will be done in time-resolved, full-field X-ray microscopy (including tomography) and X-ray spectromicroscopy.

Characterization of Cement Hydration at the Nanoscale

We have been imaging the chemical reactions in cementitious materials using soft X-ray microscopy. | **fig. 1** During the hydration process for Portland cement, the cement hydration reaction is characterized by a brief period of dissolution and reaction, during which a thin layer of hydration products forms around the cement grain. After one hour and thirteen minutes, a few needlelike hydration products on the surfaces of the grains are observed. After the fast dissolution, an induction period of very slow reaction follows. Soft X-ray microscopy is able to capture the massive precipitation of the hydration products at the end of the induction period. This technique has the potential to analyze the new generation of sustainable cements without the introduction of artifacts

Alkali-Silica Reaction: A Multiscale Study

The expansive reaction between reactive silicates present in some aggregate and the alkalis in the basic pore solution (pH 12.5–13.5) has been referred as the "cancer" of concrete. A large number of reinforced-concrete bridges have been affected by this deleterious reaction, which creates a gel that swells inside the concrete mass, generating tensile stresses that over time can crack the structure. It is well accepted that the swelling is caused by the gel's absorbtion of water, however, there is only a limited understanding of the location of the water inside the gel. We are performing a detailed multiscale characterization to develop new repair strategies for the affected structures. The Furnas Dam in Brazil developed cracks due to the Alkali-Aggregate Reaction. To improve the existing repair methods, it is necessary to develop a comprehensive characterization of the expansive gel, which was analyzed by atomic force, soft X-ray, and scanning electron microscopy. The reactive aggregates were studied by neutron diffraction.

Acknowledgments

This essay was based on work supported in part by Award No. KUS-I1-004021, made by King Abdullah University of Science and Technology (KAUST) and by National Science Foundation Grant 062464.

fig. 1 | Images of hydrating Type II–cement particles in a saturated calcium hydroxide (CaOH2)–calcium sulfate (CaSO4) solution, obtained by soft X-ray microscopy; a: at 1 hours, 13 minutes; b: at 2 hours, 49 minutes

a.

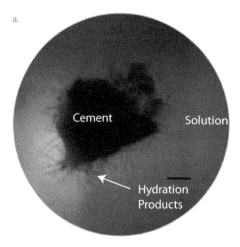

b.

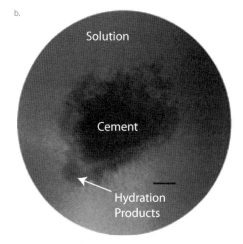

The Hypergreen Path

Jacques Ferrier

There is no such thing as a privileged material in architecture, only the privileged relationship between a given material and its architectural expression. With concrete this relationship is multiform. Its plastic possibilities and casting technology allow it to adapt to a wide range of different architectural expressions that all share a common approach: the fusion of structure and envelope. This fusion makes it appear as if the building were, in a sense, constructed from a single block, a leitmotif that has appeared frequently within the history of modernist architecture. For the Hypergreen project, I adopted a completely different approach, emphasizing a clear separation between the building's skeleton and its skin, but without relinquishing the plastic expressiveness of concrete, nor its sensuality.

Hypergreen is a research project, developed in partnership with the Lafarge Group, that aims to design a prototype that uses tall buildings as a relevant urban solution for the sustainable city of the twenty-first century. It reinterprets the skyscraper to propose an ultra-environmental project, fully incorporated into its urban context and able to provide mixed spaces adapted to new ways of living and working. The project's point of departure was an analysis of structure, undertaken by structural engineer Jean-Marc Weill. To minimize the consumption of materials, we carried out research to determine the form and orientation that would adapt most efficiently to the structure. These investigations resulted in an elliptically shaped peripheral structure, as this system was best able to resist horizontal loads and seismic constraints. This thinking concerning the structure formed an integral part of a global approach, given that the elliptical shape is also the best in terms of compactness and internal lighting, as well as allowing the building to be profiled to match the directions of the dominant winds.

As a result, the lozenge-shape structure, inspired by the metal projects developed by Russian engineer Vladimir Shukhov, was placed outside the building. | fig. 1 The system was imagined as a series of prefabricated concrete elements interconnected by post-stressing, a technique long established in the construction of bridges but which would be a first for a building with a height of 240 meters (787 feet). Prefabrication meant that the structure could be factory manufactured and then erected on-site. From the outset, the project envisioned an easy final dismantling of the building. Only the use of recently developed ultra-high-performance fibrous concretes would allow for this type of structure to be produced with reasonably dimensioned components. Using standard concrete, the substantial bulk of the structure would have significantly increased the weight of the building and caused problems for the natural lighting of the elevations.

The Hypergreen project makes use of a new technology to develop an innovative architectural morphology. As such, it falls within a historical continuity that has associated technical innovation with architectural innovation to meet society's expectations, which currently involve the need to build sustainable cities. In addition to reducing materials and using fewer pollution-producing products, Hypergreen adds certain ideas concerning the use of the structure from the point of view of energy consumption. The skyscraper's structural grid becomes increasingly dense to the south, but it remains generously open to the north and adapts as needed to the east and west to meet the needs of the site and program. It acts as a sunlight filter, reducing heat loads as well as decreasing the building's cooling requirements by 30 percent (based on a simulation carried out for a country in a temperate climatic zone). Since the mid-twentieth century, skyscrapers have generally been built as glass prisms that rarely take climatic conditions into consideration. This model of tall building has been generically replicated in cities across the world. By contrast, the density variations in Hypergreen's structural grid provide a new image, that of an oriented skyscraper with considerable materiality. | figs. 2–3

Hypergreen's materiality is diametrically opposed to that of the smooth, cold image of the skyscraper. For this

figs. 2–3 | Hypergreen project, by Jacques Ferrier Architectures, 2005

fig. 1 | Shabolovka radio tower, by Vladimir Shukhov, Moscow, Russia, 1922

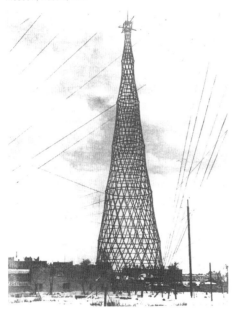

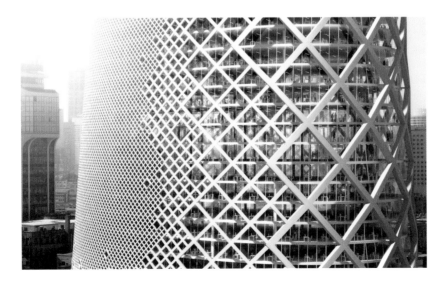

figs. 4–5 | Changsha Railway Station competition, by Jacques Ferrier Architectures, Beijing, China, 2006

project and in those that our office has subsequently worked on, I have paid particular attention to the effects of depth resulting from the structure's clear detachment from the elevation behind it. This in-between space provides a setting for an interplay of light, shadow, and reflection. Capturing these changes in daylight and in the in-between spaces creates an almost infinite number of kinetic geometrical variations, depending on the angle and the distance from which the skyscraper is viewed. It is not an architecture that immediately bares itself to the viewer. With its ability to record the subtle traces of passing time, concrete expresses its solidity and density through the paradoxical form of a delicate structural net. Its usual massiveness is replaced by a certain sensuality.

We used this concept of dissociating the climatic structure from the envelope itself for the Changsha Railway Station project in China. Here, the concrete grid permits the fusion of station, shopping center, public amenities, and office buildings, which are grouped together to form an urban mega-object. The density of the Changsha Railway Station complex varies according to the amount of sunlight it receives, and it provides a support for photovoltaic cells that also act as sunbreakers. | figs. 4–5 For both the Changsha Railway Station and Hypergreen projects, the independence of the envelope and structure provides a multitude of possibilities that are able to absorb alterations made to the project due to program changes or the replacement of elements that have become obsolete as a result of technological developments. The clear hierarchy between structure, envelope, and interior layouts is the key to the design of a building that, due to its capacity to transform itself, will have a stronger chance of lasting over time.

In these projects, the use of concrete is not restricted to structural or climatic issues. It goes further and questions the project's materiality, given the specific physicality of concrete's texture and density. It has a sensuality that makes it similar to stone, to which is added the specific aspects of its technical qualities and its formwork finishes.

We are using this same quality of concrete for the design of a hybrid structure for the French Pavilion at the World Expo Shanghai 2010. The structure, which provides horizontal stability and seismic resistance, is positioned outside the building. This external structure allows for the elimination of shear walls within the pavilion, resulting in a free and flexible space for the scenography. In compliance with the rules set by the World Expo authorities, the structure can be fully dismantled. As a result, the grid is assembled from steel elements that are bolted together. Glass-fiber-reinforced concrete cladding conceals the assembly systems and also incorporates the lighting. This indissociable construction system simultaneously resolves a number of technical and architectural questions, but from my point of view, it is above all an innovative expression of a mineral grid enclosing the building, which appears as if it were suspended over a lake—that represents its decisive impact. The building appears to defy gravity. Its geometrical curves evoke the flexibility of a fabric sail. This application of concrete introduces the theme of the pavilion: the sensual city. | figs. 6–8

figs. 6–7 | French Pavilion, World Expo Shanghai, by Jacques Ferrier Architectures, Shanghai, China, 2010

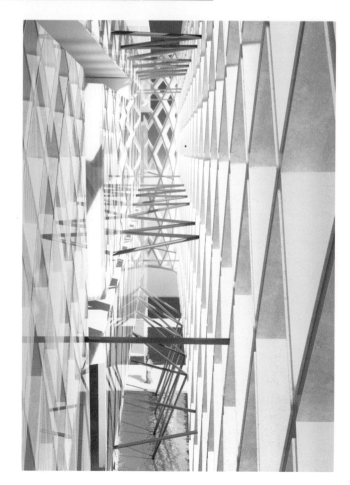

The Hypergreen Path

Jacques Ferrier

fig. 8 | The Sensual City, French Pavilion

Cultural Effects

209

Materialization of Concepts

Bernard Tschumi

218

The State of Concrete: An Investigation of Concrete in China

Qingyun Ma

227

Living with Infrastructure

Marc Mimram

234

Opportunity in Transition: Reinventing of Concrete

Toshiko Mori

242

Implicit Performance: Exploring the Hybrid Condition

Juan Herreros

250

Solidifications

Fernando Menis

255

A Building and its Double

Mabel Wilson

259

Cloaked Transparency: Land Port of Entry, Massena, New York

Laurie Hawkinson

264

Artificial Natures / New Geographies

Kate Orff

267

Concrete Becoming Plastic, Then Graphic

Neil M. Denari

Materialization of Concepts

Bernard Tschumi

In December 2007, I drove for about forty-eight hours to see a building that has fascinated me for as long as I can remember: the Great Mosque of Djenné in Mali. | fig. 1 It's built entirely out of mud and is only about 82 feet (25 meters) tall, but because no building in that part of the world is more than two stories, it seems like an enormously large structure in comparison to everything around it. The sticks that protrude—they are sublime in their expressive effect—are actually highly functional. After the rainy season, which lasts about three weeks, much of the surface mud falls off the building and has to be replaced. During a yearly celebration, the village of 8,000 people reapply the mud. The protruding sticks are used as supports for the villagers to reconstitute the mud surface. The architecture becomes a social act. The inside is stunning. If you build with mud, there are only certain things that you can do. The maximum span can be no more than 8 feet (2.4 meters), as most local tree branches, used as reinforcement devices, do not exceed this distance. The architecture has a lot to do with material—much of it the result of that act of materialization.

I have often said, architecture is the materialization of a concept, but part of the concept is derived from the material itself.

To materialize is to make, to represent as material, or to invest with material attributes—*to give material form*. A concept is an idea, an abstract notion, or a mental expression of an object. These words define what architecture has to do and what architecture is. So the questions I'd like to raise are as follows: Does architecture start with a concept or with a material? And if it starts with a concept, how is a material chosen? Why do you use a particular material for a particular concept?

For example, in the case of a building meant to be an introverted video pavilion, we intentionally reversed the user's expectations and made it out of transparent glass, including the columns and beams, in an attempt to build the ultimate glass house, but for a specific programmatic and social purpose: video-art displays for the Dutch city of Gröningen. A material can be chosen in relation to what happens inside the pavilion. In other words, the glass is not only about a technical or technological effect; it also must be appropriate in relation to the particular activities that take place in the space. The choice of material may have social implications or even a civic role.

Our design for the School of Architecture in Miami, Florida, had to be built in 2000 for only $132 per square foot. Precast concrete was the only material that could make this possible at the time, but the choice of concrete also had to do with available construction technology as well as the local culture of materials, both suggesting an understanding of concrete that you do not have, for example, in New York City. This building, made out of precast concrete, illustrates how the cheapest and most efficient strategy, in this case, could be found in the technology of parking garages with their double-Ts, illustrating one of the most basic types of construction: the house of cards. | figs. 2–3

Another conceptual issue is the differential nature of material envelopes. The mandate for the concert hall that my office designed for Rouen, France, was to build a performance venue in thirteen months. The concept is a double envelope: the outer envelope, made of steel, includes thermal insulation and black waterproofing material, while the inner envelope is made of precast or poured-in-place concrete according to pragmatic construction logic. The inner envelope supports the performance space itself (with a 6,000-seat audience). The cost and the speed of manufacture are as important as the building's appearance. Conceptually the project is about two envelopes, each having a particular material characteristic: a steel envelope, a concrete envelope, and the movement of the crowd in-between. | figs. 4–5 We pushed the materialization of this concept to the extreme, bringing in transparent seats so that the concrete would continue to appear as one of the two key starting points of the project.

fig. 1 | Great Mosque of Djenné, Mali

fig. 2 | Views of exterior construction,
School of Architecture, Florida
International University, by Bernard
Tschumi Architects, Miami, Florida, 2003

fig. 3 | Views of exterior construction, School of Architecture, Florida International
University

fig. 4 | View of exterior construction, Rouen Concert Hall,
by Bernard Tschumi Architects, Rouen, France, 2001

fig. 5 | View of interior, Rouen Concert Hall

fig. 6| View of exterior construction, Limoges Concert Hall, by Bernard Tschumi Architects, Limoges, France, 2006

fig. 7 | View of interior

When people start to move into the auditorium, they interact with the materiality of the actual concrete architecture rather than with furniture seats.

Now, what happens if we take the same concept and change the materials? Instead of having, as in Rouen's particular case, the context of a surrounding highway, in Limoges, France, we have an extraordinary forest with 200-year-old trees. Instead of steel, the outer envelope becomes translucent polycarbonate; instead of concrete, the inner envelope is clad with wood, which serves well with its acoustical properties.

The in-between structure with its movement vectors is made of concrete so that the materiality actually changes according to its role: concrete gives way to wood as you arrive at a certain height (in this instance, as at Rouen, the issue of weight played a role and we switched material at that point). | figs. 6–7 The Richard E. Lindner Athletics Center at the University of Cincinnati has a particular configuration, which includes a large overhang to preserve the preexisting facilities underneath it: mechanical rooms, loading docks, and so on. The facade itself is actually a gigantic truss, which I liked because I could avoid designing a facade. | figs. 8–9 So it's the logic of the structure that gives you the appearance of the architecture.

But things are not necessarily what they seem, since behind the precast concrete is really a steel structure. Why? We had a choice. Either we would have a concrete structure clad with steel (as in the case of Steven Holl's dormitory at MIT) or we would have a steel structure with concrete cladding. In many parts of the United States, exposed structures are prohibited, so you need to insulate it. In Athens, for our New Acropolis Museum we not only had to consider housing very precious artworks and sculptures of antiquity in an earthquake-prone region but also specific constraints: the foundations were to exist in and alongside precious archeological remnants on an important historic site at the foot of the Acropolis. | figs. 10–11 Here the building is in three parts: glass, metal, and concrete, with each part in relationship to an aspect of the site and the program. The precision of the concrete itself is very much related to one important thing: the building's contents. The New Acropolis Museum has absolutely no staging; it's not a museum that displays flashy video effects, it is simply about the marble of the sculptures. We wanted to emphasize the delicacy and yet hardness of the marble, whose extraordinary precision is placed against the homogeneity and the porosity of the concrete, which absorbs the light and serves as a backdrop of sorts. | figs. 12–17

To return to my original question—what makes people decide to have a building made of concrete or wood or steel—the reasons may be architectural but also cultural, economic, social, or political. Ultimately these reasons are what really shape our consciousness of architecture, because architecture is always in reference to a material. As Spinoza the philosopher said, "The concept of dog doesn't bark." In our case, I think architecture is the only art where the concept of dog does bark.

fig. 8 | View of exterior construction, Richard E. Lindner Athletics Center, University of Cincinnati, by Bernard Tschumi Architects, Cincinnati, Ohio, 2006

fig. 9 | View of exterior, Richard E. Lindner Athletics Center

figs. 10–11 | Under construction, New Acropolis Museum, by Bernard Tschumi Architects, Athens, Greece, 2006

fig. 12 | Interior view, New Acropolis Museum

fig. 14 | View of the Archaic Gallery

fig. 13 | Main stairs, looking from the Slopes Gallery to the Archaic Gallery prior to installation, New Acropolis Museum, by Bernard Tschumi Architects, Athens, Greece

fig. 15 | View from the archeological excavations, looking toward ground level

fig. 17 | Night view of excavations at the entrance

fig. 16 | View of on-site excavations

The State of Concrete: An Investigation of Concrete in China

Qingyun Ma

In China the on-site construction tradition and low-cost labor market have married and given birth to an unseen quantity of built masses and an unprecedented speed of urban growth. Concrete plays a major role in this state of China. Everyone hears that anything that can be designed can be built, but every architect voices frustration at the lack of training and rigor in construction labor and materials, which are imperative in achieving the highest architectural quality. Concrete lies at the origin of this frustration. Concrete has offered speed, it has offered jobs, and it has created China's current growth pattern. If one were to graph two lines representing cement production per capita and the nation's gross domestic product per capita, they would run perfectly parallel.

The fact that China has delivered buildings in so many forms and typologies and in so many regions and customs reveals two antithetical perceptions of concrete. On the one hand, concrete is seen as a homogeneous material that can be cast throughout a territory as big as China itself, and for a universal landscape; on the other, it is a material that can be covered and disguised by polyfaceted surfaces and polychromatic expressions. This paradox has generated architectural discourse that is simultaneously highly spectacular and suspicious.

Therefore, it is not likely that concrete will lead the effort, either in creating architectural icons, as seen in Beijing, or in transforming the building industry in the hands of the highly mobile but non-mechanized labor market. A typical scene: a group of workers drag shovels (with screeching noises) through the construction site under the large overhang of ccTV. The question is, are they the ones who pour the concrete or cover the concrete? Whatever the answer may be, eventually concrete will give way to other, newer materials: aluminum-glass curtain wall (AGC), expanded polystyrene system (EPS), glass-fiber-reinforced concrete (GRS), or whatever three-letter combinations may emerge later. The point

is that they will allow the separation of hand and machine, design and engineering, which may be the cause of the bankruptcy of our current engineering culture in China and the United States.

This is the state of concrete, which is actually neither technical nor technological. It's political! It is out of a fear of totality. The reason that materials other than concrete take command in the prevailing building industry is that those materials are subject to separation and assemblage, a perfect scenario for trades and disciplines that are politically dependent and intertwined. Concrete does not really work that way, or at least it's not intended to. It requires a kind of totalitarian control and a totally coordinated labor force. More importantly, it requires integrated engineering. Given the current environment—and a divided context of being—will the last hope of an integrated state be addressed by a new concrete, Ductal, or something that reverses the logics of concrete such as low-melting-point plaster (LMP), a material not to be poured, but scooped?

What follows is a portfolio of my office's work, demonstrating the confusing, paradoxical state of concrete. The first project, Zhujiajiao Administration Building, represents a kind of hiding act. It was designed for a local, traditional Chinese town. Obviously, a relationship to historical features and traditional materials is preferred, which means wood, bamboo, and removable panels. But the initial study models were made of foam, which is actually a form of concrete. What we didn't know was that, in the end, the traditional look was a must. So concrete was covered up with wood in the form and stack tiles (or louver panels). | figs. 1–2 The design process started as a monolithic, volumetric strategy, which ended up with 90 percent of the concrete lying behind the paneling. Then, is such hiding in favor of history or in the service of constructability? Both, maybe.

The next project is an even better example of undercover concrete. The project, for the local television and broadcasting agency, is located in Xi'an, a city of many dynasties, known for its city wall and moat. In a certain way, the wall is suggestive of concrete construction: it is composed of two layers of huge bricks resembling concrete formwork. When the moat is dug, the dirt is removed to fill the distance between two parallel, brick masonry walls. The project's proximity to the worshipped Giant Wild Goose Pagoda required that the building, a 90,000-square-foot (27,438-square-meter) state media headquarters, have a low height of 56 feet (17 meters), so we made a literal translation of the city wall—not in the sense of its vast landscape nature, but its monolithic, concretelike power. The strategy called for a merge of public activities with earth formations.

The main portion of the volume lies in the basement, with only two stories above ground. The walls undulate and fold in many directions, and while at one time they were intended to be different from the traditional city wall, the rest of the time, this proved to be difficult. The angled walls had to be made of cast concrete, because no one could stack bricks at so many angles, just as ancient labor with abundant hands and time. | figs. 3–4 The concrete work is of such poor quality that metal studs were used to adjust the cavity between the concrete surface and the external layer, which is, in this case, cut stone. The undulating is intentional, but the warping is not. Of course, there are layers of waterproofing (necessitated by the open joints of the stone layer), and lastly came the glazed inserts between the stone layers. There is always a hybrid state of concrete—a 1,000-seat theater is held together by a double-layered, thin-steel structure supporting the circulatory and breakout spaces. To create a monolithic surface, all the windows have rotating stone louvers. The landscape here is flat but not completely, creating complex grading problems that only concrete can form and deform.

The next project is a house for my father, where concrete becomes a means to integrate engineering, design, craft, spatial expression, and materiality. The structure is a concrete frame filled with stones from a nearby river. Handpicked and sorted by color, the stones were collected every summer (during flood season) for three years. The walls are very thick—about 19.7 inches (50 centimeters), which allows for a certain range of stone sizes on either side, with concrete poured in the middle. The floor-to-floor dimension is high, 13 feet (4 meters), and requires rebar reinforcement within the frame, tied both horizontally and vertically between frames. Vertical rebars would be easy, but horizontal ones are not so. To allow the stones to sit randomly, soft wires were tied between the vertical rebars to guide and hold the stones. Bamboo boards line the house interior as formwork, which remains after the concrete is poured—an unmistakable influence of Kahn at the University of Pennsylvania, where I studied. The stable concrete syntax allows other materials to play off variable semantics. | figs. 5–7

We move back to Shanghai with the next project, which is a mixed-use cultural facility serving a newly built community in the Qingpu district. Not far from the site of the administrative center, the building sits in the middle of a manmade lake. The idea of the project is to take the landscape around the lake up onto the roof of the structure so that it becomes accessible, useable space for the general public. The complicated roof topography, the expansive space below, and the lack of funding made concrete the only possible construction material. Conceptually the building is like a stretch of highway hovering over a bathtub in the lake—not unlike the many lifted highways of the region. One could imagine the propriety of hiring highway builders for this project because of the rare possibility of exposing concrete. In reality, the only company who could build this was a highway contractor; as it turned out, they were the only ones who could produce the post-stressed concrete required for the large span, and they could employ the amount of local labor needed. This "exposed concrete," however, is not the favored, phenomenological, rich-textured contemplative one, and it can't be easily covered up. It is the honesty of the concrete that is powerful!

Bamboo boards, the cheapest and most accessible to untrained labor, as shown in Father's House, were used as formwork, but the curvilinear form required so many different sizes of bamboo board that in the end, it did not even make sense to manage the sizes. We basically went to the

fig. 1 | Wood-panel clad Cultural Barrel upon completion, Zhujiajiao Administration
Building, by Mada s.p.a.m., Shanghai, China, 2003

fig. 2 | Wood panel detail showing folding planes and tile stacking

The State of Concrete

Qingyun Ma

fig. 3 | Metal stud system for cladding, Xi'an Centennial Media City,
by Mada s.p.a.m., Xi'an, China, 2005

fig. 4 | Stone cladding, Xi'an Centennial Media City, 2005

fig. 5 | View of pool between a double wall, Father's House, by Mada s.p.a.m., Jade Valley, China, 2001

The State of Concrete
Qingyun Ma

fig. 6 | Concrete frame filled with locally sourced stone

fig. 7 | View of interior

contractor's warehouse and dug through all the leftover, abandoned bamboo boards from countless previous projects. It became easier to compose different sizes, to approximate the curvilinear formation of the roof, and then to shave the edge when the formwork was tightly locked in place. Instead of employing a three-dimensional form-control instrument, our process was actually a two-dimensional approach brought to a three-dimensional space through human effort. The overall shape of the roof was achieved with a scaffolding of millions of steel pipes laid in a meter grid of changing heights toward the roof, yet allowing for a space of human height for error and readjustment—again, two-dimensional but intriguing in the context of parametric scripting, where humans have become blades or melters. | figs. 8–10

Obviously, the idea of a rooftop landscape required that we reverse the whole beam, which then left all potential mistakes on the roof fortunately covered by dirt and then flowers. Since it was finished, the project has truly been used as a public space, and the two undulating surfaces, intersecting at different elevations, have brought many interesting public events together. To connect back to the community, we, for the first time, designed a bridge, a realm in which Marc Mimram has much expertise, but it is hardly a bridge as much as a feeder for the pedestrian who must make the choice of going up or down, back or forth, move or not move. In building the bridge, we created a V-shaped pier that splits in the middle and changes through length to accommodate the choices.

The next project was a competition entry for French automaker Renault's truck division, outside Lyon. At that time, I was fascinated by the possibility of creating a great and "real" concrete building, given Lyon's stature in the culture of concrete. This was actually to be Renault's branding center for new models and technologies—a retro, 1950s, thin-shell concrete structure, self-supported only by a set of locations on the ground surface. The roof moves and morphs through the site, creating a continuum of forms and spaces, that aside from light conditions, are otherwise indifferent and unspecified, despite being labeled "marketing," "showrooms,"

"theaters," etc. The difficult part of the project is that moving beyond the minimalist, clean, stylishly white, universally elegant images, the design process falls well outside those descriptions. We still had to use the hands of eighteen-year-old Chinese modelmakers with long nails, who would work in a very traditional way with wood, mud, glue, and nails. What we learned was that the design and manufacturing processes were incompatible when approaching this problem, and we lost the competition.

Passing from the bridge that I showed earlier to the bridge we are currently working on takes us from being concrete junkies to becoming Ductal fanatics. This is a bridge across the Huangpu River, leading from the 2010 World Expo site in Shanghai. In the early phases of its planning, a bridge was designed by the French firm AS; it proved to be too ambitious, but the idea of a bridge remained. I suppose this was the reason why a bridge was proposed to not cross the main river but to feed it. We won the competition with the proposal of three bridges, of which one can be built out of concrete. Given our frustration with concrete or the state of concrete, I thought that a proposal to use Ductal and a collaboration with Lafarge's engineers would have a new angle for a concrete bridge.

My message to the client, the government, was that if the 2008 Summer Olympics showed confidence, the 2010 World Expo would show competence. The key is not to do traditional in a big way, but to do something new, even if small, like this little bridge. I eventually realized that this bridge won the competition because it resembles a dragon's spine. | figs. 11–13 A dragon's spine is not far from Ductal construction. The design and production could be compartmentalized and then joined in the middle through tension elements. We were in discussion with Ductal at Lafarge to actually make this the first Ductal bridge in China, but we eventually decided on steel. Ductal was not ready, but perhaps the concrete we now know is already on its way out?

fig. 8 | Construction of the roof, the shape is approximated by steel scaffolding at 0.5-meter (1.6-foot) intervals, Thumb Island, Qingpu Community Center, 2003

fig. 9 | Roofscape, Thumb Island, Qingpu Community Center, 2003

fig. 10 | Roof structure reversed to accomodate planting, Thumb Island, Qingpu Community Center, 2003

figs. 11–12 | Site of the Dragon Bridge, by Mada s.p.a.m., Xuhui, Shanghai, China, 2008

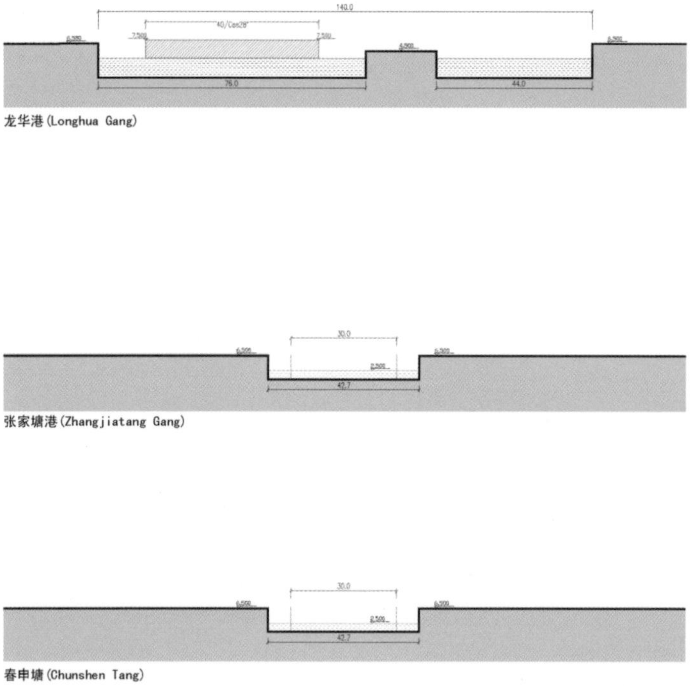

龙华港桥位置

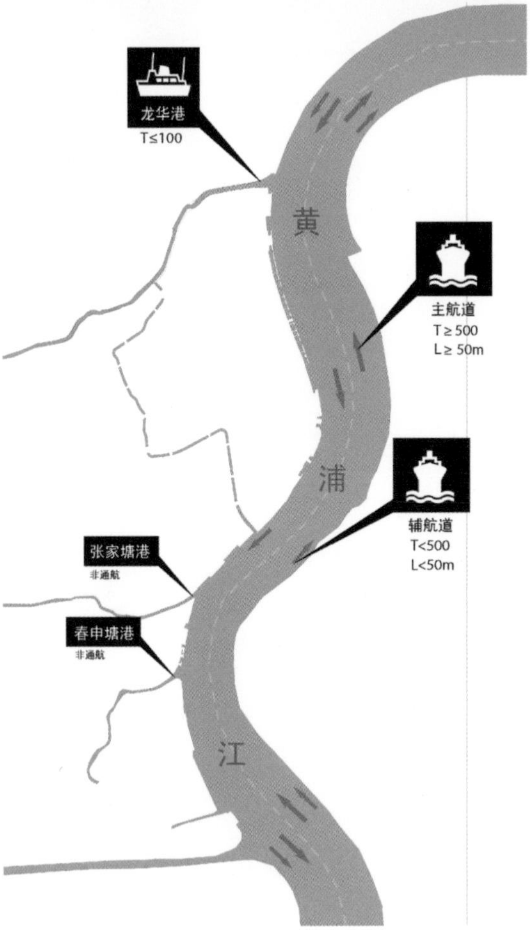

龙华港
T≤100

主航道
T ≥ 500
L ≥ 50m

辅航道
T<500
L<50m

张家塘港
非通航

春申塘港
非通航

黄

浦

江

140.0

40/Cos28°

78.0   44.0

龙华港 (Longhua Gang)

30.0

42.7

张家塘港 (Zhangjiatang Gang)

30.0

42.7

春申塘 (Chunshen Tang)

fig. 13 | Cross section, Dragon Bridge

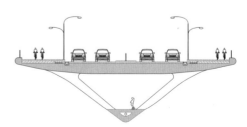

Living with Infrastructure

Marc Mimram

Infrastructure is often treated as a necessary evil—an urban scar, distributing abstract but vital flows, whether it be cars or trains for the transportation of people or goods. The city seems to turn its back on—or, at least, is forced to put up with—what actually drains or supplies it. Yet urban infrastructure also forms a part of our shared urban space, a network with the potential to combine and join together rather than disunite; that is, to link rather than separate. Infrastructural projects generate multiple opportunities that depend on the design of the infrastructure itself and its ability to move beyond its strictly defined function. Each situation is geographically and historically specific, and the unification achieved through infrastructure often means breaking barriers that may be physical, historical, and social.

The production of infrastructure also consumes vast quantities of materials, particularly concrete. We would like to focus fresh attention on the architectural design of infrastructure from the viewpoint of new materials, notably new types of concrete that combine technological progress with attention to the cityscape.

Our research program is designed to use a project to symbolize the following situations: to create local attention by considering the infrastructure's territorial scale; to recognize structure as an opportunity to create brightly lit pathways; to show how environmental commitment involves the efficient use of materials; to draw on structural innovations and other properties of materials that are incorporated into construction; and to make the city, the location, and its urban pleasures central to each project by developing them along the generous principle of shared public space.

We endeavor to make the full, urban potential of infrastructural links coherent through each implemented project. The basis of any functioning link—crossing from one side to the other—involves showing how it can be inhabited, how the inhabitant can drift away from the place without leaving the infrastructure, and how a link may be established while truly living with the infrastructure. Our work involves two complementary approaches, one based on welcoming and accommodating capacity that is latent in a given work of infrastructure, and the other by working on the physical space surrounding the infrastructure.

If works are generally seen as a part of the ground plane, they may also be designed as roofs, elements that are capable of supporting flows, while also protecting the public space below it in order to make it available to the city. Elevated trains, roadways, and bridges offer a public and sheltered level and may also have welcoming and accommodating properties, which can be appropriated by various kinds of urban activities, markets, and utilities. As a unit constructed with attention to the landscape, infrastructure can serve more than just the purpose of transit; it can offer various corridors and pathways, as well as distinctive ways of viewing the landscape. Further attention may also be directed at the bordering function of the infrastructure, where it segments the landscape and brings different parts of the site into confrontation or opposition. To the extent that the infrastructure becomes inhabitable, it may turn this opposition into a link, creating a bond through the infrastructure so that the city enjoys seamless continuity.

Inhabitable bridges have been enduring models for this conception of infrastructure; moving beyond their purely functional role, they extend, develop, and give meaning to the idea of a bond. It is possible to extend the antiquated tradition of inhabitable bridges, which once unified the urban layout across a city's rivers. Inhabited bridges from the eighteenth century—such as the Pont Neuf and Pont Notre-Dame in Paris, the Old London Bridge, or the Ponte Vecchio in Florence, as well as Sir John Soane's utopian designs for the Triumphal Bridge—mark the golden age of inhabitable bridges. It could be argued that this tradition was extended through the nineteenth century, particularly for the construction for World's Fairs, in projects such as the Eiffel Tower and Pont d'Iéna. The fascination with new forms of urban bridges was reinvented in the early twentieth century, whether in Raymond Hood's vision of elevated street bridges in Manhattan or in Konstantin S. Melnikov's project for a taxi parking garage over the bridges on the Seine. Further echoes of the inhabitable bridge appear at an even greater territorial scale after World War II, in Kenzo Tange's Tokyo Bay project or in Yona Friedman's Spatial City, Elevated Blocks project. This tradition can now rediscover all of its meaning by drawing on modern-day developments in structures, progress in new materials, and also attention to the conditions in which a city develops in relation to the rivers that first enabled it to come to life, in each case with its own distinctive geography and urban development plans.

The Rooftop Bridge, Shanghai, China

To say that a bridge has an underlying face is a euphemism. The underside needs to be considered not simply as the necessary counterpart of the vital part above, but on the contrary, as having its own status within public space, a status that exceeds the purely functional property of its surface. We can treat the bridge as a roof that covers and also enhances public space. | figs. 1–2 The roof provides a site from which the city may be admired, and it creates a meaningful place. Taking shelter on the bridge means being welcomed into a public space in an open and multifarious way. One can point to several precedents for such urban roofs.

In the manner in which it plays down the boundaries marked by its facades so as to enhance its welcoming function, is not Mies van der Rohe's Neue Nationalgalerie (1968) first and foremost a giant roof available to the public? Does not Lina Bo Bardi's São Paulo Museum of Art (1968) make this function of the roof as a public space even more explicit, turning it into the agora of the metropolis? It could be said that Paolo Mendes da Rocha further takes up this theme in his bridge buildings, such as the Brazilian Museum of Sculpture (1988) or his roofs over public spaces, such as the Plaza del Patriarca and Viaduct do Cha. Finally Behnisch Architekten's giant curtain and Frei Otto's design for the Munich Olympic Stadium (1972) might be seen as extrapolations of a pergola.

There are doubtless many more examples of this in the history of modern architecture. Treating the bridge as a roof, carefully observing places that enhance the city, and making distinctions in the layout of meaningful spaces belonging to the infrastructure means extending the basic functional status of an infrastructure that is detached from the ground to provide the city below with a service. Means of anchoring are easily found in the city, extending a simple infrastructural superstructure into a roof, thereby increasing communal spaces by unifying the most powerful public places under the roof. The canopy, drape, layer, plaque, or overhang mark are all examples of infrastructure's ability to connect to the city.

The Accommodating Structure, New York, New York

Bridges of this kind can also serve other urban functions, such as opening up the landscape in relation to the city in order to create face-to-face interactions with tall buildings, in addition to providing a physical link. We would like to explore the accommodating function that a bridge might serve, in terms of the multiplication of urban situations and the creation of functional exchanges, as well as in terms of the modularity, assemblage, and juxtaposition of elements evolving over time, all of which may be related to this kind of accommodating structure. | fig. 3 Thanks to its high degree of inertia, the structure may be more than just an opaque superstructure; it can be turned into a transparent top, with transit flows maintained inside. The structure also allows an elevated street, between two discontinuous open facades, to be carefully shaped from structures detached from the ground. This kind of tall city should not be considered as an independent organism that abandons the city below it to its own sad fate and history. On the contrary, thanks to infrastructure's bonding function, it can facilitate interaction between tall buildings, weaving another reference above ground level. Alternatively, infrastructure may be incorporated into the land, like a multipurpose tool open to the evolving city. | figs. 4–5 This city constructed around a superstructure may become relational, developing an interaction with the landscape.

fig. 1 | Views of canopy modules, the Rooftop Bridge, by Marc Mimram Architect and Engineer, Shanghai, China, 2008

fig. 2 | Section, the Rooftop Bridge, 2008

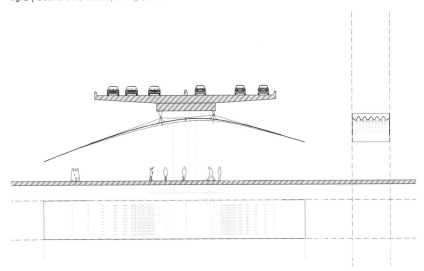

fig. 3 | General elevation view, the Accommodating Structure, 2008

The Landscape Bridge, La Courneuve, France

Even though infrastructure provides services from which everyone benefits, it often comes under criticism from people living nearby, mainly due to the disturbances sometimes caused by its use. Traffic combines with noise and pollution to create a new kind of rejection through the construction of protective barriers, such as soundproof walls or screening roofs. Such protective barriers turn the infrastructure into a sacrifice of territory, setting obstacles in the immediate vicinity; it abandons the land in which it is incorporated, becoming an abstract bond between distant points in the landscape from which it is detached. On the contrary, we might consider this kind of infrastructure as forming an organic bond that carries with it more than just traffic flows by notably introducing a new kind of landscape and ecosystem, which could take the city's landscaping to a whole different scale.

These giant bridges, deeply entrenched in cities for topographical reasons, may be seen as landscape units, inner-city parks, lungs breathing fresh air into cities—all of which would thereby be enhanced on this major territorial scale. The bridge's artifice might correspond to the artifice of nature, not through camouflage but rather as a landscape unit opening the city up to the horizon. | figs. 6–7 Taken as a means of geographical discovery and as an urban landmark, bridges have the potential to provide a landscape-oriented means of healing, enhancing the settings in which they are incorporated.

The Inhabited Structure, Moscow, Russia

This project is first and foremost generated out of the site conditions in which it is to be incorporated. The geography, layout, landscape, and history are just as crucial as the durability of the materials chosen for carrying out the project. The bridge interacts with the landscape, from which it derives its structural determinants and the various scales of its components. | fig. 8 But a bridge is not a solitary object, it enters into the land and exalts the geography in which it comes to life.

It's interesting to note that the vertical city, or the "standing city," has increasingly developed around its conditions of transport, supply, and structure. As it continues to surpass height limits, the mile-high tower that Frank Lloyd Wright once dreamt of may soon be constructed. It's time to take a look at this progress, setting these towers in a new perspective and converting them into inhabitable bridges, with the potential to satisfy local conditions. | figs. 9–10 The tradition of the inhabitable bridge has the potential to create a new synthesis of technology, geography, and urban care, setting within infrastructure its own sequence in relation to the landscape in which it is incorporated.

Endnote
This study was realized by the author in collaboration with Lafarge.

figs. 4–5 | Cross-sections, the Accommodating Structure

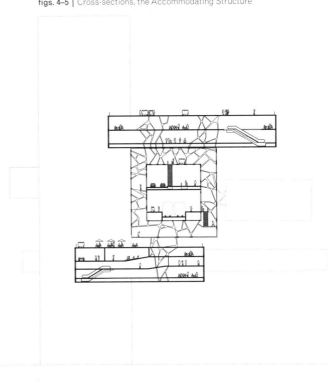

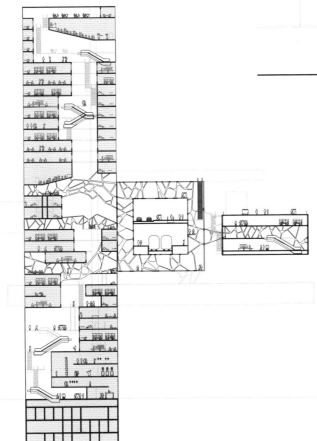

fig. 7 | Cross-sections, the Landscape Bridge

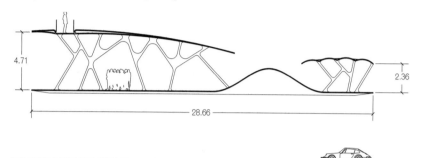

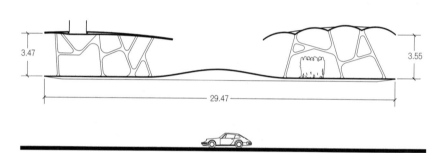

fig. 6 | Section plan, the Landscape Bridge, by Marc Mimram, La Courneuve, France, 2008

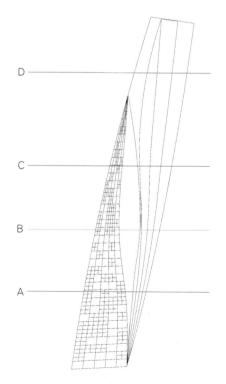

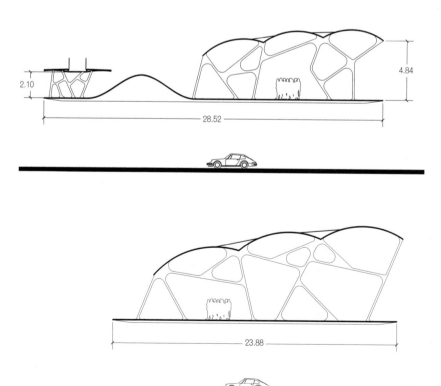

fig. 8 | Site view, the Inhabited Structure, by Marc Mimram Architect and Engineer, Moscow, Russia, 2008

fig. 9 | Cross-sections, the Inhabited Structure

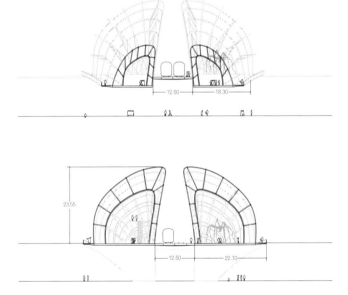

fig. 10 | View from the central circulation area, the Inhabited Structure

Opportunity in Transition: The Reinventing of Concrete

Toshiko Mori

Concrete in its liquid state is an undefined material. It is a fluid, featureless gray sludge. At first it looks malleable and pliant, yet it is slow moving, heavy, and resistant. Without an active engagement of mind and imagination to create a performative mix and cast, the material is massive and featureless, mute and lazy.

As it undergoes the phase change from liquid to solid, it achieves a miraculous transformation from an amorphous substance to a highly specific form and mass. It takes on the characteristics and textures dictated by the material and shape of the mould, and its consistency is affected by the pouring and curing methods. Achieving any set of desired effects necessitates a highly calibrated and orchestrated process of sequencing and timing. Its fluidity in its transitional stage presents the opportunity to formulate future challenges and innovations. The same basic steps hold the potential for an infinite number of permutations that combine strength, density, thickness, texture, and continuity of surfaces. It is a material we continue to reinvent by coming up with new mixtures, new molding techniques, and new pouring, conveying, vibrating, and releasing procedures.

The casting process requires extensive experimentation and testing to ascertain the visual and structural results. For architects, the process is empirical at times, but hands-on material experimentation is essential to understand the precise point of inflection between flexible fluidity and obstinate solidity.

As building design becomes an increasingly integrated and holistic process, it is especially important for material experimentation to be incorporated into the educations of architects. For a number of years, I taught the materials and construction class at the Harvard Graduate School of Design with Thomas Schroepfer and Nader Tehrani. A required course in the first year of the MArch program, it includes a hands-on, three-hour weekly workshop component. The course combines and builds upon architectonic and material exercises originally taught at schools such as the Dessau-Bauhaus, Cooper Union, and the Illinois Institute of Technology. The workshop gives the students an opportunity for tactile exploration of materials while testing conceptual and technical frameworks. To practice economy of means, each student is given an equal quantity of materials to work with, which they cannot exceed, and they have access to hand and machine tools only (no digital fabrication at this stage). The exercises are: Surface, using paper; Aggregation, using wood; Intersection, using wood and plastic; Textile Tectonic, using spools of yarn; and Modulation, using any leftover material to make a mould that simulates a small-scale concrete casting. | fig. 1

The Modulation casting exercise takes on the most complexity because the students must design the moulds as well as the objects. The exercise requires them to think about the process itself: the methods and sequencing of the pour, the speed of the pour, the shaking of the liquid material for even distribution, the release sequence from the mould, and conceptualizing the possibility of repetition and recombination for further aggregation and reuse of both the artifact and the mould. It is the most intensive exercise because it deploys the element of time, which is essential in working with concrete.

This type of exercise can be scaled up to actual construction in the mock-up stage, as illustrated by one wall of the Visitor Center for Frank Lloyd Wright's Darwin D. Martin House (2009) in Buffalo, New York. The new Visitor Center will provide 7,775 square feet (2,370 square meters) of gallery, orientation, and gathering spaces for the Darwin D. Martin House, built in 1905. Our design strategy creates a dialogue with the original house through a series of contrasting elements. Where the house is monumental, the Visitor Center is diminutive in size, low, and linear in its massing. Its transparent glass facade and open plan contrast with the materiality and introversion of Wright's design. The inverted hipped roof of the Visitor Center refers to the form of Wright's building while simultaneously demarcating its distinct public function.

fig. 1 | Experiments with concrete, Harvard Graduate
School of Design, materials and construction class; **a:**
Theodore Baab; **b:** Alda Shur; **c:** Vera Black

a.

c.

b.

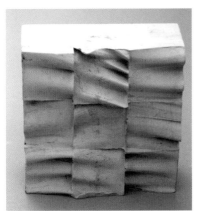

Reinterpreting Wright's lifelong attention to exploring materials, technologies, and techniques, the new building reflects the structural, infrastructural, and programmatic relationships of the original house, in a contemporary and abstract design, creating a distinct visual identity for the center.

While the pavilion has the appearance of a cantilever, it is not. An innovative structural design using slender, solid-stainless-steel perimeter columns was fundamental to achieving the illusion of a cantilevered roof, maximizing the transparency of the facade and integrating the structure with the glazing system. Engineered by Bill Baker of SOM Chicago, the entire lateral load of the structure is taken on by the four central piers encased in concrete. Below grade, these piers are further braced by deep-grade beams, which resist any rotational movement. | figs. 2–3

In terms of precision, the steel columns are 2¾-inch (7-centimeter) square, solid stainless steel. These steel columns assist the piers in supporting the live and dead loads of the roof at the perimeter. They were fabricated using computer-numerical-control (CNC) milling and a grinding system to approach absolute 90-degree corners. This slenderness is possible due to the narrow spacing of 7.6 feet (23 meters), which is quite unusual for a steel structure. Instead of having 25- or 30-foot (8- or 9-meter) spans between columns, the repetition of these delicate columns allows the facade and structure to blend perceptually.

While the main facade of the Visitor Center (facing east) is composed entirely of glass, which wraps around three elevations of the pavilion, the west facade is made of concrete. At a formal level, the deep horizontal fluting of the concrete wall is a visual reference to the raked brick pattern of the Darwin D. Martin House, creating a palimpsest of the original house. At the structural and infrastructural level, the wall demonstrates concrete's capacity to incorporate, with advanced and integrated engineering, multiple systems efficiently to optimize building performance. | fig. 4

The long, cast-in-place concrete wall acts as a load-bearing and shear wall by transferring roof loads from the shorter steel columns to the 6-foot (1.8-meter) deep horizontal, concrete-shelf cantilever. This shelf also shades the building from the afternoon sun from the west. Natural daylighting studies were done to determine the angle of the roof and depth of the shelf to ensure diffused light reflections while preventing glare. At the same time, the concrete mass acts as a thermal mass that shields the pavilion from strong prevailing winds from the Great Lakes throughout the year.

In its cavity, this west wall houses the fresh-air intake for the displacement ventilation system. This high-efficiency air-filtration system removes all the particulates, pollution, and pollens from the air, thus ensuring a consistent, high indoor-air quality. The outdoor air and ventilation is controlled by carbon-dioxide sensors, which monitor the level of carbon dioxide produced by occupants inside the pavilion. This organically responsive system optimizes energy efficiency. As carbon dioxide levels rise, more outside air is introduced into the space, increasing air exchange throughout the building. When people leave and the carbon dioxide levels decrease, the building responds by closing the outside air intakes.

To achieve all of these structural and formal objectives, the project architect, Sonya Lee, made a series of eight experimental conditions during the mock-up stage with various formworks, admixtures, releasing agents, pouring processes, and vibration methods. | fig. 5 From this, she determined the final formulation that could be poured in one day and produce structural integrity, a consistent texture, and precision of the pattern geometry. Doing a single pour provided greater quality control in terms of reducing the adverse effects of variables in temperature and humidity, while ensuring a consistent, precise recipe for the concrete mix. A single pour was also more economical. While it required more preparation and studying of the conditions, mixes, and release agents, the reduced time on-site and expedited schedule of a single pour translated into reduced construction costs. | figs. 6–7 At the same time, use of a standard-form liner and mixture further reduced costs over the originally proposed precast concrete. Wright himself experimented with the use of cast-in-place

fig. 2 | Structural diagrams by SOM Chicago, Visitor Center for the Darwin D. Martin House, by Toshiko Mori Architect, Buffalo, New York

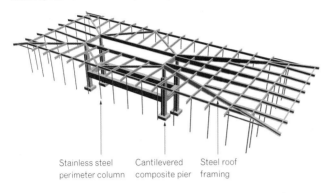

Stainless steel
perimeter column

Cantilevered
composite pier

Steel roof
framing

fig. 3 | Gravity and snow-load steel-bending moment diagram by SOM Chicago

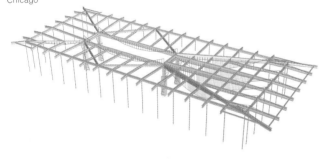

fig. 4 | East-west roof section with concrete piers

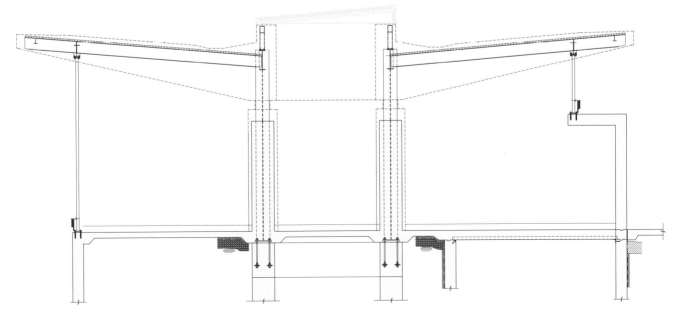

fig. 5 | Comparison of mock-ups of concrete mixtures, by project architect Sonya Lee

	1	2	3	4	5	6	7	8
Mix	4,000 psi regular	Self-consolidating concrete	4,000 psi with superplasticizer	Self-consolidating concrete	Self-consolidating concrete, less sand, more fly ash	4,000 psi with superplasticizer	4,000 psi with superplasticizer	Self -consolidating concrete
Oil	No	Used water on surface of formliner	Four types of oil: regular form oil, Armour all, PAM, cooking oil	Cooking oil on left, nothing on right	Cooking oil	Regular form oil	Regular form oil	Regular form oil
Vibrated	Internal	Light tap	Heavily every 10 in. (25.4 cm) internal	Left side only, internal	Left side tapped with thick rod, right side no	Heavily, internal	Vibrated first 2 feet (24 in.) then vibrated second 2 feet poured on top	Heavily, internal
Notes	Used original side of formliner	Flipped formliner over for smooth finish	Used smooth side of formliner	Used smooth side of formliner	Flipped formliner back to original side	Front with wood strips, snap ties at interior flutes	Spec Formliner on left, Fitzgerald formliner on right	Spec Formliner on left, Fitzgerald formliner on right
Dumped/conveyed	Dumped	Dumped	Conveyed	Conveyed	Dumped	Conveyed	Conveyed	Conveyed
Result	Matte finish with orange-peel surface, Honeycombing	Rough finish, large amount of honeycombing and laitance	Smooth shiny finish, reduced honeycombing	Tiny air pockets all over ribs	Lighter, less consistent, large amount of honeycombing and laitance	Smaller air pockets at upper flute, smooth finish	Air pockets still visible	Rough finish on left side, large honeycombing on right

figs. 6–7 | On-site concrete pouring, Visitor Center for the Darwin D. Martin House, by Toshiko Mori Architect, Buffalo, New York

fig. 8 | Interior view

figs. **9–10** | Fabric formwork experiments, directed by Mark West at the Centre for Architectural Structures and Technology (CAST), University of Manitoba, Faculty of Architecture

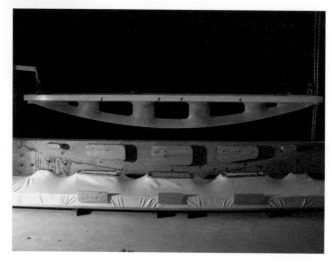

reinforced concrete, one of the earliest of which was at the E-Z Polish Factory in Chicago, built in 1905 for the Martin brothers. The west wall of the Visitor Center is a tribute to Martin and Wright, for their early spirit of experimentation with concrete. | fig. 8

Continuing this spirit of trial-and-error experimentation is essential to advancing the future potential of concrete. One person at the forefront of this material exploration is Mark West of the University of Manitoba, Faculty of Architecture, in Winnipeg, Canada. He is the director of the Centre for Architectural Structures and Technology (CAST). The Centre's work is a model for promoting ideas, design, technology, and creativity for both industry and academia. CAST operates in traditional methods as well as new geometries, materials, and techniques that can respond to various modes of production. Working in a small community and with a university that also has a limited budget, the local Lafarge Precast factory has been a collaborative partner in CAST's experiments. The Centre's hands-on approach to physical exploration combines the traditions of fine arts, engineering, and architecture.

CAST's innovative approach utilizes simple construction methods and common building materials, making new technologies accessible to both high- and low-capital building cultures and economies. Since concrete has broad applications in various modes of production, from low to high tech, adapting to different levels of economy is crucial to the future advancement of concrete technologies. Another goal of CAST's experimentation is material reduction in construction. Their primary means and methods derive from the use of a simple, flat rectangular fabric, taken right off the roll as formwork, and the use of rectangular construction tools. The full-scale work moulds are made with inexpensive geotextiles that cost about a dollar per square meter.

Prototypes and experimental models produced in the past include: precast panels in fabric moulds | figs. 9–10 ; reusable lightweight fabric moulds for column designs; methods for producing very light, thin-shell panels cast from sheets of hanging fabric by spraying fiber-reinforced concrete (the final panels are 2 to 4 inches (5 to 10 centimeters) thick, with one piece of 15-millimeter (0.6-inch) steel rebar on each perimeter); cast-in-place and precast lightweight beams using fabric moulds to form efficient, variable-section beams that follow structural curves (it would be interesting to see them incorporate high-performance textiles and their weave patterns to replace steel for tensile reinforcement); fabric-cast trusses formed from flat sheets of fabric stretched over simple rigid frames and used as mould walls, allowing for the formation of efficient truss designs that can reduce dead-weight and concrete volumes; and fabric-formed precast thin-shell funicular vaults.

Concrete demands an infusion of creative ideas, vision, and imagination by the intelligence and pragmatism of architects and engineers. Concrete's fluid state is an opportunity for continual reinvention, and its multitasking capabilities situate it ideally at the forefront of new construction technologies that optimize building performance.

Implicit Performance: Exploring the Hybrid Condition

Juan Herreros

Webster's Third New International Dictionary:

> **im·plic·it** *adj* [Latin *implicitus*, past participle of *implicare* to infold, involve, implicate, engage—more at EMPLOY] 1 obs.: tangled or twisted together : INTERWOVEN 2a (1) : tacitly involved in something else : capable of being understood from something else though unexpressed: capable of being inferred : IMPLIED—compare EXPLICIT (2) : involved in the nature or essence of something though not revealed, expressed, or developed : POTENTIAL b (1) : not appearing overtly : confined in the organism (2) of a culture : capable of being derived only as an implication from behaviour : not apparent or overt to the people it characterizes : tacit and underlying 3a : lacking doubt or reserve : UNQUESTIONING, WHOLEHEARTED b obs.: UNQUALIFIED, ABSOLUTE 4 archaic : marked by an implicit faith, credulity, or obedience

> *Hybrid* \ *1 a:* marked by heterogeneity in origin, composition, or appearance: Composite b: being a linguistic hybrid <a-term> 2: of, relating to, or resulting from the union of gametes from parents of different genotype 3: having characteristics resulting from two diverse cultures or traditions.

I belong to a generation that has grown up rejecting any sense of heroism in architecture. This attitude can, in large part, be assigned to those epic, concrete constructions in which the suffering of operators in those densely populated scaffoldings so excited our elders—all those compressive stresses, all that obesity, whose resolution was the basis of Vitruvian *firmitas*, and utterly lost its prestige in the 1970s. And concrete—with its hard-working, slave-driving, open-air chemical process, according to the believers in cables, articulated joints, and tensile structures—was largely relegated to the most professional of practices, to those who used it

as material whim for the sake of a poetic essence—a poetic essence that was neither essential, as it lacked true simplicity, nor poetic, considering what it weighed.

But this period was just a sigh. The metallic optimism of the "High-Tech" movement soon lost its sanity (or its jumper-cables), opening a new sense of loss and inviting us to take a new look at those good old construction methods. This is why looking at concrete seems to be a historical obligation, prodding us to understand why reinforced concrete has always played an autonomous role in architecture.

The division of the construction process into skin, skeleton, mechanical systems, and interior organizations was a major breakthrough in its day. Within architectural design, it triggered an expansion, where concrete practically saturated all areas of our building practices. But concrete has always been concrete; where concrete ended, something else began. Let us say that concrete has been an individually identifiable material, always a protagonist in the systems it participated in, often as the only player. Times are changing, however, and the conceptual transparency associated with the clear identification of constructive elements and materials is, nowadays, disappearing, giving way to a contentious blurred state. The old dream of the desirable compatibility between disparate components has created a new condition: the indiscriminate merger of components into one another, making it impossible to sense any distinction or boundaries between them. Concrete is a specific material with its own science and culture, but only recently has research begun to elucidate the possibilities of integrating concrete into complex systems, beyond its own applications and forms of technology. To broaden this investigation and to create an experimental platform for future applications, an integrated constructive resource, is certainly one of the most interesting programs that we can imagine today.

While surveying other areas of technical evolution, there appears to be a common interest in dissolving the limits of what had previously been thought of, designed, and used—all as perfectly differentiated applications. This trend in construction materials and resources, which can be called "crossbreeds," or more precisely "hybrids," come together to combine a wide variety of ingredients. Some of these ingredients have yet to be implemented in construction systems, opening tangible possibilities to create alternative products with properties and applications that can be applied in specific yet collaborative manners. That said, this new hybridization of materials is not merely a material or structural concern. Within this research lies a deeper interest that is generated through the integration of different fields of knowledge, methods of design, and their respective functions.

The hybrids of greatest interest are those that offer complete systems. The root of this statement makes a clear indication toward a future of numerous extraordinary possibilities in an evolving, transformative construction culture. Hybrids play an exciting role because, apart from their potencies as structural, constructive, and efficient actors, they also ought to deliver spatial, aesthetic, and adaptable properties, formulating an array of different, even incongruent situations, creating conditions in which there are no apparent limits to their use. As such, a wide and innovative range of elements should include living or animated ingredients and recycled products, as well as ingredients previously rejected or even consciously forgotten by those gilded and established design and construction practices.

This condition of potential integrations, which I prefer to call "implicit performance," will emerge through the above-mentioned hybrids, and it is clear and present that concrete must play a significant role in such an environment. But, if the objective of this debate is to explore and exploit the limits of concrete's involvement with other resources, and in order to create this new series of construction materials and applications, then concrete should in fact assume a significant role but, by definition, should not become the only element in play. Therefore all of these variables confronting us are a singular question designed to identify the multiplicity of conditions of compatibility and integration—shall we say "complicity"—where concrete and that certain something else can create a new material system, adopting a potentially infinite set of different characteristics. If concrete surpasses its original performance to the point of becoming a new material in and of itself, it will then carry inherent contemporary, spatial, and experiential consequences. It is critically important to underscore that behind the collective work that such a program requires, there is an interest in generating practical implementations of theoretical topics as a method to construct a second nature, thus creating architectural applications and systems that must reconsider the material conditions with which we construct and destroy the world.

Xurret System, 2004

A series of objects having a plantlike surface and acicular texture, which are mutually compatible due to a parametric reconstruction of their relief, developed in liquid pigmented concrete using resin formwork. They suggest different natural combinations, which invite the public to sit down, lie down, or talk. Resisting definition either as street furniture, sculpture, or as concrete pieces, the materiality of these objects remains as undefined as their use. | figs. 1–3

Inert-alive Panel, 2005

A concrete panel is impregnated with lichen spores that begin to appear according to increased levels of dampness and changes of season. Differences in lichen growth differentiate between the facades exposed to the wind and sun, those that are protected, and those that are not. Reacting with the stimuli of weather and pollution, its colors can be controlled and drawn with great geometric precision, planning an efflorescence as enthralling as the coming of spring, in order to construct an animated architecture that emulates the passing of time as an enrichment of the project, rather than as an inevitable deterioration of it. | figs. 4–5

Usera Library, 2001

This library in Madrid, Spain, was designed with a lightweight floor structure, transporting all of the building's mechanical

figs. 1–3 | Xurret System, by Abalos & Herreros, 2004

figs. 4–5 | Inert-alive Panel, by Abalos & Herreros, 2005

figs. **6–8** | Usera Library, by Abalos & Herreros, 2001

Implicit Performance

fig. 9 | Volleyball Palace, JuanHerrerosArquitectos, 2007

fig. 10 | Business Services Center, by JuanHerrerosArquitectos, 2008

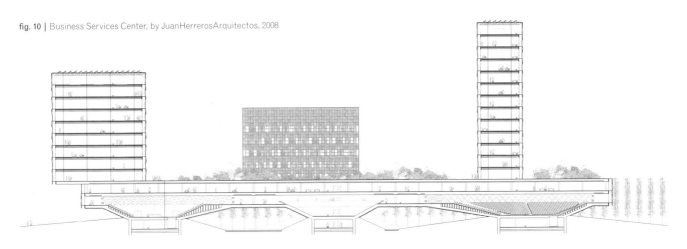

systems within it and turning the programmatic spaces into isotropic, thermal surfaces. While this might seem to be an unnecessary sophistication of the old-fashioned raised technical floor, the concept intended to make the building work in accordance to the Thermal Active Building System (TABS) energetic principles, also known as Concrete Core Temperature Control (CCTC). These principles, based on activating the building elements as energy agents, transformed the inertial value of concrete into an essential part of the climate-control systems, far surpassing its traditionally limited structural role. | figs. 6–8

Volleyball Palace, 2007
Designed for a site in Medellín, Colombia, this structure contains a section in which compressed pieces are built in concrete, while tensile pieces use steel according to Buckminster Fuller's tensegrity guidelines. The mechanical structure is the building itself; it organizes the circulation while establishing a contemporary spatial experience that omits any superfluous systems or decor. | fig. 9

Business Services Center, 2008
The foundation emerges from the ground, configuring an aircraft-carrier-like platform with three steel-structure buildings. Applying a component of low-resistance concrete that reuses aggregate materials taken from the area has created a strangely thick series of cross-sections. These sections, in turn, somehow refer to the archaeological discovery of the site's geological past, contained in layers of alluvium deposits laid down by a brook that is prone to unforeseeable flooding. | fig. 10

Implicit Performance Workshop, deSingel, Antwerp, 2008
A group of students delivered a two-week experiment dealing with the implicit performance of concrete, requiring conditions from the material not prescribed by its orthodox use. Concrete that is transparent, magnetic, plant covered, filtering, accumulating, and changeable over time, or that attracts pollution, birds, and seeds, etc. was developed. The aim of the experiments was to overflow a practice, which often limits concrete to the production of structural elements or pieces that are added to a skeleton without any greater implication than their own presence. | fig. 11

fig. 11 | Implicit Performance Workshop, by deSingel, Antwerp, 2008; **a:** conwax (concrete with wax admixture) allowing for greater insulating properties, **b:** magnetocrete (magnetic concrete), **c:** Kantcrete (concrete cast with lace-covered formwork, **d** and **e:** removing the wax from the conwax by abrasion or erosion to affect the final texture

a.

b.

c.

d.

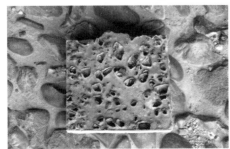

e.

Solidifications

Fernando Menis

Surrounded by a specific landscape, we try to research and to imagine the relationship between architecture and site, much like a slow and quietly moving flow of magma that solidifies and crystallizes according to the specificities of time and location. It is important not to lose the constant desire to learn from the engineers who work with us, as well as from the shuttering workers, the carpenters, and other specialists involved in the construction. Maintaining close contact with the knowledge of various specialists provides us with the opportunity to participate in the solidification of the idiosyncrasies of the various people involved in a project, giving rise in each case to a tangible element that becomes a key part of the project's future development.

Such elements do not arise spontaneously but are the product of an extensive dialogue and a keen interest in customs and culture as the heritage of a place. They take shape through comparisons with previous experiences, as well as through interferences and contributions from other investigations that are carried out in parallel at the office. The office's recent work involves developing anchoring mechanisms to ensure that our projects are impregnated with the site's local material culture from the very beginning. Inquiring about the specific uses of materials and technologies, including intermediate technologies and local craft traditions, we shape the object from an amalgam in which idea, form, and matter are originally united. Thus we talk about building a building twice: first through a back-and-forth process, a series of successive approaches that refines a project's latent concern, not unlike the shaping of raw material; and second through a formless, amalgamated, and imprecise substance that slowly molds and anchors to the particularities of a specific place and society.

As often happens in the process of working with concrete, it is the initial lack of precision, uncertainty, and unity of the raw material that allows a project to fit correctly in a place, where it acquires all of its final properties. Therefore it is not surprising that besides the convenience of reusing natural resources and the surrounding landscape, the use of concrete also supports our research.

Magma Arte & Congresos

The Magma Arte & Congresos, created with my former partners Felipe Artengo Rufino and José María Rodríguez-Pastrana Malagón, was built over a period of ten years. The building melds completely with the landscape of the Canary Islands and was constructed with materials taken directly from the building site, where a crusher was installed to produce aggregate for the concrete. | figs. 1–4

Over the years that the project developed, our skills were also increasing—a dynamic that changed our ideas. As a result we have been forced to continually modify the project; for instance, wiping out pillars or redoing the deck, another instance of a back-and-forth work process. In fact, the design of the curved deck, which follows a completely different geometry than the building's base but ends interlacing with it, was not finalized until the end of the project. | figs. 5–7

The building is tailored throughout to the extreme detail: services are carefully hidden inside boxes, surfaces carry a remarkable set of textures, and a wide range of parts, including speakers, lights, and nozzles have been meticulously planned and designed before being installed on-site. | fig. 8

Solidifications
Fernando Menis

fig. 1 | Magma Arte & Congresos, by Fernando Menis, Felipe Artengo Rufino, and
José María Rodríguez, and Pastrana Malagón, Adeje, Spain 2005

fig. 2 | Under construction, Magma Arte & Congresos

fig. 3 | Modules as broken rocks embedded in the
topography

fig. 4 | Model

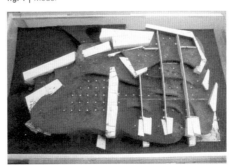

fig. 5 | Details of texture and lighting, Magma Arte & Congresos

Solidifications
Fernando Menis

fig. 6 | Music hall and auditorium

fig. 7 | Interior

fig. 8 | Variations in surface and color of cast concrete from the use of local
volcanic stone, different types of wood formwork, and manual treating after casting

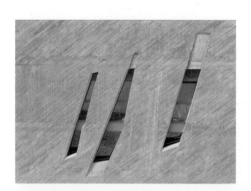

A Building and its Double

Mabel Wilson

> A cast of an object traps it in time, eventually displaying two histories—its own past and the past of the object it replicates.—Richard Shone

For her controversial site-specific sculpture *House* (1993), artist Rachel Whiteread cast the interior of a three-story dwelling located in the East End of London. | fig. 1 All of the other houses on the block—ubiquitous Victorian brick terrace houses—had been razed, leaving behind one 14-foot (4.3-meter) wide specimen, former address: 193 Grove Road in Bow. Workers excavated under the lower level of the house to underpin a foundation for the new concrete structure that the artist had proposed. Inside, Whiteread and her crew treated all the walls with a debonding agent, and proceeded to meticulously trowel concrete onto all of the outward-facing surfaces. From the windowpanes to the interior of the hearths and around the boxes that held the light switches, they worked this fine layer of concrete into all of the crevices and openings. Following this intricate process of lining the interior, the work crew veiled the ceilings, walls, and floors with a tight grid of rebar to reinforce the new structure so that each room formed a self-supporting structural shell. | fig. 2 Onto this reinforcement, gunnite, a much coarser type of concrete, was pneumatically sprayed in a series of layers, entombing the interior in a soupy atmosphere of gray.[1] Once cured, the exterior cladding of brick, wooden lathe, plaster, paint, and wallpaper was peeled off to reveal the interior space of the house, now cast in positive relief by the concrete. Through this casting method, Whiteread erected a second version of 193 Grove Road, a building within a building that turned its inside out. The building's party walls along with its front and rear facades had become its own formwork. *House* recast the private sphere of the domestic interior as a public work of art.

When *House* was unveiled to the public in the fall of 1993, it sat, a bulky light-gray monolith in an empty East London block, whose nearby houses had all been demolished to make way for Mile End Park. The project provoked immediate and divided reactions from the public and from critics. Some called it a monstrosity, alarmed by *House*'s ungainly form, and deemed its difficult topic, the destruction of a neighborhood in the name of urban renewal, not worthy of the lofty term "work of art." Other dissenters claimed it "a waste of 50,000 pounds sterling." Many were riled by the memorial's enigmatic statement and downright ugliness. The former tenant at 193 Grove Road, described in a local paper as a "war hero," told local reporters that he thought the money should have gone to buy a new house. Various art critics attacked *House* for lacking the virtues of craft and execution, defaming it as a brilliant conception, typical of this particular generation of artists, but lacking in the true genius that would make it great art. Others, moved by the work, praised it as a monument or perhaps more aptly, an anti-monument, testifying to the complex fate of London's working class communities in the rapidly gentrifying hub of global finance capital,[2] which by the 1990s was defined by the techno-sleek profiles of high rises like Richard Rogers's Lloyd's of London bank (1986) or the luxury residential towers on the nearby Isle of Dogs, rather than the steeples of the Church of England or the gothic towers of the British Parliament. While boosters lauded *House*'s power to signify loss, to remember in its ghostly presence a now absent community, whose homes had been routed by economic disenfranchisement, condemnation, and removal by the State, the project's ability to recall the white working class enclave was not without the tensions of race and class that are implicit in highly visible public expressions of cultural heritage. Whiteread's neutral grey box had ignited a firestorm of public furor.[3]

Despite these differing and passionate opinions, what they all saw was a work of art that had dematerialized the architectural threshold, delineating the public sphere from the private domain. Onlookers gained an extraordinary perspective into the Victorian interior, a rather mundane, cramped enfilade of rooms, whose choreography of working class life had been hidden by the houses on either side and buried in a block of repetitive terraces. Windows—once transparent apertures to the street—now appeared as raised quadrants chiseled into the smooth grey block. A bay window expressed its authority as it burst forward along Grove Road's once bustling corridor. The faint tinge of wallpaper and patches of fading yellow paint had been delaminated from the house and transferred onto the surface of concrete. Sectional cuts of wooden floors and walls partitioned the solid mass of *House*. And the cadence of walls and doors marked the sequence from public rooms in the lower floor to private bedrooms in the upper level. The mise-en-scène of everyday life left its traces in the liquid state of the concrete, which, once solidified, suspended these vicissitudes in perpetuity. Or at least until Whiteread's *House* yielded to public outcry and, like all the other homes that once stood on the block, fell prey to the claw of a hydraulic breaker.

As with any process of casting, the terrace house had formed its apparitional twin: *House*. A cast not only duplicates an object, but also traps it in time.[4] To cast, which also means "to throw," initiates a process of transformation in which something changes from one state to another. During the nineteenth century, the technique of casting was regularly employed in the fine arts to preserve the character of something that would be or had been lost, such as an artifact of antiquity or notable works of art deemed suitable to copy for wider circulation. Not only reserved for antiquities and works of art, casting was widely used in the creation of death masks, objects that best represent casting's memorializing capacity. In this sense, Whiteread's *House* was appropriately called a memorial, casting into the present the final moments of a demolished home.

In architecture, however, building is a prospective practice rather than a retrospective one. Instead of doubling something already present, formwork casts a new building that has yet to exist in the world. With concrete, one builds the building twice, its formwork followed by its pour. And yet, like the discarded mold, the formwork is nonetheless lost upon the completion of its cast. Thus in architecture, the formwork, like the house at 193 Grove Road, is the absent agent in the creation of the building's final form. A cast-concrete building retains the memory of its formwork. Its markings are sometimes evident in the board outlines, plank striations, and punctures of tiebacks left behind upon the final walls, floors, and ceilings. Such traces can be seen throughout Le Corbusier's midcentury masterpiece, the monastery of Sainte Marie de La Tourette (1960). | fig. 3 On a hill above the village of Éveux-sur-l'Arbrèsle, workers labored on the monastery for several years and the narrative of its construction can been followed on the interior and exterior surfaces of the myriad of forms that make up its precinct.[5] Indeed, if casting throws a building into time, it also locates it in space. The formwork functions as the shape, model, representation, and idea as imagined by the architect. The form, one could say, works to emplace the pour. The form also works to craft the resultant building. A composite term, "formwork" holds the concrete in place as it transforms over time, molecularly from one state—liquid—to its next state: solid.

The rationalization of modern construction techniques in the nineteenth and twentieth centuries allowed for a streamlining of methods toward efficiencies in production and performance. With innovations in concrete, the economics of building (time and material) could be controlled by calculating dimensions according to which standardized materials would be employed for the formwork; on-site work crews need only to erect and reuse the formwork in the process of pouring, packing, and curing the concrete. The modularity of elements is evident in the patchwork imprints registered on a building's roughly hewn walls. It also meant that the metrics of labor, or the "man hours" required to erect the formwork and guide the pour, could also be calibrated to manage cost. The regulation of labor costs, which in certain locales were held at minimum, was essential to the completion of expansive, mid-twentieth-century civic monuments realized by Louis I. Kahn in Bangladesh and India, by Niemeyer and Costa in Brazil, and by Eero Saarinen at

A Building and its Double
Mabel Wilson

fig. 1 | *House* by Rachel Whiteread, commissioned by Artangel, 1993

figs. 2–3 | Construction of the monastery of Sainte Marie de La
Tourette, by Le Corbusier, Éveux-sur-l'Arbrèsle, France, 1960

Washington Dulles International Airport in Chantilly, Virginia, and John F. Kennedy International Airport in New York, all of which required the immense mobilization of human resources. And yet despite the swarms of workers needed to erect these exquisite constructions, photographs taken shortly after their completion appear eerily vacant and sparsely populated, as if they too were already ruins of a near future.

Whiteread's turning the inside to the outside revealed the messiness of the sociocultural condition, the stains and the residues of everyday life, but also those laws of the land, rulings that enable the State to seize property, within which we situate buildings. Proposing the notion of "social-time spaces," in regard to *House*, the cultural geographer Doreen Massey describes how Whiteread's gesture "worked at the disruption of such social-time spaces. It jumped into and threw awry the 'normal' time-spaces, the ideas of time-spaces, which we construct in order to live our lives."[6] As a public artwork, it created a prism, albeit a peculiarly opaque one, through which various publics were able to project and make visible their positions on a range of contested topics about what is art, home, housing, belonging, and neighborhood. As architects cast their projects into places, whether in concrete, steel, or whatever available building material, they also produce space, often described in architectural discourse as the elegant spatial sequences elaborated by concept and execution. But what architects may be less capable of discerning is the manner in which their work will produce social space, either disrupting and destroying or extending and creating new social time-spaces through which people shape their lives. Formwork is an appropriate reminder of this hidden doubling; it creates the space for the emergence of the building and subsequently disappears. Once in place, the building as architecture creates the social spaces of inhabitation. This is perhaps the secret life of buildings, beyond the purview of the architect, where the paint meets the concrete wall and when the house transforms into home.

Epigraph: Richard Shone, "A Cast in Time," in *House*, ed. Rachel Whiteread and James Lingwood (London: Phaidon Press in association with Artangel, 1995), 52.

1 | For a detailed description of the construction process, see Neil Thomas, "The Making of House: Technical Notes," in *House*, 128–30.

2 | See the section "Compendium of Press and Cartoons in Rachel Whiteread and James Lingwood," in *House*, 132–9.

3 | Doreen Massey, "Space Time and the Politics of Location," in *House*, 34–49.

4 | Richard Shone, "A Cast in Time," in *House*, 50–61.

5 | Sérgio Ferro, *Le Couvent De La Tourette: Le Corbusier*, Monographies D'architecture (Marseille, France: Parenthèses, 1988), 43–60.

6 | Massey, "Space Time and the Politics of Location," 36.

Cloaked Transparency: Land Port of Entry
Massena, New York

Laurie Hawkinson

Material choice and integration in the design of a building have always been a primary consideration for the architect, from the rusticated stonework of H. H. Richardson's Allegheny Courthouse and Jail to the remarkable form-finished concrete at Kahn's Salk Institute.

Conflicting Agendas

The need for a secure facility for the operation of a new Land Port of Entry at Massena, New York, by the U.S. Department of Homeland Security, and the proscribed mandate of the General Services Administration's Design Excellence Program to create a welcoming and aesthetically pleasing gateway into the United States, posed a particular dilemma for us.

We thought to use materials and building systems that could accommodate and illustrate the dilemma of a politicized architecture: open and democratic, while simultaneously protected and secure.

Looking to contemporary American industrial materials and systems as components of roadside and interstate architectures, we chose glass and polycarbonates for their transparency and thermal-insulating capacities, concrete and concrete block for their opacity and economy, and corrugated steel siding and standing-seam roofing for their ubiquity.

In each of the structures at the port, the materials, in concert with one another and in ways directed by program and design intent, play multiple roles in the buildings' operations and representations.

Administration Building

At the main Administration Building, a structure whose north-facing primary facade is always in shadow, we combined a ballistic observation window, interior human-high concrete-block perimeter walls, and an exterior translucent polycarbonate skin to create a shadowbox structure, whose apparent transparency dispels the idea of an impenetrable building face.

The building appears softly translucent during the day. At night, its exterior—polycarbonate, traffic-paint supergraphic—is rendered dynamic by the headlights of oncoming motorists. The building also glows internally, partially masked by the concrete partitions, disallowing any overt understanding of the facilities' operations or program.

A clear, glazed-perimeter window wall affords visual access to public areas, which are purposely identified by a wayfinding device, traffic paint, and the industrial-safety-color: yellow.

Port Facilities Building

The Port Facilities Building is a freestanding structure that supports the operation of the port in diverse ways, providing management offices, dedicated equipment storage, and a concrete fire tank reservoir for the port-wide sprinkler system.

The exceptionally high water table at the site precluded the customary option of burying the tank.

We elected to incorporate the concrete tank into the southern facade of the building. As part of its footing and foundation, the reinforced concrete walls of the tank not only support building steel, but their location and dark gray material mix turn the tank and its contents into a huge heatsink, simultaneously self-warming and insulating. Thus the concrete tank becomes an integral component of the building's skin and physical evidence of an environmentally conscious program.

The building exteriors enjoy the same mix of exterior materials as found at the Administration Building. Polycarbonate, glass, concrete, and standing-seam metal cladding are displaced to afford daylight at the building's interior and visual access to public spaces.

Non-Intrusive Inspection (NII) Facilities Building

The NII Facilities Building, an unconditioned structure, scans commercial vehicles and provides a concealed location for their physical inspection. The concrete in this building serves

as foundation and wall for the building steel, while simultaneously acting as a radiation screen for protecting port per-
sonnel from the gamma rays emitted by the vehicle scanning
equipment.

Here, too, the building exteriors enjoy the same mix of
exterior materials as found at the Administration Building.
Polycarbonate, glass, concrete, and standing seam metal cladding are displaced to afford daylight at the building's interior.

Rendering, Massena Land Port of Entry, by Smith-Miller + Hawkinson Architects,
Massena, New York, 2009

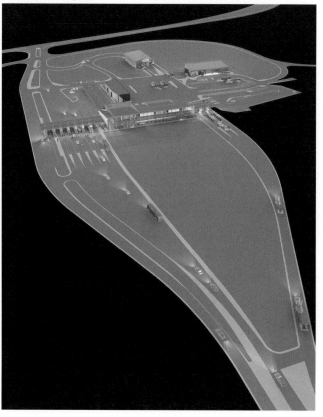

Cloaked Transparency

Laurie Hawkinson

Approach to Massena Land Port of Entry

Curtain wall and supergraphic detail

View of the approach

Passenger Inspection Plaza

Non-Intrusive Inspection and Port Facilities Building

Secondary inspection building and canopy

Cloaked Transparency

Laurie Hawkinson

Non-Intrusive Inspection Facilities Building

View of inspection bay

Interior of inspection bay

Building section

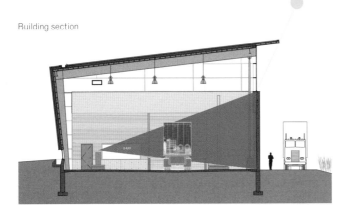

Artificial Natures / New Geographies

Kate Orff

The Turtle Creek Pump House in Dallas, Texas, could be described as a study of concrete in five ways. This project—a collaboration between Julie Bargmann and Kate Orff of D.I.R.T., Mesa Design Group, Cunningham Architects, and the client—exemplifies an attitude toward making and a joint approach to the operations of deconstruction and reconstruction, with minimal site impact.

The site is home to a former pump house and municipal waterworks. | fig. 1 Before the waterworks ceased operation, two large concrete tanks were filtering potable water before pumping it across the adjacent creek to an expanding residential district. | fig. 2 Eventually, concrete was poured on the grounds and the site became a parking lot and storage area for municipal vehicles. A new owner acquired the site with the goal of transforming it into an art and event space. | fig. 3

Turtle Creek is a tributary of the Trinity River and, like many urban streams, it has experienced more flooding and scouring at its edges due to an increase in impervious surface coverage throughout the watershed, among other reasons. Rather than demolish and haul away the material, we set out to selectively jackhammer the existing surface into different sizes of rubble, increasing the pervious area near the creek's floodplain. Some of this material was then displaced to the front of the garden to form patches of open space amidst a lush garden.

In the tanks, we kept an existing craggy wall punch and ground down the reinforcement to show the section and the materiality of the concrete walls. | fig. 4 A zone around the edges of the first tank was saw-cut and removed to form a perimeter of planting set within gravel: a mixture of brick, asphalt, and concrete, which, when broken down together, form a beautiful warm color. A new concrete floor was poured in both tanks. The waterworks were connected back into the potable system, and the second tank was waterproofed so that it could be flooded for "wading parties" and events.

At the entry to the site, a new turf-block matrix was developed with a gradient of open to closed spaces, allowing cars and people to cross it; however, while the site is dormant, it still enables water to infiltrate. The garden engages the designed deconstruction and re-placement of concrete as well as new technologies, patterns, and uses. | fig. 5

At this moment in the process of global urbanization, the discussion of concrete may need to shift from the scale of formal architectural accomplishments to the scale of collective landscape effects. Concrete is made by accelerating the geological processes of hardening—aggregates, cementitious materials, and water—to create a stonelike synthesis. On an urban landscape scale, we can witness the role of concrete in accelerating the presence of an artificial nature that supports, at least in part, human and animal life. One could speculate, for example, that entire mountaintops have been exploded for aggregate, carted to the flatlands, and reconstituted into new high-rises (or artificial mountains) as a sort of large-scale redeployment of nature and the construction of a new geography. At the same time, as coral reefs are threatened with extinction throughout the world's oceans, molded concrete reef balls are being introduced in order to try to stem the decline of the marine life inhabiting these ecosystems.[1] To engage this artificial nature, questions about the future of concrete should be broadened to include geological time and concepts of deconstruction, decay, entropy, failure, and obsolescence alongside new technologies, means, and methods.

1 | One-third of the more than 700 species of reef-building corals are threatened with extinction, according to a comprehensive survey by the Global Marine Species Assessment (GMSA): "One-Third of Reef-Building Corals Face Elevated Extinction Risk from Climate Change and Local Impacts," published in *Science Express, Science*, http://www.sciencemag.org/cgi/content/abstract/1159196.

fig. 1 | View of existing tanks, Turtle Creek Pump House, Dallas, Texas

fig. 2 | Demolition underway

fig. 3 | Demolished concrete set aside for reuse

fig. 4 | Hole punched in tank wall

fig. 5 | New garden with displaced concrete floor slabbing

Concrete Becoming Plastic, Then Graphic

Neil M. Denari

The adjective *concrete*, synonymous with *specific, real, tangible,* and *particular*, appears already by the fourteenth century as "characterized by or belonging to immediate experience of actual things or events," indicating an architectural fault line that articulates the differences between direct or concrete experiences and those that are mysterious, imagined, unknown, illusive, or hypothetical. The noun *concrete* (dating to 1656)—150 pounds per cubic foot of pure weight and intractable mass—is architecture's material delivery of specificity, formed first by intention (design and engineering), next by a provisional yet powerfully buttressed formwork of various surface systems (such as slipform steel panels and gel-released plywood), and finally by the intention to actually pour the grey, viscous, momentarily workable material into place. With concrete there is no going back. The trucks have come and gone. It flows only with the commitment to be tangible, to be real, and it would seem, the commitment to believe in the power of form. One can speculate here that concrete is not for the faint of heart, or for the architect who wishes to perform feats of magic through slight-of-hand materiality, or the architect who believes only in process, not product.

As Le Corbusier's *béton brut* phase emerged in the 1940s and 1950s, pushing well past his steel and glass smoothness into the roughness of the politics of everyday life, the term *brutalism* was invented not only to describe irregular surface qualities, but to express the tangibility of experience in a heavy way. Life is hard. Through brutalism, architecture became obdurate, even unyielding in its mass, crushing the effete project of steel and plaster with its overwhelming commitment to exist forever. Yet, with the structural possibilities of reinforced concrete in hand, the most apparently ponderous period of modernism had instantly become a discourse on architecture's most famous incongruity: the heaviest material had become weightless and infinitely plastic. No longer simply organized around grids, columns, beams, and the *lingua franca* of dry, piecemeal construction, concrete escalated a formal agenda predicated on wetness and fluidity, a material sensibility that not only defied its weight, it also defied the morals of international modernism. It did so by becoming plastic. Experience could finally be poured in place.

It would be wrong, however, to presume that concrete had somehow become a profligate construction method, capable of dismissing the rigors of geometric discipline in favor of freeform sculptural promiscuity. While in terms of image, structural system, and surface finish, the shotcrete techniques used at Notre Dame du Haut in Ronchamp were opposed to the in-situ precision of a typical Nervi project; each in its own way spoke to the emerging attitudes toward plastic form available to the architect or engineer that surpassed the doctrinaire formalisms of an exhausted prewar modernism. Ironically, at least for a time, the heavy, older material of concrete had breathed new life into the machinelike, apparently new world of lightweight materials, exerting mass and primitiveness as an antidote to the cerebral abstractions of an earlier hermetic period of whitewashed concrete construction.

As concrete passes from one material state to another—from discrete particulate matter, such as cement and sand, to a heavy liquid mixture, to inert super-solid—the nature of its workability is described in direct relation to its plasticity. It is interesting to note that the adjective form of the word *plastic* existed long before the *noun plastic* was invented; in other words, plastic was a set of qualities and properties before it existed as a discrete material. Like concrete, plastic is capable of being molded and continuously deformed without rupture. It is in the realm of workability that the adjective *plastic* and the noun *concrete* meet—a temporal state of becoming mass. In this transitional phase, the plasticity of experience can be formed, on the way to becoming visceral and quite direct. It makes perfect sense then that concrete, in collaboration with steel reinforcing, would become a sinuous, fluid, molded, and expressively shaped material, capable of a highly customized, monolithic specificity. There is no other material that could be less "off the shelf" (concrete block notwithstanding) than concrete. Just short of injection molding, architecture had finally connected with the fluid abstractions of industrial design.

In the early 1960s, brutalism evolved into quite a speculative language, over coding the rational with the soulful, a condition that rejected weight in favor of levity. The Bank of London and South America, completed in 1966 in Buenos Aires, and designed by the collaborative team of Clorindo Testa and the firm SEPRA, is arguably the apex of such a development. | fig. 1 More refined than Testa's Buenos Aires National Library (designed in 1961, another icon of Latin American architecture), the Bank of London and South America obviates the dissonance between the sense of protective permanence expected from a bank and an architectural openness, most evident in a perforated concrete brise-soleil that doesn't so much filter light as much as aggressively express plastic vitality. The bank's punch-card-like street elevations shock in their material excess, as it is clear that they hold up nothing more than their own weight, a forthright example of a post-functionalist Latin American modernism, as well as a brand of architecture that reduces the depth and plasticity of concrete into an almost two-dimensional surface of logolike figures. Who would have thought that, at its most advanced moment, brutalism would give way to a taboo agenda within architecture, becoming reduced to the status of a screen imbued with nothing more than a nonsensical semaphore, a pattern of dots and dashes that only communicates its graphic immediacy, rather than an eternal depth.

When concrete is asked to support the painted hieroglyphs of airport logistics, the airport tarmac, not unlike the facade at the Bank of London and South America, might be seen as an emblem of concrete's role within the graphic project. As a literal ground to the more informative and indeed operative language of information architecture (or graphic design), concrete is nothing more than a slab, a sort of mineral desktop supporting the lines, logos, icons, and texts that are necessarily the most important and contingent programs of airport functionality. In the process of becoming first

plastic and then graphic, concrete's directness as a material is no longer a quality in and of itself, but it appears only in collaboration with the media content inscribed into a blank gray background. | fig. 2

National Centre for Contemporary Art, Carlow, Ireland
Neil M. Denari Architects' project for the National Centre for Contemporary Art in Carlow, Ireland, explores the "forma-graphic" nature of concrete, simultaneously able to shape space and operate as a "signform" of programmatic responsiveness.

Carlow is located one hour southwest of Dublin by car. A small provincial town, it hosts the Éigse Carlow Arts Festival each year, an internationally recognized event that served as the impetus for a competition to design a 2,200-square-meter (7,217-square-foot) museum. A strict program of exhibition spaces, classrooms, and spatial adjacencies, as well as a tight, limited site surrounded by a variety of edge conditions, form the basic parameters from which to begin. As such, we have designed the building to connect to two cultures, two scales. The first is of the local situation of the site—adjacent to St. Patrick's, Carlow College—to open public spaces and to the center of town. The second is the global scale of the quality and types of art that this facility will show.

Since the program of the centre virtually fills out the site, the adjacent open spaces must flow into the building in order to make it accessible and infrastructural. To enable this, a portion of the site has been lowered by 1.8 meters (5.9 feet). Not only does this produce a more continuous landscape, the sectional configuration allows the building to be reduced in apparent height. While the building at the lower levels is transparent and dynamic, the mass of the building above is organized into four opaque bands that respond to the program inside and to the site context outside. The corrugated appearance, along with elements like the sawtooth skylights (emblems of the daylight factory), are intended to connote "production," while the softer elements, such as the higher central bay of Gallery 1, contrast with the purely extruded nature of the corrugations. This element, in particular, both

Concrete Becoming Plastic, Then Graphic

Neil M. Denari

fig. 1 | Bank of London and South America, by Clorindo Testa and SEPRA, Buenos Aires, Argentina, 1966

fig. 2 | Aerial view of the tarmac at Orly International Airport, Paris, France

figs. 3–4 | Renderings of the proposed National Centre for Contemporary Art, by Neil M. Denari Architects, Carlow, Ireland, competition, 2002

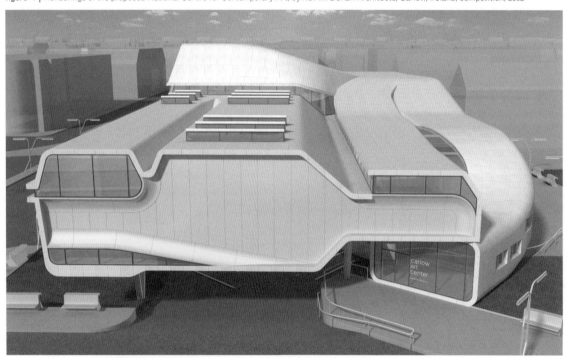

blends into the front facade and simultaneously creates a large, abstract supergraphic on the parking lot.

The overall architectural goal is to combine the flexibility of a *kunsthalle*-type building with a formal quality that attempts to deliver specificity, or perhaps legibility, in the realm of graphic resonance. Embedded within this pairing of pragmatic directness and tectonic vitality is an argument for architecture's need to incorporate the forces and logic of other media, most of which work antagonistically against architecture's role as a timeless vessel. Without recourse to obvious media systems, such as digital signage, concrete's workability as a plastic material emerges as a set of smooth extrusions, a parallel bundle of shape-specific volumes that accumulate into a formagraphic whole. In using the certainty of the material to leverage tangibility against institutional lightness, the project incorporates rather than resists the work that concrete can do across manifold dimensions.

| figs. 3–4

Acknowledg-
ments

Solid States: Concrete in Transition is the second book in the series that has emerged from the annual Columbia Conference on Architecture, Engineering and Materials. Each volume is edited from an academic conference sponsored by the Graduate School of Architecture, Planning, and Preservation (GSAPP) in collaboration with the Fu Foundation School of Engineering and Applied Science at Columbia University. The idea—for architecture and engineering schools to collaborate on a joint conference and publication series—was initiated by Mark Wigley, dean of the GSAPP, with Christian Meyer, chair of the department of civil engineering and engineering mechanics, and Michael Bell, professor at GSAPP and chair of the conference. Partnerships between the schools and a scientific committee were formed with an interdisciplinary focus linking engineering, architecture, and materials science. Each year, the material focus migrates, but the essential structure of inquiry remains the same. As with the previous book and conference on glass (*Engineered Transparency: The Technical, Visual, and Spatial Effects of Glass*), in considering concrete, we examined the degree to which we could still, in fact, isolate a single material within

the broad context of building materials, and we found that the degree to which the fields of engineering and materials science are defining new boundaries is instigating a need for clarification on what constitutes the state of the art in concrete today. New techniques for creating thinner, lighter, and stronger concrete structures; new techniques for examining concrete at the nanoscale; as well as research incorporating recycled materials, such as glass and fly ash, were crucial. These questions were not being asked in isolation; they were embedded deep within the research of colleagues, and they were situated within contemporary projects and preexisting collaborations. *Solid States* explores these collaborations and places this work in an academic context, capturing a moment when the professions of architecture and engineering, and the scholarship that surrounds and often propels them, were far more reflexive and intertwined than they had been since the early twentieth century. It was the right time to examine this shared work, in part because of the new directions it revealed.

The title of this book is a reflection on the perceived inert quality of concrete but also the factual aspects of its properties of flow, both as a material and as a global commodity. Our goal was to launch renewed inquiry into these notions of flow, and its subsequent shape, form, and plasticity. How has global trade and neoliberalized borders rearranged concrete's formerly clear boundaries and material properties? The architects, engineers, and scholars who spoke at the conference and contributed to this volume have all mined this vein, and each was given a great deal of preliminary information on the overall organization and goals of the conference.

If we were to identify each person that gave shape to the conference, the list would resemble this book's table of contents. Almost everyone who participated has stepped outside of their comfort zone, especially those that took lead roles in shaping panels and exposing their long-standing work to new directions. Others generously allowed their work to be placed in relation to that of new colleagues and engaged in conversations reframed by issues of environmental engineering and energy concerns. All of the participants witnessed their work being examined at the levels of art history and political and cultural history, forging a new kind of communication between scholars, engineers, and architects.

The conference and book also benefited from the tremendous energy and intelligent work of Benjamin Prosky. The book was shaped with insight by our partners at Princeton Architectural Press, particularly Laurie Manfra and Jan Haux. Thanks are also due to Jordan Carver and Pollyanna Rhee for their assistance with images and permissions, and to Jeannie Kim for her important advice and direction. The original graphic identity for the event was formed by Luke Bulman and his design firm, Thumb. Diana Darling and William Menking of the *Architect's Newspaper* were our media sponsors and helped situate the project's ambitions early on. The conference was accompanied by the exhibition Concrete Trajectories, curated by Rosana Rubio-Hernandez with Jesús Donaire Garciá de la Mora, who also provided advice and insight on the structure of the conference. Special thanks are also due to Lou Fernandez, John Ramahlo, Mark Taylor, and the GSAPP audiovisual crew. We would also like to extend a special thanks to Devon Ercolano Provan, director of the GSAPP Development Office and Melissa Cowley Wolf of our Alumni Office. Associate Dean David Hinkle is at the center of any project at the GSAPP, and he helped guide this work.

Solid States was generously supported by Lafarge and in particular by Chairman and Chief Executive Officer Bruno Lafont, as well as Jacques Lukasic and Pascal Casanova. With the help of their associates, we were able to reach a far wider professional audience and broaden the scope of the school's engagement with industry. This book and the accompanying documentary film were made possible by Larfarge, and their partnership creates a new engagement with industry that our professions and schools will increasingly rely on.

As a long-term project, the GSAPP continues to develop the Columbia Conference on Architecture, Engineering, and Materials, with the October 2009 conference (and forthcoming book) *Post-Ductility: Metals in Architecture and Engineering.* Mark Wigley, dean of the GSAPP, has been tremendously inventive in opening the school to new opportunities for thinking and exchange. The conference and this book would not have been possible without his drive and momentum.

—Michael Bell and Craig Buckley

Contributors

Angelo Bucci is a principal at the São Paulo–based firm SPBR Architects (www.spbr.arq.br). He teaches at the University of São Paulo, Faculty of Architecture and Urbanism in Brazil.

Jean-Louis Cohen is the Sheldon H. Solow Professor in the History of Architecture at New York University's Institute of Fine Arts. His research focuses on nineteenth- and twentieth-century architecture and planning in France, Russia, Italy, Germany, and North America.

Preston Scott Cohen is the Gerald M. McCue Professor in Architecture at Harvard University's Graduate School of Design (GSD). Preston Scott Cohen Inc. (www.pscohen.com) is based in Cambridge, Massachusetts.

Carlos Eduardo Comas is a professor in the Graduate Studies in Architecture Program at the Federal University of Rio Grande do Sul in Porto Alegre, Brazil.

Neil M. Denari is a professor in the Department of Architecture and Urban Design at the University of California, Los Angeles. He is the principal of Neil M. Denari Architects (www.nmda-inc.com).

Jacques Ferrier is the founder of the Paris-based firm Jacques Ferrier Architectures (www.jacques-ferrier.com).

Benjamin A. Graybeal is a research structural engineer with the U.S. Federal Highway Administration (FHWA) at its Turner-Fairbank Highway Research Center in McLean, Virginia, where he manages the structural concrete program.

Laurie Hawkinson is a professor at Columbia University's Graduate School of Architecture, Planning, and Preservation (GSAPP) and a partner at the New York–based firm Smith-Miller + Hawkinson Architects (www.smharch.com).

Juan Herreros is a professor at the Superior Technical School of Architecture of Madrid and the founder of herrerosarquitectos (www.herrerosarquitectos.com).

Steven Holl is a professor at Columbia University's GSAPP and the founder of Steven Holl Architects (www.stevenholl.com).

Sanford Kwinter is a professor of theory and criticism at Harvard University's Graduate School of Design. He has written widely on philosophical aspects of design, architecture, and urbanism.

Qingyun Ma is the Della and Harry MacDonald Dean's Chair of the School of Architecture at the University of Southern California in Los Angeles. He is the founder of MADA s.p.a.m. (www.madaspam.com) based in Shanghai, China.

Fernando Menis is an associate professor at the Polytechnic University of Valencia and founder of Menis Arquitectos (www.menis.com) based in Tenerife, Spain.

Detlef Mertins is an architectural historian known for his revisionist histories of modernism in the twentieth century. He is a professor and former chair (2003–8) of the Department of Architecture at the University of Pennsylvania.

Christian Meyer is a professor and chair of the Department of Civil Engineering and Engineering Mechanics at Columbia University's Fu Foundation School of Engineering and Applied Science.

Marc Mimram is a professor at the School of Architecture of the City and Territories of Marne-la-Vallée. His architecture and engineering consultancy (www.mimram.com) is based in Paris.

Paulo Monteiro is the Roy W. Carlson Distinguished Professor in the Department of Civil and Environmental Engineering at the University of California, Berkeley.

Toshiko Mori is the Robert P. Hubbard Professor in the Practice of Architecture at Harvard University's GSD, and former chair of the Department of Architecture (2002–8). She is the founder of Toshiko Mori Architect (www.tmarch.com).

Antoine E. Naaman is Professor Emeritus of Civil Engineering at the University of Michigan in Ann Arbor.

Guy Nordenson is a professor of architecture and structural engineering at Princeton University School of Architecture, and the founder of Guy Nordenson and Associates (www.nordenson.com).

Kate Orff is an assistant professor at Columbia University's GSAPP, where she directs the Urban Landscape Lab. She is the founder of SCAPE (www.scapestudio.com) based in New York City.

Jesse Reiser and Nanako Umemoto are the founders of Reiser + Umemoto (www.reiser-umemoto.com). They have lectured at architecture schools throughout the United States. Reiser is an associate professor at Princeton University School of Architecture.

Stanley Saitowitz is Professor Emeritus of Architecture at the University of California, Berkeley's College of Environmental Design and a partner at Stanley Saitowitz/Natoma Architects Inc. (www.saitowitz.com) based in San Francisco.

Hans Schober is a partner at Schlaich Bergermann und Partner, Consulting Engineers (www.sbp.de) based in Stuttgart, Germany, and president of the firm's New York office.

Matthias Schuler is the founder and managing director of Transsolar KlimaEngineering (www.transsolar.com) based in Stuttgart, Germany. He is an adjunct professor of environmental technology at Harvard University's GSD.

Ysrael A. Seinuk is a professor at the School of Architecture at Cooper Union for the Advancement of Science and Art. He is the founder of Ysrael A. Seinuk P.C. (www.yaseinuk.com).

Pierluigi Serraino is a practicing architect, historian, and PhD candidate at the College of Environmental Design at the University of California, Berkeley.

Surendra P. Shah is the Walter P. Murphy Professor of Civil Engineering at Northwestern University, where he directs the Center for Advanced Cement-Based Materials. He serves as Honorary Professor at Hong Kong Polytechnic University and at the University of L'Aquilla in Italy.

Werner Sobek is the director of the Institute for Lightweight Structures and Conceptual Design at the University of Stuttgart, Germany, and the founder of the international firm Werner Sobek Engineering & Design (www.wernersobek.de).

Heiko Trumpf is a principal at Werner Sobek Engineering & Design (www.wernersobek.de) and lecturer at the University of Stuttgart.

Bernard Tschumi is a professor and the former dean (1988–2003) of Columbia University's GSAPP. He is the founder of Bernard Tschumi Architects (www.tschumi.com) based in Paris and New York.

Mark Wigley is an architectural critic and theorist, and the dean (2004–present) of Columbia University's GSAPP.

Mabel Wilson is an associate professor at Columbia University's GSAPP, where she directs the Program for Advanced Architectural Research.

Credits

Project Credits

Congregation Beth Sholom, San Francisco
Acoustical consultant: Charles M Salter Associates Inc.
Architect: Stanley Saitowitz/Natoma Architects
Building Area: 29,000 sq. ft. (2,694 sq. m)
Client: Congregation Beth Sholom
Completion: 2008
Construction cost: approximately 11,933,000 U.S. dollars
General contractor: Overaa Construction
Interior consultant: Shelter
Landscape consultant: Blasen Landscape Architecture
Mechanical engineers: Rumsey Engineers Inc.
Project team: Stanley Saitowitz, Neil Kaye, Markus Bischoff, John Winder, and Derrick Chan.
Structural engineers: Forell/Elsesser Engineers Inc.

House in Ribeirão Preto, São Paulo, Brazil
Architects: Angelo Bucci, Fernando de Mello Franco, Marta Moreira, and Milton Braga
Building area: 1,851 sq. ft. (172 sq. m)
Client: Débora Falleiros and Alexandre Mello
Collaborators: Anna Helena Vilella, Eduardo Ferroni, Eliana Mello, and Maria Júlia Herklotz
Completion: 2001
General contractor: Paulo Balugoli
Project budget: unavailable
Structural engineer: Ibsen Puleo Uvo

House in Ubatuba, São Paulo, Brazil
Architects: Angelo Bucci, Ciro Miguel, and Juliana Braga
Building area: 2,960 sq. ft. (275 sq. m)
Client: Regina Mei Silveira e Antonio Carlos Onofre
Collaborators: Flávia Parodi Costa, João Paulo Meirelles de Faria, and Tatiana Ozzetti
Completion: 2009
Project budget: unavailable
Structural engineer: Ibsen Puleo Uvo

Nanjing University Performing Arts Center, Nanjing, China
Architect of record: Institute of Architecture Design and Planning, Nanjing
Building area: Program: 160,000 sq. ft. (16,000 sq. m)
Client: Nanjing University
Completion: 2009
Design architect: Preston Scott Cohen, Inc.
Project budget: approximately 7,032,000 U.S. dollars

O-14, Dubai, United Arab Emirates
Architect of record: Erga Progress, Dubai, United Arab Emirates
Assistants and interns: Tina Tung, Raha Talebi, and Yan Wai Chu
Building area: 299,990 sq. ft. (27,870 sq. m)
Client: Creekside Development Corporation, Dubai, UAE
Completion: 2010
Design architect: Reiser + Umemoto RUR Architecture
Design team: Mitsuhisa Matsunaga, Kutan Ayata, Jason Scroggin, Cooper Mack, Michael Overby, Roland Snooks, and Michael Young
General contractor: Dubai Contracting Company
Project budget: approximately 50,000,000 U.S. dollars
Structural engineer: Ysrael A. Seinuk, PC
Window-wall consultant: R.A.Heintges & Associates

Tel Aviv Museum of Art, Tel Aviv, Israel
Accessibility consultant: Michael Roitman
Acoustics: M.G. Acoustical Consultants Ltd.
Architect: Preston Scott Cohen, Inc.
Building area: 200,000 sq. ft. (18,500 sq. m)
Client: Motti Omer, Director and Chief Curator
Completion: 2010
Competition consultants: Ove Arup and Partners, Caroline Fitzgerald, Tom Dawes, Mark Walsh-Cooke (structural and MEP), and Hanscomb Faithful and Gould (cost estimator)
General contractor: Hezkelevitch Engineering
Project management: CPM Construction Management Ltd.

HVAC: M. Doron - I. Shahar and Co., Consulting Eng. Ltd.

Lighting: Tillotson Design Associates

Project budget: approximately 45,000,000 U.S. dollars

Project team: Preston Scott Cohen and Amit Nemlich

Structural engineer: YSS Consulting Engineers Ltd., Dani Shacham

Vanke Center, Shenzhen, China

Architect: Steven Holl Architects

Assistant project architect: Eric Li

Associate architect: China Construction Design International

Building Area: 1,296,459 sq. ft. (120,445 sq. m)

Client: Shenzhen Vanke Real Estate Co.

Climate engineers: Transsolar

Competition team: Steven Holl, Li Hu, Gong Dong, Justin Allen,
    Garrick Ambrose, Johnna Brazier, Kefei Cai, Yenling Chen,
    Hideki Hirahara, Eric Li, Filipe Taboada

Completion: 2010

Curtain wall consultant: Yuanda Curtain Wall

Design team: Jason Anderson, Guanlan Cao, Lesley Chang,
    Clemence Eliard, Forrest Fulton, Nick Gelpi, M. Emran Hossain,
    Seung Hyun Kang, JongSeo Lee, Wan-Jen Lin, Richard Liu,
    Jackie Luk, Enrique Moya-Angeler, Roberto Requejo, Jiangtao
    Shen, Michael Rusch, Filipe Taboada

General contractor: The First Construction Engineering Limited
    Company of China Construction Third Engineering Bureau

Landscape architect: Steven Holl Architects and China
    Construction Design International

Lighting consultant: L'Observatoire International

Mechanical engineer: China Construction Design International

Partner in charge: Li Hu

Project architects: Garrick Ambrose (SD/DD), Maren Koehler and Jay
    Siebenmorgen (DD), Christopher Brokaw and Rodolfo Dias (CD)

Project budget: unavailable

Project managers: Yimei Chan and Gong Dong

Structural engineers: China Academdy of Building Resarch (SD/DD)
    and China Construction Design International (CD/CA)

Image Credits

Frontispiece: © Iwan Baan

Essays
"Earth as Urban Laboratory"
fig. 1: courtesy HOK; fig. 2: courtesy Avery Architectural and Fine Arts Library, Columbia University; fig. 3: © Fondation Le Corbusier/Artists Rights Society, 2009; fig. 4: © CNAM/DAF/Cité de l'architecture et du patrimoine/Archives d'architecture du XXe siècle/UFSE/SAIF; fig. 5: Popperfoto/Getty Images; fig. 6: © Centre des archives contemporaines, Fontainebleau; fig. 7: reprinted from Affonso Eduardo Reidy, *The Works of Affonso Eduardo Reidy* (New York: Praeger, 1960); fig. 8: Jean-Louis Cohen; fig. 9: © Marc Mimram Architecte Ingenieure.

"Pervasive Plasticity"
fig. 1: Plan FLC 19209A © Fondation Le Corbusier/Artists Rights Society, 2009; fig. 2: Collection Centre Canadien d'Architecture / Canadian Centre for Architecture, Montréal; fig. 3: © Sze Tsung Leong, Courtesy Yossi Milo Gallery, New York; fig. 4: © Haubitz+Zoche; fig. 5: © Srdjan Jovanovich Weiss; fig. 6: courtesy Eero Saarinen Collection, Manuscripts and Archives, Yale University Library; fig. 7: © Archiv am Goetheanum; fig. 8: courtesy Detlef Mertins; fig. 9: Collection of Avery Architectural and Fine Arts Library, Columbia University; fig. 10: © Walter Niedermayr; fig. 11: © Hélène Binet; fig. 12: © Emily Geoff; fig. 13: © Ferda Kolatan, Erich Schoenenberger (su11); figs. 14–15: courtesy Museo nazionale delle arti del XXI secolo, Rome; fig. 16: © Courtesy Historisches Archiv der Stadt Köln; fig. 17: courtesy the Trustees of Sir John Soane's Museum.

"Concrete: Dead or Alive?"
fig. 1: © Erick Greene; fig. 2: © Time Life Science Library, 1966; fig. 3: courtesy Toyo Ito & Associates, Architects, The Taichung Metropolitan Opera House is built by the Taichung City Government, Republic of China (Taiwan); fig. 4–7: © Reiser + Umemoto RUR Architecture; fig. 8: courtesy U.S. Department of the Interior, National Park Service, Thomas Edison National Historical Park; fig. 9: reprinted from Affonso Eduardo Reidy, *The Works of Affonso Eduardo Reidy* (New York: Praeger, 1960).

"Modelmaking Rangers"
figs. 1–21: © Richard Knight.

"Reinforced Concrete and Modern Brazilian Architecture"
figs. 1–8: © Leonardo Finotti; fig. 9: reprinted from "Amorphous Metallic Form," Jan Schroers, Chris Veazey, and William L. Johnson, *Applied Physics Letters* 82, no. 3 (January 2003); fig. 10: courtesy Paulo Mendes da Rocha, photographed by José Moscardi; fig. 11: courtesy of the Archives of Joaquim and Liliana Guedes; figs. 12–15: © Leonardo Finotti.

"Notes on Weight and Weightlessness"
fig. 1–2: © Steven Holl Architects; fig. 3: © Paul Warchol; fig. 4–6: © Steven Holl Architects; fig. 7: © Andy Ryan; figs. 8–12; fig. 13: © Paul Warchol; figs. 14–15: © Steven Holl Architects; fig. 16: © Iwan Baan; figs. 17–18: © Steven Holl Architects.

Projects
"Horizontal Skyscraper"
p. 90 top and bottom: © Iwan Baan; p. 91: © Steven Holl Architects; pp. 92–95: © Iwan Baan; pp. 96–101: © Steven Holl Architects.

"Concrete or the Betrayal of Geometry"
p. 103: © Preston Scott Cohen, Inc.; pp. 104–105: © Iwan Baan; p. 105 right: © Shi Hua; p. 109: © Preston Scott Cohen, Inc.; p. 110 top: © Ohad Matalon; p. 110 bottom and p. 111: © Iwan Baan; p. 112 bottom: © Preston Scott Cohen, Inc.; p. 113 top right: © Ohad Matalon; p. 113 top left and bottom: © Iwan Baan; p. 114: © Preston Scott Cohen, Inc.; p. 115 top and bottom: © Ohad Matalon.

"Tower and Temperament"
p. 119: © Reiser + Umemoto RUR Architecture; p. 120: © Sebastian Oppitz; pp. 121–123: © Reiser + Umemoto RUR Architecture.

"A Circular Journey"
pp. 126 and 127 top left: © Stanley Saitowitz / Natoma Architects Inc.; p. 127 top right and bottom: © Bruce Damonte; pp. 128–129: © Rien van Rijthoven.

"São Paulo: A Reinforced Context"
p. 132 top right: © Nelson Kon; p. 132 top left: © Raul Garcesp; p. 132 bottom: © Nelson Kon; p. 133 top: © SPBR; p. 133 bottom: © Nelson Kon; p. 134: © SPBR; p. 134: © Nelson Kon; p. 135: © Nilton Suenaga.

Structural Engineering + Material Science

"Exposed Concrete"

fig. 1: © Christian Richters; fig. 2: © Roland Halbe; fig. 3: © UNStudio; fig. 4: © Arnold Walz; fig. 5: © Wenzel & Wenzel; fig. 6: © Brigida Gonzalez; figs. 7–8: © Roland Halbe.

"Magical Structuralism"

fig. 1: © Philips, Eindhoven; fig. 2: courtesy of Guy Nordenson and Associates; fig. 3: courtesy of Steven Holl Architects; figs. 4–5: courtesy Guy Nordenson and Associates.

"From Wire Mesh to 3-D Textiles"

figs. 1–13: courtesy Antoine E. Naaman.

"Engineering in Cuba"

fig. 1: source unknown; fig. 2: © Andrew Moore, courtesy of Yancey Richardson Gallery; figs. 3–17: courtesy Ysrael A. Seinuk, PC; fig. 18: © Reiser + Umemoto RUR Architecture; fig. 19: © Sebastian Oppitz.

"Nanotechnology in Concrete"

figs. 1–11: courtesy Surendra Shah; fig. 12: © *Nature* magazine.

"Ultra-High-Performance Concrete in Highway Transportation Infrastructure"

figs. 1–4: © Federal Highway Administration (FHWA).

"Form Over Mass"

figs. 1–2: © Schlaich Bergermann und Partner; fig. 3: © Gert Elsner; figs. 4–16: © Schlaich Bergermann und Partner.

Energy + Sustainability

"An Integrated Energy and Comfort Concept"

fig. 1: © www.thomasmayerarchive.com; figs. 2–6: © Transsolar Klimaengineering; figs. 7–8: © www.thomasmayerarchive. com; fig. 9: © Transsolar Klimaengineering; figs. 10–13: © www. thomasmayerarchive.com.

"Green Concrete and Sustainable Construction"

fig. 1: courtesy Paulo Monteiro.

"The Hypergreen Path"

figs. 1–8: courtesy Jacques Ferrier Architectures.

Cultural Effects

"Materialization of Concepts"

figs. 1–4: © Bernard Tschumi; figs. 5–8: © Peter Mauss/ESTO; fig. 9: © Bernard Tschumi; fig. 10: © Peter Mauss/ESTO; fig. 11–13: © Bernard Tschumi; figs. 14–17: © Christian Richters; fig. 18: © Peter Mauss/ESTO.

"The State of Concrete"

figs. 1–13: © MADAs.p.a.m.

"Living with Infrastructure"

figs. 1–11: © MARC MIMRAM Architect & Engineer.
Opportunity in Transition
figs. 1–7: © Toshiko Mori Architect; fig. 8: © Paul Warchol; figs. 9–10: © CAST, Faculty of Architecture, University of Manitoba.

"Implicit Performance"

fig. 1: © Bleda & Rosa; fig. 2: © Ábalos & Herreros; fig. 3: © Bleda & Rosa; figs. 4–6: © Ábalos & Herreros; fig. 7: © Bleda & Rosa; fig. 8: © Paolo Roselli; fig. 9: © Roland Halbe; figs. 10–11: © herrerosarquitectos; fig. 12: © Bureau Bakker.

"Solidifications"

fig. 1: © Roland Halbe; fig. 2: © Hisao Suzuki; figs. 3–6: Office Menis Arquitectos; fig. 7: © Hisao Suzuki; fig. 8: Office Menis Arquitectos.

"A Building and its Double"

fig. 1: © Rachel Whiteread, courtesy of the artist, Luhring Augustine, New York and Gagosian Gallery; fig. 2: courtesy Mabel Wilson; fig. 3: © Sergio Ferro.

"Cloaked Transparency"

fig. 1: © Smith-Miller+Hawkinson Architects; figs. 2–3: © Michael Moran; figs. 4–6: © Sean A. Gallagher; figs. 7–10: © Michael Moran; fig. 11: © Smith-Miller+Hawkinson Architects.

"Artificial Natures / New Geographies"

fig. 1: © Julie Bargmann; fig. 2: © Kate Orff; fig. 3: © Julie Bargmann; figs. 4–5: © Tom Jenkins.

"Concrete Becoming Plastic, Then Graphic"

figs. 1–4: © Neil M. Denari Architects.

DVD Contents

1   Sanford Kwinter
2   Toshiko Mori
3   Carlos Eduardo Comas
4   Heiko Trumpf
5   Fernando Menis
6   Mark Wigley
7   Bruno Lafont
8   Steven Holl
9   Guy Nordenson
10   Matthias Schuler
11   Christian Meyer
12   Preston Scott Cohen
13   Pierluigi Serraino
14   Mabel Wilson
15   Stanley Saitowitz
16   Hans Schober
17   Angelo Bucci
18   Sanford Kwinter
19   Toshiko Mori
20   Guy Nordenson
21   Jesse Reiser
22   Ysrael A. Seinuk
23   Benjamin A. Graybeal
24   Kenneth Frampton
25   Antoine E. Naaman
26   Qingyun Ma
27   Marc Mimram
28   Reinhold Martin
29   Juan Herreros
30   Matthias Schuler
31   Bernard Tschumi
32   Roundtable discussion

Credits

Associate producer: Rima Yamazaki
Cinematography: Mead Hunt, Allen McPheely, and Roger Grange
Editor: Joëlle Schon
Production assistants: Mary Latvis and Keith Strand
Production manager: Elinor Feist
Production company: Michael Blackwood Productions, Inc.
Sound recordist: Mark Mandler

Produced and directed by
Michael Blackwood

This film was made possible by the generous support of Lafarge.